## CATHERINE TOWNSEND

Catherine Townsend is 30 and writes the weekly sex and dating column 'Sleeping Around' in the *Independent*. Her first memoir was also called *Sleeping Around: Secrets of a Sexual Adventuress*.

Born in Georgia, USA, Catherine spent several years as a gossip columnist for *New York Magazine* before moving to the UK. She writes regularly for *Glamour, Cosmopolitan* and *Marie Claire*, has contributed to various newspapers, and has been a radio and TV commentator. She has a BA and MA in Journalism.

ALSO BY CATHERINE TOWNSEND

Sleeping Around

# Breaking the Rules

## Confessions of a Bad Girl

### CATHERINE TOWNSEND

JOHN MURRAY

First published in Great Britain in 2008 by John Murray (Publishers)
An Hachette Livre UK company

A CIP catalogue record for this title is available from the British Library

B-format ISBN 978-0-7195-6353-9
A-format ISBN 978-1-84854-000-2

Typeset in Garamond (Adobe) by Palimpsest Book Production Limited,
Grangemouth, Stirlingshire

Printed and bound by Clays Ltd, St Ives plc

John Murray policy is to use papers that are natural, renewable and recyclable
products and made from wood grown in sustainable forests. The logging and
manufacturing processes are expected to conform to the environmental
regulations of the country of origin.

John Murray (Publishers)
338 Euston Road
London NW1 3BH

www.johnmurray.co.uk

For Dad and Caroline

This is a true story.
Some names, identifying characteristics and time sequences
have been changed to protect anonymity.

*The unpalatable truth is that falling in love is, in some ways, indistinguishable from a severe pathology. Behaviour changes are reminiscent of psychosis and, biochemically speaking, passionate love closely imitates substance abuse. Sex is a 'booby trap', intended to bind the partners long enough to bond.*

*Using functional Magnetic Resonance Imaging (fMRI), Andreas Bartels and Semir Zeki of University College in London showed that the same areas of the brain are active when abusing drugs and when in love.*

From 'The Pathology of Love', by Dr Sam Vaknin

# ONE

They say that there are some landmark moments in life, and my wedding day was definitely one that I'll never forget. But when I was a kid staging the mock-ceremony in white sheets, I never imagined that my first night as a married woman would end in a threesome with the best man.

Okay, so it wasn't exactly a conventional wedding. My friend Mark and I only tied the knot so that I could stay in the UK. I was a twenty-eight-year-old American journalist based in London, and while I'd successfully landed a column in the *Independent* about my love life called 'Sleeping Around', my new gig didn't come complete with a work visa.

Although I love Mark as a friend and was hugely grateful for the sacrifice he was making on my behalf, I was an emotional wreck. Before the ceremony I almost climbed out of the window, and though I kept trying to remind myself that this was only a formality I couldn't help feeling sad as the registrar read us the vows. While I smiled and held my husband Mark's hand, all I could think about was my new boyfriend Paul (or JP for short!), and the hot sex we'd had that morning. I've never read about that moment in any bridal magazine.

And yet the day appeared very traditional from the outside: I wore white, despite the fact that several of my ex-lovers were in attendance, and no one mocked the blushing bride.

I also looked (dare I say) lovely and innocent in my very cool, vintage eighties, white strapless prom dress that I'd recently snagged from a boutique in the King's Road. However, glancing at my five-foot-ten frame in the mirror in the registrar's office hallway, it hit me that I looked like a miniature ceramic bride from the top of the wedding cake, which perhaps wasn't the look I'd been aiming for.

Somehow, Mark and I managed to get through our vows after a few glasses of champagne. Since the overriding theme of the day was terror rather than euphoria, we felt completely justified in getting totally pissed later. So after stepping out into the spring air and bidding farewell to some of our guests, the core crowd, including Mark, his hunky South African architect flatmate Russell, my two best friends Amy and Victoria, along with her fiancé Mike, all piled into a cab and headed towards Notting Hill.

Things started to go downhill at the pseudo-reception we'd organized at E&O restaurant. Underneath Mark's straitlaced banker exterior lurks a serious party animal and sexual deviant, which is one of the many reasons why I adore him.

Somehow, Mark had got hold of an Ecstasy tablet, and since he's not exactly a veteran drug user he was 'petting' Amy's velvet dress by the time we got to the table.

'Maybe we should just cut this short and head home,' I whispered to Amy and Victoria, who were seated next to each other on my right. I was beginning to feel strangely panicked myself, and – even though I knew that this was totally psychological – trapped. I'm the girl who balks at giving a credit card number to secure a dinner reservation, and I had tied the knot. I was sure that Mark was feeling exactly the same way, wondering what the hell he had got himself into.

'Darling, it's your wedding day, we're not going anywhere!' Victoria announced. Then, lowering her voice an octave, 'Besides, we have to have some convincing pics for immigration, right? So, you and Mark, squeeze together and big smiles please!'

I scrunched closer to Mark, and was already starting to sweat. I also felt uncomfortable because I'd broken my cardinal rule about drinking champagne while in tight-fitting clothing – the lining of the dress was practically cutting off my circulation.

'I love you, honey pie,' Mark whispered.

'I know you do, sweetie,' I told him.

'No, really, I seriously adore you.' He looked at me with wide eyes as he stroked my arm. 'Your skin is so soft!'

Rolling my eyes, I gave him a hug. 'I love you too,' I said. 'You are the best. Thank you. I mean that, from the bottom of my heart.'

In some ways, I was thrilled that Mark had volunteered to tie the knot with me, even if this wasn't exactly the result I'd had in mind when I'd dreamed of how my future husband would also be my best friend. We'd been so close for so long that I knew nothing could upset our friendship. We were cool.

Everyone toasted the happy couple, and after the champagne ran out we moved on to pear martinis. I know this was only a fake wedding, but, still, everything felt rather anticlimactic. Maybe I shouldn't have been surprised at that, though. My 'milestone' birthdays have all been a bit of a let-down:

I spent all night on my twenty-first in a bar in New York, knocking back tequila shots and chatting up a buff guy with a beard before my flatmate Erin and I realized that we were in a lesbian bar and 'his' name was Glenda. Then I threw up in the toilets.

New Year's Eves are generally no picnic either; ever since my dad left on the one when I was thirteen I seem to have been cursed on that day.

'Hey.' Mark nudged me in the ribs and gestured to our petite and stunning blonde waitress. 'She is seriously fit. And she keeps coming over. Do you think this whole "I've got married to someone else today" thing will put her off?'

'Mark, she keeps coming back to bring our food. See the trays of canapés in her hand?'

'So, man, how did it feel?' Russell said to Mark. 'Speech!'

'God, I was so shit scared,' he said, by now slurring his words. 'Seriously, though, I'm just so happy to have got through this whole thing without killing Cat and without pissing or soiling myself!'

The cute waitress dropped his drink in front of him and backed away quickly, looking horrified.

'How romantic,' I said sarcastically, and then smiled despite myself. 'I'll bet a lot of people feel that way when walking down the aisle, we're just the only ones brave enough to admit it!'

My phone vibrated in my lap, and I hastily pulled it from under the table to reveal the latest text from JP, who was completely unaware of the wedding fiasco. He still thought that I was having brunch with my girlfriends. When I had torn myself away from his bed that morning I had somehow managed to pull off the lie. 'How about a sleepover tonight, gorgeous? Xxx, JP', he'd written.

For a few seconds, I was utterly devastated as the reality of the circus act sank in. Some day I wanted to get married for the right reasons. How was I going to tell my new boyfriend that I'd just got hitched? And how would he ever understand even if I did explain my reasons?

To say that JP is as straight as an arrow is a bit of an understatement. This is the guy so thorough that he attended medical school to understand better the technology that his Internet company was selling. He visits his grandfather in the care home every Saturday and drives a Ford Escort, for Christ's sake. I wasn't sure that saying, 'Chill, babe, I'm only committing immigration fraud, it's not like I'm married for real,' was going to cut it.

Any way I sliced it, I didn't look like the most honest and straightforward individual. Would he still want to stay with me? I felt my stomach lurch, and this time it wasn't the martinis.

'Are you okay?' Victoria refilled my drink, while retouching my hair. 'You look upset.'

'I'm just worried about what JP is going to say,' I told her. 'I've decided that I'm coming clean and telling him tonight.'

'Honey, I know that you're all about honesty, but, really, are you sure that's a good idea today? You are very emotional.'

I knew that Victoria saw no problem with having secrets, because she essentially thinks of men and women as separate species, who have to play by different rules.

She's utterly fearless, and believes with absolute conviction that she's fabulous. My chemistry with her was instant and immediate, ever since the day we bonded at the hairdresser's, after she'd overheard me crying about my ex-boyfriend Patrick and telling the hairdresser that I wanted to cut my hair short.

She'd approached my chair with a towel on her head. 'You have gorgeous hair,' she'd said, 'and there really ought to be a seven-day waiting period before a woman is allowed to chop it off after a break-up, sort of like there is to buy a gun in the US.'

I still owed her for that reality check, since I have naturally wavy hair and the only thing worse than getting dumped would have been hitting the singles scene resembling Rod Stewart.

'I'm from Georgia,' I'd told her, smiling despite myself. 'You can get a gun in ten minutes. It's only abortions you have to wait seven days for.'

Victoria and I love and perfectly complement each other, because when I justify bad male behaviour she snaps me back into reality. And I like to think that I advise her to see the good in people.

Women, she's always telling me, should maintain mystique – a lesson she has learned from her impossibly glamorous French mother. It has clearly worked for her, because she's happily engaged to Mike, but I know that I have to be true to myself. Besides, I have verbal diarrhoea and would only blurt out the ugly truth at a later date.

'I have to tell him the truth, no matter what, if we're going to have a real relationship. Imagine how shitty he would feel if I wait months. I can't handle the guilt!'

While Mark went in search of our waitress, Amy, who had overheard the turn in our conversation, sidled in closer. 'Look,

Cat, I don't want to lecture you on your wedding day. But if you were going to tell him, you probably should have done it before today. Haven't you ever heard the expression that it's easier to ask for permission than forgiveness?' This was typical Amy. Unlike Victoria she is scruples all the way. Her sweet, virtuous nature exactly suits her perfect, Barbie-blonde, doll-like proportions.

I laughed. 'My mum used to tell me the same thing in high school when she caught me sneaking back in through my window at dawn.'

'My point exactly.'

'But if I had listened to her I would have missed all the best parties,' I said. 'Besides, I actually don't think that I should have to ask permission for this.' I hoped I sounded more convinced than I felt. 'I love him, and I want to make him happy. I'm just in a crazy situation.'

Suddenly I had a desperate longing to see JP right away. I wanted him to hold me and tell me that everything was going to be okay. Somehow, I had to make him understand. I texted him and arranged to meet across town.

'Well, good luck, sweetie,' Amy said, giving me a hug.

I said my goodbyes to the rest of the table.

Suddenly, I couldn't wait to see JP, so to save time I gave Victoria my share of the cash and asked if she could sort it out. She pushed a pink cocktail into my hands. 'Here,' she said. 'One more for the road. Sounds like you might need it.'

Tears filled my eyes as I thought about the timelines that my girlfriends had drawn in school: great career by twenty-five, married by twenty-eight, kids by thirty . . . Logically, I know that not everyone's life moves along in a perfect little linear pattern – more often, it's a tangled matrix that takes years to unweave. Mine was definitely the latter, which I had always thought was more interesting. But after all the excitements I'd had since coming to London, I suddenly craved a little simplicity.

I needed to dab my eyes, since a quick glance at my profile in the spoon on the table showed that I was in danger of morphing into Courtney Love on a bender.

My head was spinning as I pushed past the bar and stumbled towards the loo, colliding headlong into a group of well-dressed men in suits. The drink in my hand spilled all over the nearest, who was wearing a cream-coloured tie that quickly turned crimson.

'God, I'm so sorry,' I said, dabbing at it with a cocktail napkin, which only made him look more like a stabbing victim. 'Your tie is ruined.'

'Don't worry about it, it was no great loss,' he said, laughing and looking down at my festive white dress. 'Congratulations, by the way!'

'Oh, um, thanks,' I said awkwardly. Mr White Tie bought me a glass of champagne, which I attempted to accept graciously. As he started to make small talk, I didn't have the heart to tell him that it was only a marriage of convenience and that I was technically about to commit adultery. Why ruin everyone else's perfect illusion?

I downed the champagne as quickly as I could, and after a quick dash to the toilets to repair my make-up I was out of the door, and into the fresh air. I felt relieved to be getting outside, and to clear my head away from all the drama.

Then I remembered that I was the cause of the spectacle, and my heart sank as I thought about what I was going to say to JP.

Now that I was married, it was time to ask my boyfriend if he wanted to get serious.

# TWO

I met JP at Shoreditch House, where he'd already ordered me a Southern Comfort on the rocks, my favourite bevvie since high school. He looked amazing in his jeans and blazer combination that was more father figure than fashion forward. For some reason, I found his staid dress sense a real turn-on.

JP wasn't a metrosexual. He was the kind of guy who kept a lone bar of soap and shampoo in the shower, not mango body wash. Everything in both his Chelsea flat and his north London house, which he was designing himself (he had a passion for architecture and the project had taken him two years so far, but he wasn't stopping until it was perfect) was in its place. His surgical precision in organizing his life wasn't that surprising: his company dealt with medical technology, and a lot of his best friends were doctors.

Also, I knew that he'd almost got married before, to a woman he'd lived with for more than a decade, so obviously the decision was something he took very seriously.

God, I adored him. I had butterflies in my stomach, and I knew that it wasn't the liquid lunch causing my digestive angst.

'You look gorgeous, babe,' he said as he gave me a hug, looking rather perplexed. 'But your choice of ensemble is a bit, um, unorthodox. Was this a fancy dress brunch?'

I took a deep breath. 'I need to talk to you about something,'

I told him. 'But it might be best if we don't do it in here. Can we go outside?'

This proved to be a bad idea, since in my buzzed haze I had forgotten that the roof terrace was the destination of choice for all the club's pissed-off smokers. If this had been the movies it would have been deserted, like the Manhattan skyline in *When Harry Met Sally*. As it was there were three City boys, including one screaming into an alien-like headpiece about interest rates.

'So,' he said, draping his blazer over my shoulders. 'What's going on?'

I fished in my handbag for my pack of Marlboro Lights, which I always keep on hand for tense situations. I keep my smoking in check, though, since it's all about the detox and the re-tox. If I find I'm not getting a head rush every time I light up, it's time to cut back.

'Well,' I said, taking a drag. 'The thing is, I haven't told you about something that's really important to me. And you know that I'm all about total honesty – well, it's what I aspire to at least. It's nothing bad,' I said, wincing as I uttered the words because that obviously means that whatever is coming is going to be horrific, 'but, the thing is—'

Just then, one of the traders suddenly held up his palm in a 'talk to the hand' gesture, inserted his earpiece and made a shushing sound as he started yammering about the 'studio greenlighting my next project'. 'Tell them I won't even *think* about taking anything under fifty mil,' he barked, as his sheepish-looking girlfriend cowered beside him.

'That's probably his mum on the other end of the phone.' I giggled nervously.

'Maybe we'd better go back downstairs,' JP said, taking my hand. 'Are you hungry?'

I slid into the booth next to him. Being in close proximity to him, and after the adrenalin rush of the afternoon, I felt myself beginning to get turned on. I put my hand on his thigh and debated moving it higher, but the absence of a tablecloth meant this would have looked a bit obvious. For the next few minutes we chatted about random stuff in the pause before we ordered tomato and mozzarella salad, fried rice balls, sausages, and chips with mayonnaise.

'So,' he said, 'what's the big secret, Ms Townsend? Robbed any banks lately? Or are you secretly a man?'

I laughed, not so much because I found his rather lame joke funny but because I suspected that it might be the last light relief we had for a while. I was completely crazy about JP, but as it was we were hovering on the precipice of the early days, limbo period of our relationship, where things could go either way. I simply had no idea what to expect.

'I don't know how to say this, so I'm just going to tell you straight.' I looked him directly in the eye and took his hand. 'Honey, I didn't have brunch with the girls today. I got married.'

He sat upright and widened his eyes as I spilled out the whole story, about getting stopped repeatedly at customs by the woman with so much hair on her chin that she resembled a mountain goat, about how I had to get a visa in order to work legally in the country, about the groom being my best male friend. He sat for several minutes in silence.

'So you're telling me that you're married, and this is the first I'm hearing of it?' he said. 'How the fuck did this happen?'

I suspect that you can tell in the first few minutes of any

argument how things are going to pan out according to body language, and his crossed arms and inability to meet my eyes weren't good signs.

The tirade continued, and he wasn't giving me any time to answer his questions. Which, I must admit, were all legitimate. 'Why the hell didn't you tell me that you were having visa problems? How do you expect me to react to this?' He pulled his hand away, but I grabbed it again and held on tight.

'Look, baby, I know this sounds bad but please just hear me out. If at the end of it you don't want anything more to do with me, well, then I'll accept that. But at least let me explain.' My life was turning into an episode of the *Jeremy Kyle Show* – though with better dental work – and I desperately wanted to halt the train crash.

Over the next ten minutes, I explained the intricacies of visa law.

'If I'd been a structural engineer or dentist, I would have been in clover,' I told him. 'But this country has way too many journalists already, so my chances of staying here as a freelancer were between slim and none.' I drained the last of my Southern Comfort. 'And slim just left town.'

He didn't even crack a smile, but he did look calmer as he said, 'Well, I think it's obvious what we have to do.'

I allowed myself to exhale. He had a solution! Maybe everything was going to be all right.

'I think it's obvious that we have to break up,' he said.

It's safe to say that I was shocked. I knew that my situation was unusual, and maybe I'm an incurable romantic, but it's not like I was married for real, or had leprosy, or seven illegitimate children at home that I'd neglected to mention.

I was also having a horrific case of déjà vu. This couldn't be happening to me again, in another bar, with another man who'd once professed to love me now telling me that he had to bail out.

This time was supposed to be different! JP had already given me his house keys. He'd bought me an electric tooth-brush, not just a regular one, damn it, and I had my own bathroom wall socket, for God's sake. And I'd really begun to believe him when he told me that he loved me. He'd even taken to uttering those three magical words in moments not immediately following mind-blowing orgasms (which as everyone knows don't really count).

'You said that you loved me for who I am, and that I could say anything to you,' I murmured, my eyes filling with tears.

'Yeah, but Cat, there's a limit,' he said. 'I don't want to date someone who's married. I want to settle down myself in the next couple of years!'

'This wouldn't affect us. It's not like I live with him! This is only short term, and I promise you that if we wanted to take our relationship to the next level I would divorce him in a heartbeat so that we could.'

I tightened my grip on his hands. 'I love you. I haven't felt this way about anyone in ages. It just feels so comfortable and right between us.'

'I felt that way too, Catherine.' He raked his fingers through his thick black hair.

My heart sank. 'Felt? As in . . . past tense?'

'Well, I can't be involved with someone whose life is so complicated. Don't you get it?'

'Well, no, not really. Because the truth is that Mark would

14

have been my preferred choice for this marriage even if you and I were more serious. I made the decision months ago that I would never want to do this with a boyfriend because it would put too much strain on the relationship. I've had two friends of mine get married partly for visa reasons, and both times the marriages have fallen apart within a year. When I get married, I want it to be for the right reasons, because I absolutely want to be there with every fibre of my being. Er, I mean, next time, obviously.' I was starting to sweat. This was a disaster.

'And you didn't think to include me in this decision?'

'Honey, I promise I would have, if we had known each other a little bit longer. But I was down to the wire with the visa situation, and the wedding was already planned when I met you. How could I know that everything between us would happen so fast? Can't we work something out?'

He looked as if he might bolt at any second, but fortunately I was saved by the arrival of the waiter, who presented our dishes with a flourish and made a point of explaining every morsel in intricate detail as I dug my thumbnail into the flesh of my palm. I didn't give a shit about the composition of the organic sausages, I just wanted some privacy.

After the waiter left, I tried again to explain my logic. 'I did think about telling you, every day, but I just didn't think it was fair to put that kind of pressure on you this early in our relationship. I think you just have to chalk this one up to really bad timing.'

Suddenly the room went blurry, and the first of the tears that had been welling finally slid down my cheek. I dabbed at the corners with a cocktail napkin, blinked furiously and looked upwards.

Crying in restaurants is an art, and I should know because I've done it enough times. It's horrible because everyone who sees a heterosexual couple speaking in whispered tones suspects that they are breaking up.

The key to scraping back public dignity is to make it seem that I'm crying for reasons unrelated to the guy sitting beside me – that way passers-by would think that I had a dead relative, or just got diagnosed with cancer and my boyfriend was being hugely supportive. They would not, under any circumstances, think that I was a loser who was getting my ass kicked to the kerb yet again. So I forced down a rice ball, using the muscles of my oesophagus to stifle a sob, and almost choked.

'I love you, JP, and I'm so sorry for not telling you sooner, but I'm not going to apologize for who I am. I know I'm not perfect, but sometimes you get dealt some shit cards in life and have to make the best of what you have. Can't you look for something positive in this situation? It's not my dream scenario either, but I'm a believer in dealing with the rough stuff head-on, not hiding from it.'

'I'm sorry, what exactly is the positive side? And why should I care about your position?' He speared a sausage.

Men. I swear most of them could see a relative dismembered by a chainsaw and eat a four-course breakfast the next day. Meanwhile, I can't digest so much as an Altoid when I'm upset. It's so unfair.

I tried again. 'I mean, it's obviously not an ideal situation, but if I hadn't planned what I did, I couldn't have stayed in the country and I would never have met you!' I smiled at him and tried to keep my tone light.

'Maybe that would have been for the best,' he said bitterly. 'What would my friends and family think?'

'Babe, who says we have to tell them?' I pushed the mozzarella around on the plate, suddenly feeling hopeful. We were coming up with a game plan together!

'I can't have people knowing this about me,' he said. 'All I want is a normal life.'

'I want that too! I love you, and I would always be completely faithful to you. In that sense, I'm totally conventional.'

'I don't doubt your loyalty, Cat, but I mean, your job, the column, and now this . . . it's just all too much. It's not worth the drama.' He pushed his chair back. 'I should get going.'

'Honey, you don't mean that,' I said, stung. But then I started to feel a bit pissed off. Why did he have to drag my column into this, especially when he had previously raved about how proud he was of me? 'Look, I know that you are upset now, and I totally understand,' I sputtered. 'But please, just for a second, try to put yourself in my shoes. Things happen in life. But if you're saying you don't care enough to make it worth at least trying to work through this problem together, then I guess that's all I need to know.'

From the beginning, one of the things that I had found most attractive about JP was the fact that he brought structure to my life. But I wanted real stability, not the kind based entirely on appearances. He talked about loving me 'no matter what', but faced with an actual crisis his cool-as-a-cucumber façade was crumbling like a house of cards. And I couldn't help noticing that his main concern seemed to be what other people would think.

'I don't know, Cat. I do love you, but . . .'

'If you really love someone, there's just "I love you",' I insisted. 'There's no "but" at the end.'

'I can't handle this situation,' he said. 'You have too much baggage.'

'Please think about it,' I said, hating myself for begging but unable to help it. It seemed so unfair: five minutes ago we'd had this idyllic relationship, until I told him the truth.

Looking around at other couples holding hands in the buttery lighting of the bar, I allowed myself to wonder bitterly what secrets they were holding back. Maybe the petite bottle blonde in the skinny jeans and turtleneck had had a secret abortion, and the curvy girl feeding bruschetta to the older Hugh Grant look-alike checked his mobile phone every time he turned his back. Yet they all looked as happy as pigs in shit. Maybe Victoria was right, and the fantasy world was best after all. Why couldn't I have kept my goddamned mouth shut?

He threw money down on the table, said, 'I'm sorry,' and was gone.

I watched him walk away, letting the tears flow freely now, and then slumped forward to let my head rest in my hands.

Suddenly, the copious quantity of drink that had been sloshing around in my anxious gut all afternoon expanded outward, and when I stood up the lining of my delicate dress ripped very audibly.

I whipped around quickly. 'That wasn't what it sounded like,' I said to the couple next to me, who looked at me in alarm. 'My dress just tore.' They probably saw my tear-streaked face and thought that I got left at the altar for being flatulent.

I staggered out of Shoreditch House and desperately checked my phone for a text from JP telling me that he'd changed his mind. No such luck. But I found a message from Mark: 'Hi, we are back at my flat. Everyone asking where the old ball and chain is . . . you in or out?'

I went out into the alleyway and hailed a minicab. This night had to get better. Because it definitely couldn't get any worse.

# THREE

Once, when I was eight, my dad took me to an illegal cockfight. He worked in a hospital as an administrator, and one night a guy he knew got rushed into the emergency room with chest pains.

Two hours later, he died, but not before begging my dad to take custody of his fighting cock, which was aptly named Champ.

Despite the fact that the psychotic chicken woke everyone up at 5 a.m. with his crowing, Dad had a soft spot for him. So after taking custody, Dad had to explain to the guys running the fights that Champ was retiring.

But they were persuasive and insisted that the chicken have one last retirement fight. I'm not sure why my dad took me with him, but he had always loved boxing. So did I, but as my dad always pointed out, the men chose to pull on their gloves and climb into the ring. The poor animals had no choice.

I remember everything about that fight: going into the basement of a backstreet bar, where beer tabs crunched in the sawdust under my feet and the ring was spattered with blood. The cocks unleashed hell, and feathers flew until one of them stopped twitching. It was probably the most brutal thing I've ever seen.

But the bloodletting I saw that night wasn't a million miles from the viciousness that my friends inflict on their loved ones' exes after a break-up. After months of telling me how great JP was, they turned on him after realizing that he'd broken my heart.

I know that they are biased, but, God, I love them at times like these.

By the time I got to Mark's flat near Earl's Court, the party was in full swing, and JP had gone, in one fell swoop – after an update text I'd sent en route – from being a nice guy who everyone adored to 'a boring, pretentious twat'.

Mark was wearing a toga, which appeared to be nothing more than a hastily draped bed-sheet, and blasting house music from his computer. Victoria, Russell and Amy were bumping and grinding in the living room, and the girls were so wasted that they were dropping ash on the already decimated carpet. Amy had draped some ivy that looked like it came from outside the house around her head.

'Here. Drink it. Now.' Victoria handed me a glass tumbler full of green liquid. Thinking it was a half-melted frozen margarita, I downed the whole thing in one gulp. Then I saw the bottle on the counter with the menacing-looking eye staring back at me. The green stuff had been absinthe. I knew then that I was totally screwed.

My head was spinning, but luckily the party was winding down. Before long only Mark, Russell, who had a notably sculpted chest, Amy and Victoria remained.

'So, Cat, you must have done almost everything,' Russell said. 'Is there any fantasy that hasn't come true?'

I pulled a sorry-for-myself face: 'To be honest, my hottest

sex ever was with JP, because we were in love and I felt really comfortable. At least, I thought we were.'

'Look, you have all tomorrow to be depressed,' Mark said, putting his hands on my shoulders and looking me straight in the eye. 'But you have to be thankful for what you have. As of now, you're a legal resident, baby!'

Victoria and Amy gave me a hug, because their cab was waiting outside. But I stayed, because I wasn't in the mood to go home alone. Besides, after running on adrenalin all day, I was wired.

I couldn't help smiling as the three of us sat down to play 'I never', the drinking game where you have to take a shot every time a player names something that you have done. There was obviously a conspiracy going on between Mark and Russell, because they kept targeting their phrases to ensure that I imbibed the maximum amount: i.e. 'I never slept with my French teacher in high school' or 'I never took Viagra'.

'This is SO not fair,' I slurred.

'You have to admit, Cat, you have done a lot in the name of research for the column,' Russell said. 'Come on, there must be something that you haven't done!'

'I'll tell you what my hottest fantasy is, but it's really dirty,' I said, rubbing my knees together. The absinthe was making me seriously horny, and despite the day I'd had I could feel myself getting turned on. 'I remember there were a few times when I saw you coming out of the shower, and I fantasized about you letting the towel drop to the floor, and what would happen if you came into the bedroom with Mark and me.'

Mark and I have had plenty of racy encounters in the past, and though we're mainly platonic friends now, we know each

other's secrets and fantasies. I knew that my chances of luring
Mark into what he affectionately called 'the wrong kind of
threesome' were remote at best. But I'll admit that my reply
was hopefully suggestive. You never know . . .

So, I was heartbroken, but I figured maybe a bacchanal
night would be just what the doctor ordered. After all, when
was I going to get another golden opportunity like this one,
with two people I trusted completely, when we were all single?
It would be like winning the lottery.

It is one of the top life lessons I've learned from Beatles
and Stones lyrics: right under 'You can't always get what you
want' is 'If you can't be with the one you love, love the one
you're with'.

'Why not?' Mark said, laughing. 'It's marital sex, so technically, morally, we're in the clear.'

'I'm not so sure about that.' I laughed back.

I wondered if the Ecstasy was still having an effect, because
even though I wasn't looking directly at his crotch I could
spot the bulge in his trousers from the corner of my eye. The
more I tried not to look, the more my eyes were drawn – and
the more flushed I got.

'Well, it's been a long day, boys. So I'll tell you what, I'm
going to go and take a hot shower. Come and join me if
you feel like it. I'll leave it up to you.' I gave them my best
pout over my naked shoulder and sauntered into Russell's
bathroom.

Unfortunately, it didn't look like the movies, where triple-
headed showers rain down on pristine marble surfaces – his
showerhead had a cracked, yellowing hose and the only accessory for bathroom fun was a half-melted bar of green soap.

Not very sexy. So I quickly scurried across the hall into Mark's bathroom, which was scrubbed clean despite the fact that he's very messy. I guess his cleaner must have come that day.

Dirty sex should be limited to the acts performed, never the surfaces. No matter how deviant my behaviour gets, doing anything near a pile of crumpled laundry can totally kill the mood for me.

I put the water on as hot as I could stand, opened the glass door and stepped inside the shower. It was definitely roomy enough for three, though it might be a bit of a tight squeeze.

I wet my hair and lathered up, starting to massage the body wash into my D-cup breasts before soaping further down by sliding my hand between my legs. As I closed my eyes and felt the water beating down on me, I could sense the stress of the day slipping away.

The door clicked and I was aware of Mark stepping in past me and kissing the back of my neck.

After a few moments I saw Russell appear in the bathroom doorway, naked to the waist. He still seemed a bit uncertain, and I knew that, much as I might love it, there was going to be no guy-on-guy action.

Social conventions really annoy me sometimes. I know that even if I didn't have lesbian tendencies, which I do, I would have no problem being titillated in an FFM three-way, probably partially because it's socially acceptable for women to swing both ways.

Meanwhile, men whose gazes linger a bit too long at the urinal get given a hard time (no pun intended). Bisexual men are viewed as gays who haven't left the closet, which is a great shame given the range of sexual behaviour throughout history.

Lots of straight men in ancient Greece and Rome took male lovers, and it was something of an upper-class phenomenon. But I didn't want to debate ancient Roman sexual practices, I wanted to get fucked.

'Do you want to come in?' I asked Russell, feeling myself getting wetter in more ways than one. I was a bit shy about all this, but at that moment my horniness outweighed my embarrassment. I pressed my breasts against the glass, and as Mark's hand reached between my legs I could see Russell unzip his trousers and pull his cock out. Without wanting to sound clichéd, it was a bit shorter but much thicker than Mark's. I turned my head and kissed Mark, not sure what to do next. Somehow I knew that I had to take the lead, so I opened the door and told Russell to come inside.

I closed my eyes, stayed facing Russell and focused on kissing him. I sensed that he was less practised than Mark and since I'd never kissed him before I relished the feeling of his tongue exploring my mouth.

He kissed down my throat and started sucking my nipples as the water poured down on all three of us. I pulled his head into my chest as Mark continued to kiss the back of my neck in the spot that he knows drives me crazy, while reaching around to massage my engorged clit at the same time.

Russell was pushing my breasts together so that he could continue to suck my nipples, which felt heavenly, and I loved the sensation of his callused hands groping my breasts (though I fleetingly wondered how a white-collar architect got such rough hands, something told me that now wasn't the time to ask).

I think the boys were trying to avoid being at eye level

with each other, because the next thing I knew Mark was kneeling behind me, licking me out from behind with his thumb massaging my G-spot and his index finger on my clit. Not wanting Russell to feel left out, I kept kissing him and stroking his cock, and could feel from his urgent moans that he was getting very close to coming. So was I, but the cramped and slightly awkward conditions were going to make this a bit unrealistic. 'It's a little bit squished in here, isn't it?' I said and we all laughed.

I didn't want the action to end there, so gently suggested that we move to the bedroom, and grabbed a bottle of baby oil that Mark kept in his medicine cabinet on the way out.

We all climbed on to the bed, and I cupped Russell's face in my hands and kissed him, while Mark fished a condom out of the bedside dresser drawer. 'Sweetie, I don't think that I'm going to be able to have full sex with both of you guys,' I said. 'And I want to make sure that everyone is cool with that.' Having two men at the same time was one of my ultimate fantasies, though I've always found the idea rather threatening. Luckily these guys were my friends so I felt totally comfortable taking things at my own pace.

'Whatever you want,' Russell said. 'Let's just play around and have a good time.'

I'm always shocked when my girlfriends tell me that they rate performing oral sex on their partners as a chore somewhere behind folding laundry, because I genuinely love giving blow jobs. I licked the tip of Russell's cock, teasing him, while Mark continued to lick me out from behind. I could feel my orgasm building as Russell grunted and thrusted all the way into the back of my throat.

Suddenly I broke the embrace, and turned around to face Mark. 'I want you to fuck me until I come,' I said. Mark's wall is lined with a full-length mirror, so when I returned to sucking Russell's cock I could see Mark spread my legs from behind, and push into me. The naughty sight of two ripped men moaning and getting completely turned on by me was one of the most exciting feelings I had ever had.

Sex with JP had been amazing, but this was like starring in my own live porno. I could feel the inside walls of my pussy tightening as Mark slammed into me while still massaging my clit, and Russell's rhythmic movements grew more insistent. Then, as my orgasm started to build again, I felt Russell spurt into my mouth. Mark pulled my hips to him as he came inside me, while my contractions seemed to go on for ever in an overwhelming orgasm.

Eventually, I came to, and lounged back on the bed, a man on each side of me.

'Wow, three people having a simultaneous orgasm,' I said, wiping the sweat from my forehead. 'Seriously, what are the odds?' Highly aware that I was wedged between two naked, very sexy flatmates who had probably just seen each other's penises for the first time, I steered the conversation over to the house repairs. 'So, Russell, have you talked to those contractors yet?' I asked. We made small talk for a few minutes until he kissed me on the forehead and went off to his room to sleep.

Mark and I lay there together for half an hour, until I could hear his measured breathing turn to snoring. I turned and saw the digital clock read 5.12 a.m. The sun was already starting to break through the clouds.

I didn't have a change of clothes and Mark's sweats were

five sizes too large, so, lacking another option, I slipped into my wedding dress again and walked out to the communal back garden.

Sitting on the wet grass in my ripped wedding dress, I realized that I eventually want a monogamous, traditional marriage. But in a strange way, the intimate encounter with such a close friend as Mark – built on trust – had reinforced my sense that my ideal relationship will be based on how we feel about each other, not outward appearances.

I had to laugh, though, because this wasn't how I had envisioned my first night as a married woman. Then again, it certainly wasn't the first time that I'd broken all the rules.

# FOUR

Since my break-up with JP, I'd been doing a lot of soul-searching. I loved him, and even though I knew in my heart of hearts that I'd had to be honest, and I think he walked away too easily, I couldn't help replaying our conversation in my mind and wishing for a time machine to transport me back to the moment before I'd opened my big mouth.

Maybe he was right, and I should have told him sooner. But there was no going back now. I had to accept the consequences of my actions, and after two polite texts and an email elaborating on what I'd said in more detail, and asking him to consider meeting me for coffee, all with no reply, I knew it was time to let go.

I was also stressing, because I was about to deliver the final manuscript of my first book to my publishers. They wanted ideas for a second, and I was feeling so heartbroken that I seriously considered calling the next instalment 'I'm Going to Die Alone'. Instead of a cheeky and sultry half-naked illustration of me, the front cover would feature my torso being stripped of flesh by Victoria's cats, which would have turned feral after watching me perish from a heart attack (probably brought on by ingesting several tonnes of Ben and Jerry's).

I knew that I was being overly dramatic, but I couldn't

help feeling distraught. The first few days after a break-up are horrific, and after my one sexual indulgence I felt I had to go through a total dating detox.

I knew that I would pull out of my sadness, because a) I refuse to be that much of a fucking cliché and b) I believe that, in limited doses, wallowing in misery can actually be therapeutic. It allows women to cry and move on, while men who dull the pain by drinking and drowning in pussy find that the ghosts of past relationships come back to haunt them months later.

The thing that's most difficult at the end of the relationship is not just letting go of the actual person, it's the hopes and dreams of an idyllic future that you had wrapped up in them – in my case, in a dark-haired, six-foot-one-and-a-half-inch package.

But even in the depths of despair, I amused myself with the idea of my mum having to go through my belongings after the cats ate me and finding my stash of lesbian anal porn and my twenty-four-carat gold-plated glass dildos.

I had to recover and learn to love again, or risk the post-mortem horror of Mum sifting through my butt plugs at a later date. It was just that simple.

During the early post-break-up stages, I can't stomach saccharine chick flicks or clichéd romantic comedies. There's only one channel that fits the bill: the Sci Fi Channel's horror movie marathon. If I'm feeling nostalgic for a bit of couple time, I check out classic flicks like *Friday the 13th* or *Halloween* where sex equals death – it's always the virgin who survives until the end.

When I thought about how I might one day have had

children with JP, *Children of the Corn* was the best bet. There's nothing like watching a creepy red-headed child on a murderous rampage with a sickle to cure any residual broodiness.

For once, being celibate wasn't difficult. I wasn't even masturbating, and had actually replaced my remote control batteries with the ones from my vibrator, rather than the other way around.

The only hot action I was getting was from the Domino's pizza guy. I had a simple rule: once he started to recognize my voice when I asked for a Hawaiian pizza with jalapeño peppers, it would be time to pull myself together and get out of the house.

Letting go of JP was especially tough for me because I had allowed myself to believe that he could be my destiny.

A few months before I started dating him I had literally placed a cosmic order for him. I know it sounds cheesy, but after reading a magazine article about Noel Edmonds getting his dream job after he read *The Cosmic Ordering Service: A Guide to Realising Your Dreams* as recommended by his reflex-ologist, I scrawled my 'order' on the back of a cocktail napkin. The idea is to write down a wish list of things that you want to come true and submit it to the Cosmos and wait for it to happen.

So, shortly before I met JP, I wrote: 'at least five years older, over six foot, not married and sane!' as a joke. On some sub-conscious level, when he pulled up in a taxi in the pouring rain just as I was leaving a party for Gordon Brown, I'd believed that he was my knight in shining armour – brandishing an umbrella instead of a sword.

31

Like most poor souls deluded in the first flush of love, I thought that our meeting was fated.

I left a message on my political journalist friend Michael's voicemail: 'I'm wondering, if I placed a cosmic order, do I get to ask for my money back? Call me if you're around for drinks tonight.'

I had just been reading that hiring a 'sober best friend' is the must-have accessory for the post-rehab celebrity who wants to stay on the wagon. The pal – not a real friend, in fact, but a well-paid member of one's entourage – accompanies the Hollywood wild child day and night and encourages them to stay clean.

I think that we need the same thing post-break-up: the 'sexually sober friend' who stops us from toxic behaviour, such as drunk-dialling an ex or – worse still – having sex with them.

Michael also understood that the last thing I needed after being dumped was to spend time with loved-up couples. He's always the one who motivates me to hit the gym instead of crying alone and he's my walker at parties. His cynicism and wit are a breath of fresh air. But since his dry sense of humour can cut close to the bone, I also invited Amy along, figuring that I could use her aura of positivity to counterbalance his bitchy comments.

She's a glass half-full girl who is sensible and balanced. When I'm depressed I see the glass as half-full too. The trouble is, I usually try to empty it as quickly as possible.

'Cosmic ordering, huh?' he said, laughing as we downed pomegranate margaritas at Crazy Homies, my favourite local

Mexican joint. 'Apparently you forgot to include balls on your list of must-haves.'

I tried to turn the subject of conversation to Amy's recent promotion at her film production company, but couldn't concentrate on anything else and within three drinks I was in tears. 'I can't stop thinking about him,' I told them. 'I really thought that this relationship had a chance of working out.'

'Give him a bit of time,' Amy said, putting her arm around my shoulder and pulling me into a half hug. 'Maybe he's just in shock and trying to get his head around things. Who knows how he'll feel in a week?'

'Look, I don't mean to sound harsh, but I don't think he's coming back,' Michael said. 'And anyway, why would you want someone like that? If he can't handle a bit of a legal hurdle, how would he cope with a really serious problem, like cancer?'

'Thanks, that's a cheerful thought,' I said, checking my phone – yet again – for an apologetic text. Of course, I had no missed calls. 'I guess what I really need is for some horrible illness to strike, so that, if I suddenly got leprosy or all my hair fell out, this break-up stuff would pale in comparison!'

Amy shot him a warning look, but Michael was ruthless. 'All I'm saying is, the guy may have loved you. But he didn't love you *enough*. Time to move on.'

Amy signalled the waiter for another round and turned on Michael. 'That's really not helpful right now, Michael. I think it's totally normal to be sad, Cat. But tell me, why are you so devastated about this guy in particular?'

I dried my eyes and took a sip of margarita. 'What do you mean?'

'Just that there were things about JP that rightly concerned you. He seemed very set in his ways—'

'Well, I did marry someone else,' I said. 'That could have played a role in this.'

'I think you should look for someone a bit more open-minded. We create our own reality, you know.'

'Great,' I said, laughing and drying my tears at the same time. 'For my next romance I'll have to remember to create one where I don't get totally screwed over.'

'No, seriously,' said Amy. 'You only live once so it's important to take the right path. Life should be a process of self-discovery. And people should use whatever tools allow them the best guidance, be it therapy, self-help, spiritual advice, or whatever.'

'Yeah, whatever,' said Michael. 'Forget all that self-help shit. As we only live once you might as well get back out there and enjoy it.'

But I wondered whether Amy did have a point. I wanted someone who loved me the way I was, both the lost little girl part and the dirty slut part (and sometimes, in the right lacy pink baby-doll dress and black patent heels, both at once).

If it was true that my unconscious thoughts, emotions and actions attracted positive and negative experiences, was there something wrong about me?

Just then, my phone vibrated. It was Mark, asking if I was 'up for it'.

'I told you, sweetie, last night was the last time,' I wrote back. 'Welcome to the wonderful world of a sexless marriage.'

I caught a glimpse of myself in the loo mirror and – determined to channel Amy's positive thinking – thought I wouldn't kick myself out of bed. I've got a slim figure and glossy brown hair. And these days it's coupled with a well-cut fringe which accommodates my freaky wide-spaced eyes, which were the butt of jokes in high school.

And yet, the only suitable candidate for sex on the horizon was my own husband. Clearly, something had to give. I had to stop feeling sorry for myself and get to the bottom of what was really bothering me.

# FIVE

I'm always amazed by the fact that, no matter how much of a train wreck my own love life is, I'm constantly getting letters from people asking me for advice or praising my upfront attitude towards dating. But occasionally my email turns up something more sinister.

Normally, I brush off hate mail. I've long accepted that a thick skin is a necessary accessory to this job, and I'm secure enough in myself to handle it: besides, most of my mail is overwhelmingly supportive. But every once in a while, I get something so idiotic that I have to share it. After finishing this week's instalment of the column, I checked my emails, and found one that was pretty disturbing.

> No man will ever settle down with you, you do realize that, don't you? Read some evolutionary psychology.
>
> You, my dear, are what is known as a fling. Sperm is cheap, so there is no reason why a man would pass up the opportunity to have sex with a slut – but he would never marry her. Men will read your articles and run a mile.
>
> Now, most genetic sluts were selected out by evolution over the past hundreds of thousands of years. Men never settle down with sluts because the cuckoldry threat is far

*too great – they can never be sure the children they are raising are their own genes. Hence the Madonna-whore complex. So for 99% of human history, women who slept around would usually not have the resources to raise their children to adulthood, as no man would assist them or marry them, so their children died off and eventually their slut genes were selected out, i.e. limited chastity was selected among human females. The welfare state has made this more problematic, as women who sleep around and have children without a man can just marry the state, but in the generality it still holds, and men would never ever settle down with a slut. But some slut genes probably endured.*

Now, I didn't want to believe the vitriolic ranting of a guy who, in the words of another loyal reader who got in touch after I'd posted the correspondence on my blog, 'probably wanks in his mum's basement reading your material and would crumble to dust at the sight of a real woman', but in my post-break-up fragile state, I was bummed.

Logically, I knew that the right guy would understand what a loyal girl I am and not judge me on the basis of my columns. He would be proud of my success, not resent me for it.

Still, a nagging self-doubt ate away at me as I thought back to JP. Was my unflinching honesty poisoning my relationships? Maybe it wasn't just a question of men leaving me? Perhaps I was doing something to bring it on? Since I love investigative journalism, I wanted to know why.

I've never been a fan of one-size-fits-all dating advice. When I get letters asking what the 'secret' is to pulling men, I'm tempted to add the same caveat that appears on the bottom of the screen at midnight during those 'make £1,000 a week from your living room' infomercials: 'Individual results may vary'. That's why I wrote a dating memoir – not a manual.

But of course I can still understand the temptation to test the waters of a guidebook when it comes to finding a soul-mate, especially in the depths of despair. Like diet books, dating guides often seem to rely on self-loathing to sell lots of copies. Trying to adhere to a strict set of rules is probably as fruitless – and miserable – for most of us as for the four-foot-ten pear-shaped woman who thinks that the cabbage soup diet will give her legs like Naomi Campbell's. And yet, we do it anyway, for the same reason as we devoured the story of Cinderella finding Prince Charming. We desperately want to believe.

Besides, women are into punishing themselves – especially when it comes to their looks and their love lives. It's never ceased to amaze me that men, even Ricky Gervais clones with bad comb-overs, generally leave the house winking at themselves in the mirror and thinking that they look pretty good. Meanwhile, women berate themselves for not looking like Elle Macpherson clones and pinch their imaginary five pounds of fat. I think it's because men compare themselves to their best self – say, the body they had when they were boxing at university, for example. Women, on the other hand, compare themselves to the idealized perfection of airbrushed celebrities in magazines. Then they beat themselves up when they fail to match it.

I felt my time for watching horror films and eating ice cream should be coming to an end, and I needed a new project anyway. In spite of my reservations about dating guides, I decided to see once and for all what useful advice, if any, they had to offer. If nothing else it would be interesting background research for my column.

As I thought about it, a bigger idea began to take shape. I would set myself a self-styled research task. I would be receptive to whatever different forms of relationship guidance and self-exploration came along. Instead of resisting guidance, I'd test everything out and assess whether it had any substance. I'd be the Bruce Parry of the dating trenches – bring it on! But I wouldn't just blindly accept the different advice proffered. Instead, I would subject it to a searing investigative critique worthy of a Pulitzer!

Now all I needed was a name for my mission. I chewed a pencil then a smirk spread across my face. I fired up my Mac and opened a new folder – title: *The Anti-Rules*. Just pissing about, I continued with: *agent – Catherine Townsend; status – undercover; field – the dating trenches; mission – journalistic research, self-exploration, understanding what makes men tick, getting Amy off my back, finding my destiny etc, etc, etc!* Okay, it was all quite tongue in cheek but there was something genuinely pleasing about my new project. Maybe I'd even find all the answers and a new lease of life. If not, at least it would be a fun research project to get me out of my lull.

I cleaned out the self-help book section of the Waterstone's at Notting Hill Gate. I wore sunglasses (telling myself that I was channelling Audrey Hepburn rather than simply covering my embarrassment), and when the cashier shot me a sympathetic look as she scanned *He's Just Not That Into You, Women Who Love Too Much, Men Are from Mars, Women Are from*

*Venus* and *The Rules* all in one go, I was ready with my justi-
fication: 'I'm a journalist, and I'm researching a book.'

Then I smiled in an ironic way that suggested that I was
fine, thank you very much, in a contented and settled relationship and not at all freaked out about feral cats eating my
disembodied corpse.

I paid for the books, and noticed that she double-layered
the semi-transparent plastic bags the way they do at the chemist
when I'm buying laxatives and tampons, to 'make sure that it
isn't too heavy for one bag'. Yeah, right, I thought, but still
appreciated the gesture. I cheered myself up by reminding
myself that the research project would be fun.

Thumbing through the relationship guides later that night,
I realized what pissed me off most about them: they encourage
passivity, and assume that anyone who has managed to convince
an upright-walking mammal to walk down the aisle with them
is someone to be revered.

The mother of all dating guides is *The Rules*, which caused
a frenzy when it was published in 1995 because it recommended that women go back to 1950s rules when it came to
dating – basically, not agreeing to a Saturday night date if the
object of your affection calls after Wednesday, acting busy
when you are not, and turning the entire courtship into a
game.

I've always hated *The Rules*, not really for the premise that
women must be passive (though I hate that as well), but more
for the authors' patronizing attitude towards anyone who isn't
married. One drunken night, Victoria and I had ceremoni-
ally burned a copy, and I had taken perverse pleasure in
watching Ellen Fein's face melt. The bitch got divorced, and

instead of admitting that she's human and fallible, blamed her crumbling marriage on her book tour – it seems that she forgot her own rule about surrendering her personality and dreams and being a constant yes woman!

The point is: just because someone is married does not make them a relationship expert who has 'won' some sort of game. Don't get me wrong, I would definitely go to someone like my grandma, who was married to my granddad for fifty happy years, for words of wisdom, but *The Rules*' reasoning seems to infer that even people suffering in miserable marriages that last for years are somehow superior to single people, which is totally illogical.

I wasn't going to pretend to have a life and 'act busy' in order to get a man. No, I wanted actually to have a thrilling life, and let the right guy come along. But in my temporary, anchorless state, I did find it reassuring to have a plan of action in researching what these guides had to say for themselves.

After an evening's reading in bed, the only thing I found that sounded reasonable so far was the bald, slightly folksy American psychologist Dr Phil's suggestion: doing something called a 'relationship autopsy' to find out what went wrong. The idea is that I try to examine past relationships and find out what sealed their fate, including the problems that I had a role in creating.

To go forward, maybe I needed to look backward to spot the patterns that spiralled my past relationships out of control. If so, I knew where I had to start: with Jean-Claude, my mad, French first love, on whom I hadn't laid eyes for a decade.

Our break-up happened in a very public spat in Charles

de Gaulle airport after he had suddenly proposed to me. I gave him back the diamond ring and hopped on the next flight to New York. I hadn't seen him since, and the ocean between us, along with the language barrier, had always stopped me from contacting him on a regular basis.

After all that, it was surprisingly easy. I Googled him, got his work email address and sent a chatty message telling him that I was coming to Paris on business in a few weeks' time and asking him if he wanted to meet for coffee.

I was thrilled when he instantly replied that he would love to see me, and signed off with 'big kisses'. I would have read more into it but I know that the French send big kisses to everyone, even their worst enemies. Speaking of which, I couldn't help myself signing off rather differently as I fired off a response to the Darwin dickhead on my blog: *If anything, female promiscuity encourages survival of the fittest; do some research on sperm competition – you misogynistic WANKER!!*

# SIX

As the train raced through the French countryside, I sipped a glass of chilled Laurent-Perrier and thought about how far I'd come since my first love.

I had met Jean-Claude, a dead ringer for the actor Robert Downey Jr, when I was seventeen and working as a waitress in Paris. I'd needed an escape hatch from my tiny hometown in Georgia after my affair with my college French teacher got a bit too hot to handle. I was only having a fling, but my teacher seemed to have developed an infatuation and was waxing poetic about getting married after graduation.

Even though he was in his late twenties at the time, he was behaving like a lovesick teenager. Despite my repeated warnings that we were about to get busted, he'd also started taking stupid chances, like coming to my house in the afternoons in a town so small that licence plates were as familiar to friends as phone numbers.

Sitting in the front row during French class, I'd always fantasized about Paris, where gorgeous architecture and winding streets would take the place of matchbox painted houses in identikit suburbs. Like every American girl, I wanted to find love in Paris, with a real, cultured man who wasn't either a spotty teenager or grading my exams.

I found out about a new exchange programme with a lycée

in Epernay, which sounded incredibly sophisticated because it was in the Champagne region of France. Having no idea what I was in for, I immediately signed up, and exactly eleven days later I was on a flight from Atlanta to France.

But during my first week of classes, I realized that I'd made a horrible mistake. This wasn't an Ernest Hemingway experience where a writer finds herself. This was solitary confinement. And it was miserable. As an American, I suppose I'd idiotically assumed that everyone would speak English, so I was totally isolated by my appalling attempts to butcher the French language.

Which was no surprise, since my French in the previous year had focused more on tonguing the teacher than concentrating on the ins and outs of grammar.

At the same time, I was mesmerized by the French students: the brazen way they would sit on each other's laps and let their hands wander over each other in the hallways (meanwhile, holding hands was frowned upon at my college), the girls' effortless scarf-tying abilities and the blasé attitudes towards sex. Back at my college, I'd been the bad girl, and now I was surrounded by debauchery. Looking back, I can see why Victoria has always told me that she's so proud of her French mother's influence.

But the upsides of frisky Frenchmen were soon outweighed by the downsides. The sky was grey, the cliquey girls excluded me and while I had finally blossomed into popularity at my college in Georgia, here I was starting to feel like even more of a loser than when I inadvertently got a mullet haircut in elementary school. Once again, I was the outcast.

I had only one friend, a Dutch guy named Hans who was

a gap-year teacher and spoke perfect English. 'Come on, it can't be as bad as you think,' he teased me over yet another watery yoghurt, the only food I could bring myself to digest in the cafeteria since an ill-fated experience with *boudin noir* literally made me retch into my plate. 'You have to know a few French phrases. You are a smart girl, give it a try!'

'Well, I do know one; it's from a disco song . . . how does it go: "*Voulez-vous coucher avec moi ce soir?*"'

He put down his fork. 'Seriously? That's the only phrase you know?'

'That's it,' I said.

'Well, you were right then. It is as bad as you thought!' He laughed heartily while I put my head in my hands.

I leaned over the table. 'I have to tell you something, but you have to promise not to breathe a word.'

'Sure, Cat. What's going on?'

'Well, Hans, I'm breaking out tonight and I need your help.'

'What the hell are you talking about?'

'There's a 10.43 train tonight that leaves the city centre for Paris, so after the lights go out at 10 and you do your rounds I need you to prop open the door to my hall from the outside. Then I'm leaving.'

'Cat, this is crazy!'

'Look, all you have to do is leave a book or something in the door when you are doing the final check. Then go to the guys' halls and make sure that you are in your room talking to someone when I'm leaving. That way you'll have an alibi and won't get into trouble.' Tears filled my eyes. 'I've really got to get the hell out of here. You're my only hope.'

He sighed. 'I'm not worried about myself; I'm worried about you. What are you going to do when you get to Paris? Where will you live? And we've already established how, sorry to say it but, shit your French is . . .'

I cracked a smile. 'I've got one phrase under my belt, and it may be more useful than you think. Either way, I'm going over the wall tonight.'

So, at exactly 10.03, I crept through the lime green and white tiled utilitarian halls for the last time, dragging my little wheelie suitcase behind me. Hans had left the glass side door open, as promised, so I slipped it open and stepped out into the cold night air, my heart pounding in my chest. The door clicked behind me. There was no way back, and it hit me at that moment that this was the most insane thing I'd ever done in my life.

Even through my steamy affair with my teacher, I'd maintained the pretence in school of being a good girl, the slut with the perfect grade point average.

Now I was a rebel. I was going off piste into my new life, and it was terrifying – but also thrilling.

Suddenly I felt a hand on my shoulder, and stifled a scream as I turned around to find Hans.

'Jesus! Don't you ever watch horror movies? You never creep up behind someone and put a hand on their shoulder without saying something first! You scared the living shit out of me!'

'I'm sorry,' he whispered, 'but I just wanted to make sure you get out okay. It's going to be tough getting over that wall alone. And to give you this.'

He put a bottle of Southern Comfort in my hands. 'For good luck.'

I gave him a hug as we walked to the brick wall and iron gate. 'Are you sure that this is a good idea?' he asked me.

'Honestly? No. But I've reached the point of no return on this one, and I can't go back now. I'm going to Paris!'

I climbed on Hans's back and he gave me a boost up the wall, then handed me my wheelie case. As I threw it over he walked back to the main building, and I jumped down to the grass below. It was about a six-foot drop, but I landed softly.

I must have tripped an alarm, though, because suddenly I heard a piercing siren, and the iron gate started to open while a yellow light flashed. I grabbed my case and ran like hell – pausing only to grab the bottle of booze that Hans had slipped through the gate's bars, kind of like when Indiana Jones always grabs his hat.

I made it to town and was on the night train to Paris with two minutes to spare. I had exactly 200 US dollars and three changes of clothes with me, so I took a few discreet belts out of my bottle as the train sped through the night.

# SEVEN

Once I got to Paris, I checked myself into a cheap hotel and put in a grovelling phone call to my mum. She was amazingly understanding about my urge for adventure and said she'd give me two days before the money ran out to find a job and a flat. If that failed she was hauling my ass back to Georgia. Bless her, she even called the lycée to square things with them.

I spent the next two days determinedly scouring the 'wanted' ads at the American Church near the Eiffel Tower. Despite the fact that I spoke no French, a pseudo-Tex-Mex joint called the Mustang Café was hiring, and they were desperate for 'American' waiting staff who weren't actually Scandinavian.

On the plus side, being easy on the eye and having a Southern accent gave me the edge, but the brutal downside was that I had to work from 7 p.m. to 5 a.m. five nights a week.

Every dinnertime, usually after I asked the customers if they wanted 'blankets with their nachos' or something equally random, hilarity ensued.

I spent my days off exploring the city, and in intensive French classes. But my real education came at night, mainly post-midnight after the place turned into a disco, and I learned bad chat-up lines. I soon realized that the flowery language of

love I'd so romanticized was just the same lame pick-up crap
delivered in a cute accent.

Still, I'd never had so much male attention in my life. I
had five boyfriends, one for each night of the week I worked,
and the place would get so crazy that on more than one occasion there were several in the restaurant at the same time. And
I was definitely a quick learner when it came to talking dirty
in French.

I saw all the relationships as casual flings, because I couldn't
speak enough of the language to progress things further, and
not having a first language in common made it much easier
to lie, shrug sweetly and blame everything on miscommuni-
cation. Though I thoroughly enjoyed the new-found freedom
and anonymity of taking lovers, I didn't love any of them.

The night I met Jean-Claude, I was in hell. It was the
hottest day of the year, 21 June, and because we had no air-
conditioning the kitchen was already like a sauna by the time
I arrived at 6 p.m. (I always had dinner at the restaurant, being
so broke that it was my one meal of the day.)

The crazy Colombian chef, Sylvio, was already throwing
knives at the wall and screaming that there were too many
people, plus something about a government conspiracy
involving vats of meat (at least I think that's what he said. To
tell the truth I was never 100 per cent sure).

I was already miserable. In addition to the infernal weather,
my period was due and I could feel the sweat trickling down
my back and gluing my thin white cotton T-shirt (standard
issue, courtesy of the management) to my bloated skin. It was
the Fête de la Musique, a day where everyone is allowed to
play music in the streets. It sounds great in theory, but once

I'd served three or four guitar-strumming non-tipping hippies who stayed for two hours after ordering a glass of water, I was so over the festival.

Marie, the Swedish hostess, came up to me while I was cleaning menus. 'Catherine,' she said, 'I have a problem with one of the customers in my section.' I looked over and saw the man she was pointing to, who to my shock was the actor Robert Downey Jr. He looked gorgeous, like he'd finally kicked the heroin habit, so I offered to sort things out.

When I approached the table and heard him cursing in French, my heart sank. He was just an average French guy, but he was absolutely beautiful. I flashed him a smile, and stood up straighter to accentuate my breasts. 'Excuse me, sir, *quel est le problème?*'

'The beer,' he said. 'I ordered a Budweiser, and it came in an Amstel glass.'

Jean-Claude and I would laugh about this later, but at the time I didn't know that his friend Pierre, sitting beside him, was the president of Budweiser, which was doing a promotion at the bar that night, and I could feel my irritation grow that he would complain about something so stupid.

Gesturing to the packed bar around me, I tried to smile. 'Well, as you can see, we're totally full and one of our dishwashers is broken,' I said, in French. 'Is there something wrong with your beer?'

He looked down at the glass, and back up at me. 'It's in the wrong glass. This is a serious problem, is it not?'

I felt a flash of anger building in me. The place was heaving, it was hot and I had PMS, and now some annoying

French asshole was complaining about his beer glass. 'No,' I said. 'World hunger is a serious problem. Just drink your beer.'

I walked away, hands shaking with fury, which strangely mimicked arousal. Later Jean-Claude admitted that at that instant he'd turned to Pierre and said he was going to marry me.

For the next two weeks, Jean-Claude was a constant presence in the restaurant, where he always requested my section, and I always switched with someone.

This wasn't like college, where the boys took no for an answer and walked away. This was a man, and he knew what he wanted.

Finally, Pierre made Jean-Claude's appeal. 'Catherine, he has forced me to come here twelve nights in a row and I hate the food. So please, go on a date with him. He's a good guy.' That, plus the thirty-franc tip (a definite rarity with French clientele), finally got me to give in.

The night of our date started out as a comedy of errors after I accidentally locked myself out of my flat. But we shared a beautiful meal at a tiny family-run Vietnamese place in Belleville, off the beaten tourist track.

Afterwards, we strolled through the Louvre, and across the bridge to the Ile St Louis to have a *digestif* at a tiny café. I could see why American girls have a reputation for being totally easy in foreign countries, because the gorgeous accents combined with the free sightseeing treks make us cheap dates. The moonlight glinting off the Seine reminded me that I was a hell of a long way from Georgia, as Jean-Claude and I traded stories of our lives in muddled Franglish.

He was twenty-nine, and worked for the government. I listened in earnest as he told me about his secret 'missions' to Israel for the purposes of national security, and his work for different politicians. I wince when telling this story because my older self wants to bitch-slap my seventeen-year-old self for being so naïve, but, believe me, in the circumstances I would have believed anything Jean-Claude said. 'I've had a difficult two years, because my wife died,' he told me, and spilled the tale of how they had honeymooned together, and she'd had some sort of tragic scuba diving accident in the South Pacific.

I listened with rapt attention as he explained how he tried to rescue her (or exhumed her corpse; as I've said, my French wasn't great) but failed. My heart went out to him.

We went back to his flat in the Marais, after I mimed my lost keys predicament with a 'key-in-the-door' movement (which I realize now he may have misinterpreted as something altogether more lewd) and climbed the four flights of wickedly steep stairs.

Not wanting him to think I was a total slut, I asked for some nightwear to lend credibility to my lockout story.

'I don't have any pyjamas, sorry, Cat, but you can borrow this,' he said innocently, handing me a tiny T-shirt that clung to my breasts and barely covered my crotch. (Weeks later, I found out that he had an entire stash, and that this wasn't the only thing he'd lied about!)

We lay next to each other and he kissed me, tenderly at first and then with more urgency. His body was amazing: he was fit and muscled without the pumped-up look of the football players at my school, and though he was only five foot ten, the same height as me, his presence made him seem much taller. For the first time ever with a man, I felt really protected.

The T-shirt was off in seconds, and he kissed his way down my stomach and started sliding his hand inside my panties. I stopped him in his tracks, because at seventeen I was still a bit shy about men going down on me if I hadn't showered first – later I would find that far from putting them off, my natural scent made men go crazier – and slipped my hand down his trousers to unearth his cock.

What I saw almost made me leap back in surprise: he was very large, but his penis looked like a wrinkled Shar Pei puppy.

'Oh, my God,' I murmured, taken aback.

He laughed. 'Yes,' he said, 'I am not – how do you say – *circoncis*?'

I got the point. But despite feeling incredibly turned on, I could not quite figure out the mechanism. Worried that he would be offended by my hesitation, I gingerly started giving him a blow job. It didn't really work, because he wasn't fully hard. His penis felt like one of those squishy little stress balls that they sell at airports, and was about as erotic. I'd never read about this in any of the romance novels I snuck from underneath the cookbooks in the wicker basket next to my mum's bathtub. (I'd always noticed that, despite their protected placement, they were the only ones yellow and watermarked.)

'Are you okay?' he asked, staring down at me with his gorgeous blue-green eyes and long lashes. 'We don't have to do anything else, we can just lie here and hold each other.'

Fighting the urge to roll my eyes, I didn't tell him how many times I'd heard that before. 'How does this work?' I said, cautiously pushing the foreskin back to reveal the glistening pre-cum. I'd seen my share of male genitalia, but this was alien to me. But, as ever, I was a very eager pupil.

After some quick thinking, I decided to take the easy way out.

'Show me,' I said, lounging back on the bed in my black lace panties. 'Touch yourself.'

This was also covering my ass, because I didn't know the French word for 'condom'.

He started to stroke himself, and as the skin pushed up over the head, getting more and more taut, I could feel myself getting more and more turned on.

I licked my middle finger, slid my hand down my knickers and started to play with my clit, and as his breathing got heavier we looked into each other's eyes then I watched, fascinated. At that stage in my life I hadn't ever had an orgasm, but seeing him explode all over himself was one of the horniest things I had ever seen. We fell asleep in each other's arms.

Over the next few weeks we fell in love. I was so smitten by his bad-boy allure that I ignored his erratic behaviour, such as disappearing for days at a time, saying he was 'working for the government', when I found out later that he actually had a desk job with an airline company. When I questioned him, he blamed stress over losing his wife, or one of his 'missions'.

Then, just as the cracks in his story were becoming increasingly hard to ignore, he presented me with a platinum and diamond rock and asked me to marry him.

He had whisked me off to the airport saying he was going to surprise me with a secret romantic getaway. Before I knew it I found myself about to board a plane to Jamaica as he announced we were going there to exchange vows. I was only eighteen, and much as I adored him I also knew that my entire future time-line hinged on that instant. I was desperately in love, but could not shake the horrifying vision of myself in ten years' time, my dreams of going to New York or London to become a writer sacrificed to become a French housewife, eating truffles in a remote chateau and waiting in vain for him to come home. I never got on the plane and I hadn't seen him since.

# EIGHT

I continued to daydream as the train sped past green fields and nestling villages. I couldn't help revisiting my past decisions. What, I wondered, would life have been like if I had made Jean-Claude my destiny? What if I'd got on the plane with him to the Caribbean rather than boarding the next flight to New York?

Somewhere in the back corner of my mind I had always thought of Jean-Claude as the 'back-up guy', the guy who I could seek out if I wasn't married by thirty. Now that I'm nearing thirty, of course, I've moved the age of marriage up to forty. At seventeen, thirty seemed ancient!

My palms sweating, I walked into the café in the Marais that was one of our old haunts and saw him sitting at the bar, smoking a roll-up cigarette and looking sexier than ever. His face was still the most beautiful I'd ever seen, down to the cleft in his chin and his perfect teeth, a rarity among Frenchmen. Far from ageing him, his salt-and-pepper hair only made him hotter.

It's so unfair. Grey hair on a man and we think 'distinctive', while on a woman it's more *Driving Miss Daisy*. Bastard.

'Catherine,' he said, looking me up and down and kissing me on each cheek, then full on the lips. 'You look so beautiful, exactly the same!'

We moved to a quiet table in the corner, and after we discussed the obligatory 'how's your family/job/ house' questions for about the first fifteen minutes, he took my hand. I knew that he'd had a live-in girlfriend for the past two years, a relationship that he'd described via email as 'on-off'. Which, considering his rocky history, probably meant that she thought it was on when he thought it was off.

He was as intense as ever, especially when we started waxing nostalgic about the past. 'I have so many regrets about lying to you,' he said, 'but I made up the story because I had just got fired from my job, and didn't want you to think that I was a loser. I wanted to be James Bond,' he said, laughing bitterly. 'I was drunk when I said those things about my wife, and once I was in deep I didn't know how to tell you the truth. I was scared. And at first, I thought that you would be a fling. I never dreamed that we would end up falling in love.'

'At the time, I wondered if I was in love with a man who didn't exist at all,' I said, squeezing his hand. 'But since then I've thought that I may love the honest guy more.'

'I was so in love with you then,' he said. Then, gazing into my eyes, he added: 'This may sound crazy, but, seeing you again, I'm starting to think I'm still in love with you now.'

For a moment, I swooned. Had the perfect man actually been there all along, while I was too young to appreciate true love?

Here he was, sitting in front of me, still beautiful, and now the proud owner of a stunning new chateau in Burgundy. Not that I'd actually let that influence me. Besides, knowing Jean-Claude's penchant for excessive exaggeration, his photos of his new pad could be something from a French guidebook pulled from the Internet.

Reality kicked in after I asked him whether he had split up with his girlfriend.

'Well, after buying the place in Burgundy I don't have the money to buy my own house in Paris too, so for now we're under the same roof,' he said, shifting his eyes in that all-too-familiar manner. 'But we don't sleep together. I'm sure you understand.'

Well, no, actually – because I would never settle for that. I realized in that instant how far I've come from the rather naïve teenager who used to iron this man's shirts and ignore the lipstick stains on his collar. Dr Phil would be proud.

But after several glasses of burgundy I let him walk me back to my hotel on the Champs Elysées. When we paused he moved to kiss me and I didn't protest. In that instant all the chemistry came flooding back.

Before I knew it, I found myself asking him if he wanted to come upstairs. 'I would love to,' he said, cupping my chin. 'But I have to tell you, if I come upstairs I will never leave.'

So, just like I did when I was eighteen, I walked away. Falling in love requires some detachment from reality, but I worried that Jean-Claude would spend his entire life in some sort of euphoric fantasy world where infidelity doesn't count.

I was glad I'd seen him, because his type of unrealistic obsession is what entire romantic movies are made of, and for too long I had probably compared every other man's devotion to his, and penalized them when they came up short. But I've grown up enough to realise I want a relationship based on reality not fantasy.

Real love is about honesty, even when the truth is that you are too depressed to get out of bed and have a shit job. It's trusting your partner enough to love you at your worst. It's not putting them up on a ridiculous pedestal, shielding them from real life, while offering promises that don't actually stack up.

And I couldn't help thinking about his poor long-suffering girlfriend at home. I wondered what she would say if she could see him telling me that I'm his 'one true love in life'.

I'm not a love-struck teenager any more, and for me, at least in this case, with age comes wisdom. His emotions may have stayed frozen in time, but I have definitely outgrown him.

On the Eurostar home I glanced at the book peeking out of my handbag. In some ways, perhaps, Dr Phil and his 'relationship autopsy' project did give me a few insights. I certainly wasn't about to repeat past relationship mistakes. But I had to wonder whether I really needed Dr Phil to tell me that. I was in a different place to my eighteen-year-old self. I didn't just want to analyse the past: I wanted answers for the here and now.

When I got off the train at Waterloo, I ditched the book en route to the Tube. After all, I still had plenty more of these crazy guides to wade through back in my bedroom.

# NINE

My next source of relationship advice turned out to be worlds away from folksy Dr Phil and co. But still, it was all valid evidence to be stored away in the Anti-Rules research file in my head.

Despite my best intentions to remain professional, I could feel myself getting turned on as I watched the petite half-naked blonde giving her boyfriend a blow job in the shower. I was on a porn set. Not acting, just observing. I'd been working on a TV show called *How to Have Sex After Marriage*, where I, along with a feisty, dynamic psychologist called Anjula Mutanda and handsome and charming Aussie dating expert Sam Van Rood, was helping couples who were having problems with their marriages.

On the whole, I loved the women involved and relished the experience. Anjula, Sam and the entire crew were incredible people. But it was also incredibly tough emotionally to spend my days trapped, like a caged animal, with women whose marriages were in danger of breaking down. I wanted to help them, but at times I felt like the Hungarian dancing bear, unable to display my natural behaviour or get any time out of the glass goldfish-bowl walls of the studio flat that we were filming in. I was being driven mad from an excess of oestrogen! Despite Anjula's reassuring words that I was doing a great job with the women, I did worry that I was out of my depth. After all, my own relationship was in tatters; how the hell could I help anyone else?

But soon, I began to come into my own, and really get into the whole process. And some breakthrough moments made the whole experience worthwhile, mainly because I really felt that on some level the programme was genuinely helping the women.

Case in point: I'd definitely connected with Debbie, who had also come along to the porn set with me, and John, her lovely teddy-bear husband. They obviously cared a great deal for each other and were desperate to reconnect. But they had fallen into the habit of taking their marriage for granted. To rejuvenate their sex life she wanted to become more daring. The show's creators felt that directing her own erotic video would be just the inspiration she needed, and the experience clearly worked in the end, since John and Debbie raved about the programme, and seeing how happy they were was very gratifying.

I broke the news to Debbie on camera in the car that she would be visiting the set, and reassured her that none of her own clothes would come off and she wouldn't have to do anything that she was uncomfortable with. She seemed pleased. I wondered whether Debbie was secretly voyeuristic but, like so many, inhibited about admitting her sexual instincts.

At the same time I was thinking that I would have loved to have had someone facilitate my first-time porn set experience.

I'd stumbled on to my first set as a reporter, sent to interview first-time male porn actors, and ask them why they were hoping to get into the business. It turned out that some of them, like the guy who said he could do a good Marlon Brando accent but stripped down to reveal a scrawny chest, were deluded. But others, like the guy who told me that 'even with the shrinkage factor' of his leather trousers he still had a 'solid eight inches, with a G-spot curve', seemed to have real potential.

The car pulled up to a lovely period house in West Hampstead, and the curvy and vivacious brunette director chatted to Debbie as I nosed around. Other than the fact that the sofas were covered with sheets, which I suppose could have been camouflaging either bodily fluid or the evidence that they had seen better days – probably both – and the fact that half-melted candles lurked on every solid surface, I never would have guessed that the place was a bona-fide porn palace.

While Debbie got a crash course in DVD mini-cam filming, I chatted to the performers about their relationships. To my surprise, it seemed that the porn stars had rock-solid partnerships – and were rewriting the rules for monogamy at the same time.

One of the cameramen, whose girlfriend is a performer, told me how he handles his partner's day job. 'I'm not the jealous type, which is pretty necessary considering that she shags guys for work. But when I edit her stuff on screen, it can be tough.'

I tried to picture myself remaining detached while watching my boyfriend frolic naked with another girl, and couldn't imagine it. Screw the colour contrast; I would be ripping the girl's hair out. But maybe these guys had a point: after all, unlike the creepy guys trolling for sex on adultery websites, everyone was being open and honest here. Maybe an open relationship was something that I should consider.

The other performers, Richard and 'Paradise', looked

nothing like the well-oiled, silicon-enhanced leads I had imagined. Though he had a muscular chest, Richard must have been only five foot six, while Paradise was a diminutive curvy blonde who appeared to be totally natural.

They explained that they were amateurs, but only have sex with each other and get off on being filmed. I asked him how he handles the fact that everyone sees his girlfriend naked, and for tips on avoiding jealousy.

'The best thing to do is be honest with whoever you're dating about what you can handle,' he said. 'Who knows, they may like it.'

(The cameraman also taught me the cardinal rule of porn sets: 'Always label your water bottle because, well, you wouldn't want to take one a performer has used!')

I walked out to the kitchen, where one of the assistants was calmly smoking a cigarette, and another was eating a sandwich.

The director came into the room. 'Our leading man has gone a bit soft, so we're going to need to give him a bit of time,' she said. Then, without missing a beat, 'Lunch?'

She fished through the kitchen table drawers and pulled out a clear plastic bag full of Viagra and condoms. Apparently, this is totally normal and happens constantly on porn sets, and she was a total professional and made everyone feel really comfortable.

While the director shot what she called the 'soft stuff' (which I presume referred to the lack of penetration onscreen, not the lack of the guy's erection), the crew ate sandwiches and chatted among themselves.

I stuck to my canned soda and PowerBars, especially once

we went into the back bedroom, which was slightly humid from the shower steam and sweaty exertion. The thought of chowing down on an egg mayonnaise sandwich at that point was a bit much for me.

Even though I was exhausted when we finally called it a wrap, back at home that night my mind was whirring. Amy had advised a journey of self-discovery but she hadn't specified where the guidance should come from. Maybe those porn stars had something to teach me – and not just in terms of technique. Even with all my sexual experimentation, it had never occurred to me that I could have an open relationship with a serious boyfriend. But speaking to the porn stars, it was as if a light-bulb had flickered on in my head. So long as both parties were happy, maybe open relationships were the future.

I fired up my Mac and typed in the opening lines of that week's column: *Is a long-term monogamous relationship really the right solution for me? Or are happy endings obsolete outside of dodgy massage parlours?*

# TEN

It wasn't long before I had a chance to put my new theory to the test and dabble with an open relationship. On the day I turned twenty-nine, I eschewed a traditional party. Instead Victoria, Amy and I went to a gig in a dive bar in Whitechapel where my friend Alan's band was playing.

Twenty-nine isn't supposed to be that old, but it felt like the end of an era. My career was stable, I had a great group of friends and I had learned enough bedroom techniques to make years of monogamy infinitely more interesting. All that was missing was the right guy to share it with.

But in other ways twenty-nine wasn't all it was cracked up to be. By this age, my mum had been married for almost seven years and was pregnant with me. The cynical side of my brain had always screamed, 'Fat lot of good it did her, because he left her in the end anyway!'

But lately, my mind had started tricking me into perceiving them as the good years, when she believed that she had a loving husband and a stable home. That would be nice.

In some respects, I suppose that I date like a man. I think of dates as friends and a bit of fun first, not as the potential father of my as-yet-imaginary children.

But on another level, I suppose that I wonder if each guy is the One: the only difference between me and my friends is that I tend to shag the ones I'm attracted to even though they may not be 'marriage material'.

After Alan's folk-rock band left the stage, a group of very fit late twenty-something guys took the stage. They seemed to be some sort of cross between heavy metal and Goth, because their music was loud and shouty but they were wearing eyeliner.

The lead singer, despite his screaming and wild arm gestures, had chiselled features and a hot, slender, sinewy body that looked as if he spent his weekends climbing rocks. And he seemed be staring right at me when his face wasn't totally obscured by a mass of black hair.

'Do you think I'm too old for PVC trousers?' I asked the girls. For someone who'd spent her entire life hanging out with an older crowd, suddenly all those *Daily Mail* headlines, 'Lamb Or Mutton', screamed out at me. I was heading into a whole new thirty-something age bracket.

I don't think I look particularly haggard, but suddenly I was freaked out to see so many baby-faced Hoxton faux-punk types. I remember going to these sorts of clubs when I was fifteen and thinking that musician equalled 'creative genius' rather than 'likely to be living on a friend's couch'.

'Please.' Victoria rolled her eyes. 'You've got great legs. Anyway, clothing styles are limited by body type, not age. I've seen some out-of-control muffin top going on this summer – on teenagers!'

'Well, I can say with certainty that I'll never develop a PVC or latex fetish. These things are hot as hell!'

A friend had recommended that I try synthetic trousers instead of leather because they don't stretch, but I remembered that night why I never wear them for dates. It reminded me of the time I'd spent with a guy who loved me to dress in latex. Unfortunately, I sweat so much that I had constantly to douse myself in baby powder to fit into the outfits, which aggravated my sinuses. So instead of a latex goddess, the guy got a wheezing mess. I know some guys love the poured-on look, but for me it was just too much effort in the end.

I could feel rivulets of sweat pouring down my legs, and the room, heaving with fans, was so hot that my carefully layered smoky eyes were starting to run down my cheeks. So much for the rock-chick look.

'Speaking of great legs,' Amy said, draining the remainder of her Corona and pointing to the lead singer, 'Cat, he's gorgeous. And he's totally checking you out!'

She was right. The guy had to be at least six foot five, with a huge tattoo of a praying mantis down his right forearm. Possibly due to my hygiene fetish, I don't tend to go for unwashed musicians, but this one was undoubtedly hot.

'Why don't you throw your underwear on stage?' Amy yelled in my ear.

'I don't think I could pull these trousers down even if I wanted to!'

We laughed and I tried to grind seductively, despite the death metal tunes. No matter how hard I tried, I couldn't really make head-banging sexy.

After the set, we hung around at the bar until the singer, whose name I'd learned was Jamie, emerged. He was sweaty and sexy in his Metallica T-shirt and – wait for it – black leather trousers! We matched! Maybe next we would be wearing vials of each other's blood and getting matching sinister tattoos! Victoria and Amy encouraged me to make my move.

So I waited for the perfect moment, when he slipped outside to have a cigarette. Although I'm only an occasional smoker, one look at him was enough to kick-start my craving for nicotine, among other things.

'Hi, you wouldn't happen to have a light, would you?' he asked.

'No, I, um, just came out for a smoke,' I lied, smiling, 'but I seem to have run out.'

After giving me his last cigarette, he introduced himself and told me about his music. As we chatted, I noticed that there were loads of cute men outside, all puffing away.

I've always been an occasional social smoker, never more than three cigarettes per night. But since the ban started I've been smoking more than ever, and it's had an amazing effect on my love life. Smirting was definitely working for me!

I'm not exactly a shrinking violet, but it can be intimidating to approach men in bars, especially if I don't know their status. But cigarettes give conversations the perfect opener, and work for the same reason as speed dating: the built-in time limit. The verbal exchange only has to last as long as the cigarette, so if the guy is boring I can get it down to two long drags. I also have an innocent 'out' if he has a girlfriend, since I can claim I wasn't hitting on him – just getting a light.

My shared cigarette with Jamie gave us an instant bond: suddenly, we weren't just two losers huddled outside in the rain. We were rebels, taking a stand against the establishment. Just the right atmosphere for seducing a wannabe rock star.

Still, I stopped at one smoke. Buying a little black dress to improve my love life is one thing, but I wasn't prepared to risk a black lung. As I ground the half-smoked ciggie out with my shoe boot, he confessed that he read my column.

'It's very funny,' he told me.

'I'm flattered,' I said. 'Some guys think I'm scary because of my job.'

'Not me,' he said, raking his hair back – which allowed me to see that he didn't have a receding hairline, which was a definite plus. 'Actually, I'm a bit of a sexual adventurer myself. My last girlfriend Rachel and I had an open relationship, and it was amazing.'

I would agree with scientists that the bohemian lifestyle of creative types means that they are sometimes more open to sexual impulses and opportunities. After all, I'm a writer and drunken carousing and the pursuit of hedonistic pleasure are two of my favourite pastimes. But these days, I'm much more drawn to buttoned-up guys and revel in helping them find their wilder side.

Still, considering what happened with JP, maybe that wasn't working so well. Meeting an attractive, available advocate of the open relationship so soon after the porn actors' advice made me wonder whether fate was perhaps trying to tell me something.

'I guess that works for a while. I mean I've done multi-dating, but what happens when you want to settle down?'

'I'm hoping for two wives,' he said.

I waited for laughter, but it never came.

'Seriously, I don't believe in monogamy.'

We got into a spirited debate about whether humans were meant to be faithful to one person, and I was impressed to see that he had views on everything from the Mormon leader

Joseph Smith (himself a renowned polygamist) to the very promiscuous Bonobo chimps.

What I liked about Jamie, other than his ass in leather, was his view on female sexuality. He believed that women's sexual appetites could be just as voracious as men's, 'but sometimes,' he said, 'women don't realize it, or they don't realize that they've got all these hang-ups because of social conventions. Which is a shame, because women have much better orgasms than men!'

'Well,' I said, coyly sipping my Corona and licking my lips afterwards, 'I think it's safe to say that I'm definitely not repressed!'

I wanted to strip him there and then, but my PVC trousers and loyalty to my friends stopped me from going further. We made a date for the next night, where I looked forward to testing his theories further.

It was three hours into my date with Jamie when it struck me that I might have drunkenly overestimated his conversational abilities.

I tried to initiate conversation several times, but we'd already had several painfully long silences. But my ears pricked up when he told me that he played the saxophone, and considered himself an 'expert on the staccato double-tonguing' technique.

There is only one phrase uttered during the course of a date that has more significance than the pick-up line, and I call it 'the closer'. This is the phrase that convinces a woman, who may still be undecided, to go back to his place.

So when he went on to ask, 'Want to come back to mine and have coffee?' my mind was already made up. Jamie and

I might not have had a meeting of minds, but this sounded too good to resist.

I wasn't disappointed: Jamie had a fetish for going down on women, without them reciprocating. At first I found it strange, but I have to admit that, after years of dealing with certain men who only occasionally boarded the downtown bus, it was amazing to have someone who treated it as a daily commute, especially when he asked me to lie horizontally on the bed, and did something with his fingers that basically involved exposing my clit with one finger so that he could lick me up and down, which sent shivers down my spine, while gently pressing against my arse with another. I didn't know what he was doing, but it was driving me wild. 'God, that is so intense,' I gasped. 'How are you doing that?'

He looked up at me and grinned. 'Just relax and enjoy,' he said, kissing my pussy lightly before going back to the matter in hand. 'God, you taste amazing. I could do this all night.'

My orgasm was out of this world, but I have to confess that the spell was broken afterwards when he grabbed his guitar and insisted on singing me one of his new songs. It was truly awful, but I smiled and pretended to be touched.

The fact was, his music sounded like cats being strangled. But later, after I Googled his sex trick and found out that it was something called the Kivin technique, which originated in Thailand, I decided that I was happy to get hooked on the encore oral sessions.

Back in the bedroom his conversation had suddenly come back to life too. He seemed to access some kind of dirty talk stream of consciousness, which made for some pretty full-on commentary. I was intrigued to put this guy and his chat to the test. Had I finally met a man as horny as I was?

After a couple more dates, which had successfully concluded back in his bedroom, he texted one afternoon to ask if I wanted to hear his band again that night. I already had early evening plans so I suggested we meet in a bar afterwards instead.

'It's the groupies, isn't it?' he asked. 'Don't be intimidated, honey, I only have eyes for you!'

I didn't have the heart to point out that, of the half-dozen people in the audience at the last performance I'd seen, only two had been female – and they were the waitresses. I guess heavy metal doesn't really appeal to women.

After half an hour of waiting for him at the agreed bar, I began to think I had the wrong address. Finally, he called me at 11 p.m. with a lame story about how his phone had run out of credit.

He sounded pissed, and invited me back to his flat. With the men I usually date, who have day jobs and responsibilities, I would have kicked them to the kerb there and then. But the chemistry between us was intense, so I agreed.

When I got to the door, he embarked on a long drunken diatribe about his 'place in the universe', saying that he could never get a normal job because he 'didn't have the right head space'.

I talked to him for about an hour until he calmed down, then went to sleep cuddling him. There were no screaming orgasms that night, but I felt strangely protective of him. I could relate to the freak-outs that happen when you create something that's personal, though for the life of me I couldn't really understand his lyrics.

Yet it seemed that, to date a musician, I might have to morph into a mix of fan-club president and psychiatrist. Much as I love creative men, I knew that with one insane artist already in the relationship (me), it was always going to be tough to add another one to the mix.

On the bright side, Jamie was fun, had some serious oral skills, and looked great in tight jeans. I resolved to buy myself some earplugs.

# ELEVEN

With summer here, my book launch approaching and a new, albeit probably temporary, guy on the scene, perhaps everything was finally falling into place. That was certainly my mantra every time a stray thought of JP slipped into my mind.

I was also cheered up by the fact that my mum was coming over for a visit. Not only is she my best friend, but she's lovely, friendly and a fantastic conversation starter who builds me up at every opportunity – in short, the perfect wingwoman. Which was exactly what I needed.

I often have anxiety nightmares about suddenly realizing I'm naked, but in the days leading up to the launch of *Sleeping Around: Secrets of a Sexual Adventuress*, I faced a far more terrifying prospect: being in a room full of my ex-lovers.

My mum's flight was scheduled to arrive on the day of the party. I met her at the airport and, as the flowers, music, drinks and guest list for the party at Soho House were all already taken care of, we decided to go out for a catch-up tea and some window shopping to settle my nerves.

As we wandered home after tea we passed a vintage shop and simultaneously spotted a gorgeous strapless 1950s prom dress in the window. I had been stressing about what outfit to wear that night and she insisted on buying it for me then and there to resolve the dilemma. I tried to tell her she needn't but she said the dress was a present to mark how proud she was of me, so I ripped that sucker right off the mannequin. Problem solved.

I was relieved that my mum was so supportive of my book, even given the subject matter. Later that night I overheard her cheekily telling people that I put Post-its over the risqué bits of the book to let her know when she should stop reading.

Back home it was a treat to put on the dress again. But, as I dried my hair and touched up my make-up, there was no getting away from the fact I was about to enter a confined space with Andrew the married ex, Mark, my husband, and David, who once scored me some Viagra pills – not to mention several friends I'd hooked up with casually.

When I told my mum about my guest list complications, she replied, without missing a beat, 'Don't worry, darling, if you get stuck with anyone you don't want to talk to I can always distract them.'

When Mum wasn't around, I decided that I would use the techniques I'd honed in New York while multi-dating. The most important task was to find my nearest exit, and memorize the club's layout so I could hide in the loo if necessary.

To avoid embarrassing mishaps during introductions (and crying out the wrong name in the heat of passion), I long ago mastered the art of calling every guy 'sweetheart' and 'honey'.

I would also concentrate on using appropriate snippets of information if the men met: e.g. saying, 'This is Mark, he works in banking,' not, 'I once used a vibrator on him!' This would be easier said than done after my fourth cocktail . . .

*   *   *

As I surveyed the scene I spotted Mark busily plying my mum with white wine. He caught my eye and mouthed, 'Your mum is hot,' and I briefly started to worry that he was being a bit too friendly!

The evening was going beautifully. After a few glasses of Pimm's, I was back in my stride and had been chatting animatedly with all sorts of people. I had decided to stop worrying, and stop feeling guilty about possibly offending anyone. My crazy exes are an amazing part of my life, and I should be happy that they were there for me and happy to celebrate my success.

As everyone seemed to be having a fantastic time and mingling happily I thought I'd have a moment of time out. To take advantage of the lovely, warm evening I headed out to the roof terrace. My heart stopped when I saw my ex-boyfriend Andrew, who had practically been the star of *Sleeping Around*, standing out there alone.

Our break-up had been painful, so we had stayed out of contact for several months out of necessity. But I had mailed him an invite because we were definitely due a reunion.

I had been madly in love with him; in fact he was the first boyfriend ever to make me consider the eventual possibility of settling down. But he was separated from his wife, with three kids. Forget baggage, the guy was carrying steamer trunks full of emotional angst.

'Cat, I was hoping to catch you alone. I've read your book,' he began ominously.

I sighed, and looked him directly in the eye. This was the moment that I'd been dreading because I knew that even though I'd disguised his name and profession so that no one could identify him, he would see the dialogue between us and recognize himself. 'What did you think?'

He smiled. 'I loved it. It was funny at times; sweet; sad at times. A lot like life. And like us.' He touched my bare arm. 'Mostly I just felt so proud to be with someone so brilliant. So many times in the last year I've wanted to call you—'

'Andrew, I—'

'Let me finish, Cat. But then I read the book and read how happy you were with JP . . .'

My heart lurched. When I'd written *Sleeping Around* I was still with JP. Now that happiness was a distant memory.

'JP broke up with me,' I explained.

His eyes met mine. 'My wife and I, that's not really working either. The truth is, I'm still in love with someone else. It's you I think about all the time.'

I sighed audibly, sick of the drama. 'But you still live together, right?'

'Yes, because of the children. But it's nothing more than that.'

Part of me felt sorry for Andrew. But the other, stronger part of me knew that I had a right to want someone who was thrilled to be with me, instead of battling constant guilt. I didn't regret a second of my time with Andrew, but I knew that to have better relationships in the future, I was going to have to set boundaries on my terms.

I smiled. 'You know all those times when we were holed up in luxurious hotels where someone else cleaned up after us, or eating in Michelin-starred restaurants where someone else did the dishes, it was amazing and perfect but do you know what the common denominator was?'

'What do you mean?'

'I was escapism for you, from your marriage. But I've grown up. I want the whole warts-and-all reality. God help me, I do want to live with someone, and maybe even pick up their socks on occasion. I want real intimacy. Even if the price I have to pay sometimes is boredom.'

'But, Cat . . .'

I looked into his lovely blue eyes and took his hand.

'Listen, Andrew, I did love you very much. But the bottom line is, you've made the choice to stay in the house with your wife, and no matter what you said I couldn't have lived with that. Our break-up wasn't about my not loving you,' I said, 'it was about me wanting to have my needs met in a relationship, and realizing that I have the right to ask for that.'

He looked downcast, but managed a smile. 'If you insist. But listen, Miss Townsend, that other guy, may I just say that any man who isn't sure that he wants to be with you is insane.'

'Thanks, Andrew. That means a lot to me. Really.'

I hugged him, and just at that moment my friend Michael stuck his head out of the door. 'Cat?' he said. 'They want you inside to make a speech.'

During my mini-speech, I thanked my mum, my friends and my publisher. I even thanked the male cast of characters, both the good ones for enriching my life and the bad ones for giving me funny stories and teaching me what I didn't want.

At the same time, looking at all my aborted relationships up close filled me with a sense of pride. How could they ever be considered failures? For instance, Andrew and I had changed each other's lives: he knew that he had to live authentically, and I'd realized that I wanted a life partner. I like to think that we both influenced each other for the better.

In another sense the night was a little bittersweet. It was Victoria's last official night at home – she was moving in with Mike. But I kept reminding myself that we were celebrating the next stage of her life – and going out with a bang. 'Don't worry, Cat, we'll still hang out lots,' she assured me, but I knew that things would inevitably change. There would be no more New Year's Eve parties where I snog the Serbian bartender and take Polaroids of his arse as evidence of how toned he is. Girls' nights out would morph into lunches and coffees. But even though she was moving to a different phase in life, I hoped that we would always be great friends.

I ended the night taking tequila shots with the boys – and my mum – and was on my best behaviour. But wedged between Mark, Andrew and David, three amazing, trusted old friends who I'd once shared incredible sexual adventures with, I thought about my wedding night threesome, and one dirty corner of my mind wondered if I could ever go one better!

# TWELVE

'Are you sure you won't reconsider staying with me for a while?'

I was chatting to Mark from Victoria's nearly stripped bedroom, explaining the hurdles I'd encountered when looking for a new flatmate. Victoria had already gathered most of her stuff and moved it to Mike's new house in the country.

'Thanks, sweetheart, but it might be a bit awkward living with two men I've slept with,' I said. 'I'm not ready for my entire personal life to turn into a non-stop porno!'

I could hear his deep, throaty laughter. 'Point taken. But come on, do you really think you want to live with a stranger?'

'Not really. But I can't afford to live alone yet, and this place is still dirt cheap – dirt being the operative word,' I said, scraping the brown gunk surrounding our ancient boiler with a bleach-coated toothbrush. 'Besides, it doesn't have to be for ever.'

'Well, you know that you always have a place to stay if you need it. Don't feel that you have to rush into anything. And, Cat, are you sure that you want to stay there? Don't you want to live somewhere where you don't hear rats scraping behind the walls every time you turn on a light?'

'Hey, it could be worse. At least we don't have giant mutant insects, like I saw in that movie last night – the ones that developed lungs and started chasing people through the Underground—'

'Okay, I get the point! Look, just be careful, okay? There are a lot of nutters out there.'

I knew that it would be tough to find a new flatmate, because I've lived with my share of lunatics since university, and finding someone sane and sanitary has proved to be rather a challenge.

I was a bit nervous too, because I hadn't lived with someone who wasn't a close friend for several years, and the flat was so tiny that our lives would inevitably become entwined.

In the past, when I've needed to find someone to live with, I've often sent an email around my office, figuring that at least the people responding were one degree of separation from someone who was gainfully employed.

Unfortunately, this backfired at the *Independent*, because everyone who responded seemed to be intimately familiar with my column.

After seeing three guys who I'm convinced were looking to get into my bedroom rather than their own, I knew that I would have to branch out. One weedy twenty-three-year-old even enthusiastically told me that he was a trained masseur, and would be happy to dole out corporal punishment in exchange for a roof over his head.

'Why would you possibly think that I would be into that?' I asked him.

'Well, you wrote a column once about how you loved spanking, and you are well fit, so I was just thinking that we could come to some type of arrangement.' He grinned, revealing a cavity-ridden mouth that should successfully settle the fluoride in water debate once and for all.

'Just because I like sex doesn't mean that I don't discriminate,' I told him, ushering him towards the door.

He looked at me in confusion. 'Huh?'

'What I mean is, sometimes I think I should change the column's title to 'Sleeping Around, But Not With You!'. Have a nice night.'

I shut the door firmly behind him and put my head in my hands, trying to get the icky image of his undoubtedly hairless concave chest covered in oil out of my head.

Though I had lived with men before, I was really looking for a clean, sane, normal girl – unfortunately, they seemed to be in short supply.

By the next morning, I was about to give up when I wandered into the Starbucks on Old Street and saw a scrap of paper posted to their billboard that looked fairly promising: 'Professional, thirty-two-year-old single female seeks local accommodation, am open to all offers but would prefer to share with same,' followed by a mobile number.

I called the girl in question; her name was Emma, she worked in HR and seemed fairly pleasant.

Later that evening, she sat on the end of my sofa, chatting over a cup of tea. 'So,' I ventured, 'why do you need a room?'

'Well, I've just sold my flat, and switched to a part-time job,' she admitted. 'Over the next few months I'm thinking of branching out and doing something different. Maybe teaching yoga, or working in TV. I'm not sure.'

Looking back, I realize that this should have caused alarm bells to ring. But considering the transitional phase that I went through when I moved to London from New York and was temporarily homeless, my heart went out to her.

Besides, none of my other options was really panning out, and I was so crazy busy that I didn't have time to look.

The Spanker kept leaving eager messages, but unless I wanted to take my rent in whacks I figured that I should give Emma a shot.

I was excited. I'd had enough of smug settled couples lately; surely someone going through a soul-searching phase in life would be just the fix I needed. We could inspire each other! Maybe she could even become my Anti-Rules co-agent!

She asked when she could move in, and I smiled, took her deposit and handed her my extra set of keys.

# THIRTEEN

Since the summer, Jamie and I had continued seeing each other casually. One-on-one, we were playfully pushing our sexual boundaries with stuff like role-play. But after his fighting talk that first night about open relationships, he'd said nothing more on that front. In fact, I was starting to worry that he might just be happy to let the relationship slip into domestication. That wasn't the direction I wanted to go with him.

As the cold weather set in I was given an opportunity to weigh up matters. The litmus test of whether I want to take things further with a man happens when one of us gets sick. Do I long to stop by, brandishing chicken soup and the promise of sympathy sex? Or do I want to avoid the germs? With Jamie it was definitely the latter.

Case in point: when he called me and jokingly complained about a case of 'man flu'.

'Do you need anything?' I said sweetly, in a way that suggested that of course he didn't want me to drop everything and race across town just to bring him the same carton of orange juice that he could have picked up at his local corner store.

'That would be great, if you don't mind, darling,' he said, hacking pitifully. 'I'm really hurting here.'

So I was a good girl and picked up some Lemsip and various bottled smoothies from the local organic grocer's before heading over to his flat. But only after dousing myself with hand sanitizer.

On the way over I considered my relationship with Jamie. It had hit the 'awkward' phase. It had been a while since we had started sleeping together on a semi-regular basis, but still viewed calling each other the next day as optional. I definitely didn't want anything serious. But the 'Are you sleeping with anyone else?' conversation can be tricky if you want the answer to be in the affirmative.

Mind you, Jamie had been the one to bring up the subject of open relationships so I hoped he'd understand. I decided that I had to take the plunge and make sure that we were on the same page.

Despite his open-minded attitude, I felt a bit shy about bringing up our status. He had been down ever since his band failed to get their record deal, and I didn't want him to think I was not being supportive. Our dynamic was bizarre because even though we'd agreed to have a casual relationship, I'd become the one who answered his calls at 2 a.m. I didn't want our fling to become serious by default. Part of me thought that I should end things altogether.

'So,' I said, ruffling his hair and avoiding a kiss on the cheek. 'How is the patient?'

'I'm okay,' he said, gesturing to the computer on the desk in front of him. 'I've been finding ways to distract myself, browsing porn.'

I pushed his hair out of his eyes and arranged myself on his lap.

I leaned over to the computer and typed in Craigslist, the website where people post messages telling the world whatever they're looking for. I had long been secretly fascinated by its 'Casual Encounters' page and it seemed a good way of broaching the subject of our relationship status.

It caught his attention all right, and we scrolled through it together, giggling at some of the more extreme requests.

'Check this one out,' said Jamie. 'S&M fetish enthusiast needs a toilet slave, just sit on my mouth!'

'I don't shock easily, but that is seriously foul,' I said. We both laughed.

'Have I ever told you that you are the sexiest woman I've ever met?' he purred, nuzzling my neck.

'Coming from someone with carnal knowledge of the entire Asian subcontinent and probably most of Europe, that's quite a compliment.'

He pushed his chair back and immediately flew into a coughing fit that lasted the better part of five minutes. After I handed him a tissue, he took my hand and smiled.

I looked him straight in the eye and grinned. 'The thing is, Jamie, while we're sexual soulmates I'm not sure that we'd be right for each other long-term. While we could have lots of fun together, I don't want either of us to get hurt. I think we should keep things casual, maybe even introduce others into the mix like you suggested?'

He pulled me back on to his lap. 'Listen, honey, I promise you I'm cool with that. But until Mr Wonderful comes along, a girl's got to have a bit of fun, right? Weren't you the one who told me that you attract more men when you're getting laid properly?'

I had to admit, the man did have a point.

As I sat on his knee Jamie continued to browse around the Internet. I noticed that he'd scrolled to an escorts page, and as I looked closer I felt myself getting excited. He hesitated, then asked if I would be interested in picking up women together. I was intrigued. Now that most of my girlfriends had settled into more serious relationships, multiple-partner sex sessions had been few and far between.

'I might feel weird about other men,' he said, 'but I would love to watch you getting it on with another girl.'

He tried to kiss me, but I pushed him away, stood up and lifted my skirt, balancing myself against the wall as I looked over one shoulder.

'Fuck me hard, from behind,' I murmured. Before adding, slightly louder, 'But don't give me any germs!'

I leaned over slightly and bent my knees while Jamie came across and began to finger me. He teased me for ages before finally plunging into me. I came almost instantly, biting my lip as I orgasmed. When I slumped back on his sofa, my legs were trembling – and not just from holding that position.

As I pulled my panties up, I felt that our plans for three-ring circus sex would probably be a good thing. One-on-one with someone who I suspected wanted to be more than casual fuck buddies wasn't really something I could handle at that moment in time.

If someone I felt passionate about came along I doubted I would feel so happy about the sort of open dynamic the porn actors recommended. But Jamie was a sexual soulmate rather than anything else and I wouldn't mind exploring more fantasies with him. It seemed a good way to ensure things stayed casual. I'd done my Florence Nightingale bit but I didn't want to fall into the trap of domestication with a guy like him.

In the afterglow, Jamie and I went back online and found an invitation to a make-out party, promising that participants would 'lose clothes and inhibitions'. I put our names on the guest list to receive information about upcoming events. I must remember to take my own water.

# FOURTEEN

Our sexual awakening would have to wait, however, because now that winter was unmistakably on the horizon Jamie skipped the country to 'find himself' on a trip to Goa, which roughly translated to 'running around a beach shouting and dancing half-naked, which will seem like a mystical experience because of the huge amounts of drugs consumed'.

He invited me along but I politely declined the invitation. Now I was wondering if I should have taken him up on it, because I was seriously suffering from the lack of sun in London.

Even before I'd flung the curtains open to let in the light, I could make out the evidence of last night's excess on the bed. There was a torn box of frosted doughnuts, and peeling back the edge revealed several pastry carcasses with the icing licked off. But there was no man in sight, just a bunch of rainbow sprinkles scattered on the sheets. It could only mean one thing: the winter blues. And, unfortunately, I've been much more interested in making love to a box of Krispy Kremes than an actual partner.

My girlfriends tell me that my November to February hibernation period is a symptom of what they call 'Sexual Seasonal Affective Disorder'. While most of them are planning their New Year's resolutions, detoxing and doing yoga, I've been inhaling carbohydrates like there's no tomorrow. If it's cold and miserable, aren't we suffering enough?

Being alone during the holidays sucks and, to be honest, I was really depressed. Victoria had called the night before to announce that she and Mike had finally set a date for the wedding – next autumn. I was made up for her and we chatted for ages. But after I put the phone down something happened. Out of nowhere an image of me and JP popped into my head. Before I knew it all my memories of him had come flooding back.

Besides, I fucking hate Christmas.

Like many singles, I'm in my element during the long days of summer, when sunshine elevates endorphin levels and glimpses of tantalizing bare flesh rev up our libidos. At the moment, the idea of exposing milk-white skin that hasn't seen the light of day in months didn't exactly appeal.

Since my sugar levels were crashing, I met Amy in Starbucks, and was immediately inundated with Christmas music and snowflake montage coffee-holders, despite the fact that it was only the first week in November.

I'd been secretly dreading meeting up with Amy, because even though I love her dearly, I wasn't sure that I could listen to her bright-eyed excitement over her upcoming ski trip with her lovely new boyfriend, Richard, who was whisking her away to a Swiss chalet for the holidays. He's tall, very handsome, loaded and a sweet and sensitive guy, so she's really hit the jackpot there, and no one deserved it more. But seeing both her and Victoria so loved-up was tough. I hadn't seen Amy for ages and I didn't want our paths to diverge massively. I was really happy for them both, but at the same time the selfish, evil part of me was wondering, Why not me?

Meanwhile, it looked like I was going to be spending the big day watching horror movie marathons. But I wasn't bitter. I was just really, really sad.

Now the floodgates had opened, and without the distraction of Jamie I just couldn't get my mind off JP. Part of the fun of the holidays is a sense of childhood wonder, and I've always dreamed about getting a tree and creating traditions with the man of my dreams. Jamie's idea of a Christmas present would probably be picking up a holiday-themed hooker wearing red and white crotchless undies for a three-way. With JP it would have been special in a different way.

'. . . sunglasses, or will ski goggles be enough?'

Suddenly, I snapped back into reality, and into the conversation with Amy. She was going on about her holiday with Richard.

'Um, I think it depends on the weather,' I said. 'Though, you know, I've only been skiing twice.'

'Forget the skiing, it will just be nice to get some proper alone time,' she said. 'Even if we're just sipping hot chocolate next to the fire in the lodge.'

My mouth opened, and I was ready for a witty response, probably a pun on the fireside shag carpeting in their room, but nothing came out. Instead, I burst into tears.

'Cat, oh my God, what's wrong?' Amy said, fishing in her handbag for a tissue. 'Was it something I said?'

'I just can't help thinking about JP. What it would have been like to spend Christmas together, and I can't help wondering what I could have done to fix things. Doesn't he still love me? Doesn't he still think about me?'

She sighed, and fiddled with her scarf. 'Okay, I'm going to be honest with you. Can you handle it?'

I looked up at her with a tear-streaked face. 'I couldn't feel any worse. So yeah, give it to me straight. You always have.'

'Okay, well, on the one hand it's totally understandable to have lonely feelings over Christmas. But on the other hand . . .'

'On the other hand what?'

'Now that Jamie is away I think that you're suddenly fixating on JP, and I don't think it's logical,' she said. 'I'm not sure that this sadness you feel is really even about him.'

'Well, of course not,' I told her, wiping a tear from the corner of my eye. 'Love isn't logical.'

'That's not what I mean,' she said. 'I mean that I don't think this depression is all about JP. You can't seem to let him go, and I think it may go back to something in your child-hood. Or rejection issues from your past. But I think that once you figure it out, he may become less important.'

'What, you mean you think it's all about my dad? That is so obvious. Look, if I'm going to have a mental breakdown, it's going to be from some really cool illness that no one has ever heard of, or taking a massive drug overdose and jumping off a building believing that I'm Jesus Christ. Not having a breakdown because my dad left. I'm not that clichéd.'

'See? That's what I mean. You always try to be funny about everything, which is great, but you don't have to bounce back from a break-up right away if you don't feel ready.' She put her hand on my forearm and gave me a reassuring squeeze.

'Life is not made up of one-liners. It's okay to exist and not be "on" all the time. What about the journey towards self-discovery we talked about? And this research mission you told me about, which by the way I think sounds really cool? Maybe you should consider therapy?' She looked down when she said it, but I knew that she, and the rest of my friends, had probably been thinking it for months after hearing me obsess.

Even though it's tough, I love the fact that my friends are strong enough to point out the obvious signs that I may be missing, whether it's helping me dislodge an unsightly piece of spinach in my teeth or an emotionally unavailable man. They are basically therapists who help me believe in myself, but maybe I needed more than that. Maybe I needed someone who, instead of helping me pick up the pieces, could help me avoid shattering my relationship in the first place. Or show me how to pick up someone less fragile.

In my new spirit of open-mindedness, I allowed myself to wonder whether Amy might have a point. At the very least it could be an interesting new phase in my Anti-Rules research task. I'd done some dating guides, I'd done advice from porn stars – why not throw a bit of therapy into the mix!

I had always resisted therapy, because I resent the idea of spending £70 an hour to witter on about my crushing insecurities, only to have someone say at the end of the hour: 'Well, what do you think you should do?' If I had all the goddamned answers, I wouldn't need to pay someone, would I?

Perhaps hanging out with a tortured artist had also helped open my mind to therapy. After all, if Jamie was so blind to his insecurities, maybe I was too. It's always easier to recognize pathologies in someone else – maybe that's why I'm so great at giving advice! It's much easier to tell other people to stop smoking than to do it yourself. The first rush when the nicotine enters your lungs is like a slipstream, and all tensions seem to be exhaled with the smoke.

Amy suddenly gave an excited jump. 'Did you bring it with you?'

'It' was a review of *Sleeping Around* in *Observer Woman* that I had been sweating over for months. I had carried a dog-eared copy around in my bag ever since it came out.

The piece had been my first bit of press for the book, and I have to say that I found the interviews a bit terrifying. I'm much more comfortable in the position of the journalist, the intrepid reporter sent out into the sexual wilderness to chronicle the behaviour of the deviant natives. Suddenly, the spotlight was turned on me, and I felt like I was being interrogated in a gritty back room while detectives shone a 1,000-watt bulb in my face.

I told Amy about the day when Louise France came up to my tiny fifth-floor flat and I could tell that she was looking around to see if there was anything out of place, mentally or otherwise.

I confuse people, I suppose, because I don't fit their image of a total sex fiend. I don't dress in an overtly sexy way, and I'm a nice person. I'm not a pneumatic blonde with inflatable breasts, not that there's anything wrong with that. I'm just not what people expect.

My hour and a half with Louise was great, and she was friendly and genuine, but I couldn't help thinking that I kept my voice just a bit too effervescent, in an attempt not to be psychoanalysed. At the time of the interview JP and I were still blissfully happy, so her comments about me really wanting a steady boyfriend were laughed off. But now I took them a bit more seriously.

I handed Amy the rolled-up and battered copy of the magazine, and sipped my soy latte while she read. She looked up at me. 'But, Cat, this is great. She loved the book. You are way too hard on yourself.'

Amy had a point. Though the article was full of compliments, I had immediately zeroed in on the criticisms: 'Dressed in skinny jeans, grey T-shirt and court shoes, it's not immediately obvious why men fall at her feet. She is neither buxom nor blowsy. In fact she is as skinny and tall and angular as a stick of celery.'

But the line that made me sit up and take notice was the one about my family, after I'd told Louise that my dad left when I was thirteen, and I played detective for my mum during the divorce.

'It doesn't take Freud to work out that being abandoned by your father – as it might have seemed to [Catherine] at the time – just at the point when you start to get all hot and bothered about sex could be significant.'

After hugging Amy and leaving the coffee shop, I walked the entire way around Hyde Park, my sightline following the swans, and eventually the gluteus maximus of a very hot Lycra-clad guy on a bike. Cyclists always have the tightest asses.

*. . . Suddenly I stumbled across his path, causing his bike to shudder to a stop, before he helped me up and took me behind one of the stripped bare trees where I slid my hands up the bulge in his shorts, tasting the tangy sweat on his skin as he bent me over and . . .*

This is what I do, use sexual fantasies as escapism. There have been periods in my life when I've been forced to go without sex for more than a week. These include the time I was lying in a hospital bed with kidney stones (though I did manage to flirt outrageously with the hot radiologist!); another one after a bad break-up when I was crying in my tracksuit while listening to the Smiths; and occasions when I've been visiting my super-conservative, gun-collecting dad in the American South. But I can't remember the last time in my adult life when I went more than a week or so without sex – of any kind – of my own free will. My break-up with JP, and the dating desert that followed, was the one exception to this, which is why it freaked me out so much. When I have a willing partner present, nothing beats the glow that I get from good sex – or at least an orgasm. So when I'm stressed out, I don't meditate, I masturbate.

Maybe sex was starting to distract me from real intimacy?

To my surprise and delight there had been quite a few favourable articles about my book, which tended to analyse me in the process. I reasoned that if everyone in the country was going to have access to my innermost soul, I might as well call in a professional, as Amy had suggested.

# FIFTEEN

Two days later, I found myself outside a nondescript house tucked away in a quiet north London mews. My charming new therapist, Sarah, had a mid-Atlantic twang that sounded as though she'd spent several years in the States.

I planned my outfit carefully that day; I wanted something that said, 'I'm confident enough about my life choices to dress casually, but still a bit vulnerable, and definitely don't have anything to prove about my rampant sexual urges,' which roughly translated to jeans and a black sweater.

Sarah was a tiny blonde with perfectly placed buttery chunk highlights and sculpted arms that had obviously done time at a Pilates studio. She was wearing a pencil skirt and cashmere vest top, and carrying a button-up sweater, probably for good reason.

I wondered if any of her male patients experienced trans-ference and fell madly in love with her, or fantasized about her. That was probably what the dowdy cardigan was for – a sort of cashmere chastity belt. Little did she know that I've slept with several women, and am not immune to letting my imagination run wild!

We went upstairs to her office, and I sat in one of the cush-ioned chairs across from her. Even though I thought I felt fine, just seeing the tissue box in the middle of the table made me want to cry. I tried to calm myself as she asked me why I was there.

I told her everything, about JP, the escapism with Jamie, the stress of the book, the hate mail, and how lately I felt like the Grinch who stole Christmas. Even though I knew that she was there to help me, I was conscious of the fact that I tried to spice up my stories and make them more interesting.

Just because I was paying someone for their time didn't mean that I needed to bore the poor woman to death.

'How is your relationship with your parents?' she asked.

Ah, this question again. I'll never forget the day my dad left. Until the age of thirteen, my childhood had been idyllic. Christmas was a magical experience, at least on the outside: my dad would cut down a giant tree from the woods and haul it home, and my mum would spend ages decorating it, but as I got older I realized that he spent more and more time away from home, and that when he was there something was off.

Spending time with my dad became like watching a badly dubbed Japanese movie: the words didn't quite match the actions. Even when he was helping me with my homework, I sensed that he always had one eye on the door. I knew that he was hiding something. He was the cardboard cut-out man.

Still, when he told me he was leaving, I was totally floored, and resolved never to let anyone do to me what he was doing to my mum. She had prioritized everyone else over herself, and look what happened.

I remember looking at my reflection in my brand-new lit-up make-up mirror and, not for the first time, talking to myself. 'You are strong, and you are going to be fine,' I said, and took a full ten minutes to pluck the remnants of my unibrow neatly before going in to confront Dad.

I might have been facing the dissolution of my family unit, but there was no reason why I had to deal with it looking like a werewolf. Weakness was unacceptable. Control was everything.

Over the next few weeks, I saw my mum suffer a complete breakdown. She took me and my sister halfway across the country, sold everything she'd ever known and loved, and told us we would have a 'new start'.

'Our parents give us the templates for how we view life and relationships.' Sarah was scribbling furiously in her legal pad. 'What do you think you learned from that incident?'

I could feel tears welling up in my eyes. 'Never to be weak in front of a man. Because, eventually, they leave.'

'So you feel that it's important to maintain control of a relationship?'

'Well, obviously I'm not that in control, because I keep getting dumped!' I tried to keep my tone light-hearted, but started to cry.

'Right, but you can't control someone else's behaviour. Just your own, and our choice of partners is unconscious. Often we're trying to finish something started by our parents, or get a different result. There is obviously something about your relationship with JP that feels unfinished, so you need to think about what you have to do to let it go.'

I walked out of her office in a daze, wondering why I hadn't seen the truth sooner. In so many ways, many of my ex-boyfriends have been similar to my dad. They are lovely guys, but scratch the surface and you would find someone who is afraid of real intimacy. Every time we get close, they push me away.

I sighed in frustration.

'So why did my last boyfriend feel like my soulmate? I hate to sound like a cheesy country music song but why does something so wrong feel so right?'

She looked up from her notebook, 'Often we get feelings of intensity with certain people because things feel familiar. We repeat patterns.' She looked at me again. 'It's natural to do what feels familiar.'

'So you think I'm trying to recreate a happy ending I never got from childhood?'

She was silent.

So,' I said to Sarah as I was about to leave, 'what do I do to start feeling better?'

She scrawled an address on a sheet of paper and said, 'When you feel ready, go to one of these meetings.'

I looked at where she'd written 'Sex and Love Addicts Anonymous', and put the sheet of paper in my handbag. Was I really ready to go that far in the name of my Anti-Rules research project?

According to the therapist, I'm unconsciously choosing people because they can't give me intimacy. And yet I couldn't stop hoping for a happy ending, because I wanted it so badly. I know that the definition of madness is doing the same thing over and over and hoping for a different result.

And yet, I'm hooked.

# SIXTEEN

I wasn't quite sure whether therapy was giving me any answers or just making me crazier. But, speaking of madness, I'd begun to wonder whether my new flatmate Emma was insane.

It started with small things, like the fact that she would always be over-familiar with my pals when they rang the house.

Amy had ventured that perhaps she was 'just being friendly', while Victoria was more brutal. 'She sounds totally mentally unbalanced,' she told me bluntly while I was walking home. 'I called to talk to you, and she kept asking all these questions about my wedding and saying she felt like we were sisters already. I'd lock up the kitchen knives if I were you!'

Victoria, who despite her dry sense of humour is actually very warm and friendly, had noticed Emma's behaviour first after I invited Emma to join us for dinner. Now, I happened to know that Emma had plenty of money, because her HR job paid loads and our rent was so cheap, plus she had the proceeds of her flat sale in the bank. In fact, she had a lot more than I did.

Anyway, we ordered drinks, while Emma stuck to tap water, saying that she wasn't used to buying her own drinks. I could feel Victoria's gaze burning into the side of my face, so I kept the conversation light.

'Wow, is that passion fruit?' Emma said when my martini came. I offered her a taste, and she gulped half of it down and kept sipping.

The waiter came to take our orders, and Victoria and I both had the tuna burgers – she got chips and I had salad on the side. Emma said she was 'dieting' and ordered nothing.

The incident happened after about ten more minutes of pleasant chat when Emma reached out and grabbed several chips off Victoria's plate – without asking – drenched them in her ketchup and kept talking.

A sort of Mexican standoff ensued, with Victoria looking on in shock as Emma continued to scarf her chips. Eventually, she finished almost everything on the plate.

Victoria was shocked. 'It wasn't that I was skeeved out about sharing food,' she explained later. 'You know that you can lick my plate if you want. But you're my friend. She's not. Cat, the girl does not know where to draw the line!'

'It was just a few chips, for God's sake,' I retorted.

'I'm telling you that the girl does not understand boundaries. Did you hear her talking about how she wanted me and her to be best friends too? I'm telling you, watch your back!'

Victoria had been in a bad mood that night thanks to her family pressurizing her to firm up her wedding plans so at the time I just put it down to that.

A few nights later, I came home shattered after a heavy night with Michael at the House of Commons, schmoozing with MPs. I could feel the beginnings of a migraine so just wanted to sink into my bed and sleep it off. I jostled around in my handbag trying to find my keys, before preparing to climb five storeys. I tiptoed upstairs, sucking in my breath in the hope that Emma might be asleep or out. Once I got to the top my heart sank when I saw a crack of light under the door.

In truth, I had guessed she wouldn't be out. She was never out. To be honest I hadn't exactly seen much evidence of her having other friends. I seemed to be her only social outlet, and she would inevitably trap me on the sofa to 'have a girly chat'. This was always entirely focused on her life and how she was ready to 'live up to her potential'. She'd given up on the yoga idea, and now wanted to write a novel, or 'maybe become a journalist', as if this was something that happened by clicking magical shoes together a couple of times.

At first I had tried to help her by suggesting that she email editors, or write features, but it soon became clear that she had absolutely no intention of changing her life.

She wanted me to validate everything she said, which was basically that her dream life would fall into place without her lifting a finger.

'Hi, Cat,' she said. 'Do you want a glass of wine? I was thinking about what you said about emailing editors to get work, so I finally took action today!'

I shrugged off my coat, hung it behind the door and sat on our sofa. 'That's great, I'm happy for you. Who did you email? Features editors on a few magazines?'

'Well, I decided that TV was really more my thing, so I looked in your address book and found the number for the Sky News people you work with. Anyway, I called the editor and told him that I was your flatmate, and that I wanted to have lunch with him!'

I felt the blood drain from my face. I'm all for living in a fantasy world, but this chick really was unbelievable. 'You mean – Martin at Sky? I've only been on Sky News once, I barely know him!'

'Yeah, yeah, I know. He said he couldn't make lunch but we chatted for a while anyway, and he seemed to be a really nice guy,' she said, settling down across from me in the chair and grinning. 'I asked if I could be on the news to talk about my experience with a big corporation working in HR, because you know we really do see loads of crazy characters; it's even weirder than *The Office*! He didn't commit to anything, but I could tell that he was interested. Thanks so much!'

'So let me get this straight. You went through my address book, and called someone I barely know? Why would you do that?'

'I thought we could be on TV together! Wouldn't that be fun?'

I went over to the de-facto 'bar', which was really just some bottles of spirits and a half-empty bottle of tonic lined up on the kitchen counter, next to the boiler. I poured myself a shot of bourbon over two ice cubes and drained it in one sip.

I didn't know whether to feel sorry or scared. Looking at her, happily munching on pesto in the candlelight, I realized that she had absolutely no idea that she had done anything wrong.

I was enraged, but didn't know what to say. On the one hand, she exuded childlike innocence; then again, on the few nights she'd been out with my friends she was always the one who never had her wallet. Or, worse, she would nag me to chat to men so that they would buy us drinks. She always came out ahead.

Not knowing what to say, I sat down on the sofa again.

'Look, Emma, we need to talk,' I said gently. 'I know that

you didn't mean anything by it, but you have to understand that this is my career. I would have been happy to refer you to someone if you had asked me, but my flatmate making calls to my contacts out of the blue is going to make me look weird. Can you understand that?'

'Oh, I'm so sorry, I didn't mean to fuck things up for you,' she said. 'I feel terrible.'

'Don't worry about it,' I said. 'Just next time, if you want a phone number, ask me for it, okay?'

'I promise,' she said, smiling. 'Look, let me make it up to you. I've got an extra invite to a Christmas fashion party, so why don't you come with me?'

'Thanks, but I'm meeting Mark and his new girlfriend Samantha tomorrow. I didn't know that you were into fashion stuff?'

'Oh, well, it's not me really. I used to live above a journalist, and since we had about ten mail slots in the hallway, I occasionally nicked her invites and RSVPed to events as her. I got loads of free booze that way!'

She looked very proud of herself, and seemed oblivious to the fact that the poor journalist, whoever she was, would have to go without her post and probably get bitched out by PR people, wondering why her promised press coverage of the parties that her doppelgänger had attended never materialized.

'Right, I'd better hit the sack,' I said, secretly resolving to check the mail first thing in the morning.

'Oh no, that's a shame. Before you go to bed, let me give you this. I made something for you,' she said, handing me a box.

'Oh, thanks.' I was confused. Had she knitted me a scarf or something? This was turning into one bizarre night.

I opened the box and pulled out a cloth doll that looked like a miniature version of Emma, with beady little black eyes staring back at me from underneath a mop of curly red hair. The mini-Emma was even wearing one of her signature rhinestone pins. What the hell was this? Was it meant to be a voodoo doll?

'Thanks,' I said, backing towards my bedroom door. 'You, um, made a doll?'

'Yes, I collect them,' she said. 'They're like my little friends. And now you can be reminded of my friendship wherever you are!'

'Well, I'm really tired right now, so I'm going to bed,' I said, feigning a yawn.

'So she made you a doll of herself?' Victoria screeched.

I was huddled on my bed, my knees to my chest and the duvet pulled over my entire head.

I had to whisper because of the thin walls. 'It kind of reminds me of a voodoo doll, but she called it a friendship doll,' I said. 'I'm not sure if she wants to have sex with me or wear my skin, but either way it's not good!'

'Look, you have to think about getting out of there. What about Mark's offer?'

'Living with my husband? That might be a bit awkward.'

'What's going on with that anyway?'

'Well, he's got a new girlfriend. He even wants to introduce me to her, which sounds pretty serious for a guy with his track record. I doubt she'd be best pleased if I rocked up as his new flatmate. On the plus side, I'm very close to having my passport, and being an official divorcee,' I told her, 'but for now I'm just going to bide my time in this flat. I don't think things could get any weirder!'

Later, ready for sleep, I pulled up the duvet and stared at the doll on my nightstand. The truth was, I pitied Emma, but lurking underneath the pity was fear. I was afraid of ending up like her in five years, with no real friends to speak of, living in a delusion of my own making.

Besides, I couldn't blame Emma for assuming that our relationship was close. Crazy room-mates seem to be a rite of passage in modern life; it's bizarre.

In my grandmother's generation, the only person you lived with outside of family was your husband. It is an odd arrangement nowadays to be able to hear a complete stranger having an orgasm through your cardboard walls.

Still, Victoria is right. I have to get better at setting boundaries. Otherwise Emma is in very real danger of an attempted stabbing with a stolen chip!

# SEVENTEEN

I spoke too soon about things not getting weirder with
Emma. It was only a matter of time before our next strange
encounter. I had got a surprise call from Jamie in Goa. I was
touched that he'd gone one better than email and wondered
whether perhaps there might be something more to this guy
after all. Especially when he revealed the surprise he had in
store for me!

'I didn't want you to get lonely while I'm away so I've
lined up a little treat for you. I think you should meet my
ex-girlfriend Rachel. She's gorgeous. And she's dying to fuck
you. I've set you up on a date.'

The conversation soon got pretty steamy. But we had to
cut off before we had finished because of the cost of the long-
distance call.

Feeling frustrated, I went into the bedroom and pulled out
my secret box of toys from under the bed. Since I often have to
do research stories and road-test new products, I have everything
from anal beads to triple-ended vibrators down there, but my
prize possessions are the gold-plated glass dildos. They are
gorgeous, thick and very satisfying. With one hand down my
tracksuit bottoms, I found the dildo I was looking for, but noticed
something odd: it wasn't in its velvet pouch. I know that this

seems minor, but I am meticulous when it comes to the cleaning and storage of my sex toys. I'm as careful as a gun collector who keeps his prize possessions in pride of place on his shelf.

Slightly freaked out, I went into the front room. I could hear Emma coming up the stairs and putting her key into the door, so I started nonchalantly flicking through a magazine as she came in.

'How was your day?' she asked breathily.

'Great,' I said. Then, to test the water: 'I've been sent a whole new load of sex toy products to try. I have so many under my bed I can't keep track of them all!'

She hesitated, then started putting away her groceries.

'Hey, I meant to suggest, if you ever have any extras, I'm happy to take them off your hands.'

I dropped the magazine and watched her putting a cucumber into the fridge. 'Really?'

'Totally. And if you have any that you want to loan me, I'm happy to take those too!'

Despite her cheery tone, I could feel shivers going down my spine. 'You mean, you would want them – second-hand?'

'Well, I know you mentioned in one of your articles that you could sterilize them in the dishwasher, so I just thought—'

'No,' I said, 'sorry, but vibrators are strictly for me and my sexual partners.'

We both laughed, but inside I was terrified. And bummed out, because I knew that I could never ever use any of my beloved sex toys again.

Later that night, I called Mark from my bedroom, with the Smiths playing as background noise.

'So, what's the problem?' he said. 'I used to keep one in my drawer in case a girl wanted to use it.'

'Whatever, Mark, vibrators are not like teacups!' I hissed. 'They are personal use only. Can't you understand how deeply freaky it is that she wants to use something that I've had inside my vagina inside hers?'

I heard him giggling. 'It may not have been her vagina, Cat!'

'Eew! I might need to do a runner after all.'

'Look, you know you're welcome to come and crash at mine. You and Samantha really hit it off the other night. I almost felt left out, the way you guys were whispering and giggling and downing shots together. She's totally cool with you – and our situation. We have the spare bedroom, you pay rent to use it as office space and half your stuff is in there anyway. You know you're always welcome.'

'Thanks, honey. You're a lifesaver.'

But I knew that Mark was just being a bloke and failing to see how our unorthodox circumstances might be a problem for his new squeeze. I liked Samantha and didn't want to mess things up between them.

A few weeks after their first date, Mark had told Samantha the whole story of our marriage, and she'd taken it remarkably well. I had taken her out to answer all her questions, and she'd been very cool about the whole state of affairs.

'I'm not thrilled that if we get married it will be his second wedding, but to be honest I can't hold his past against him,' she'd said. 'Besides, why would I be angry at him for helping a friend out? His generosity is one of the reasons I love him.'

At the end of the day, Samantha's attitude also made me stop blaming myself for my circumstances when I met JP. When you love someone, you work through problems. Period.

I put the top on my box of tricks. 'I wonder if glass dildos are recyclable?'

With a heavy heart, I threw away my toys, because I knew that even if I sterilized them in thousand-degree heat, I would never again be able to use them with the same degree of carefree, reckless abandon as before. I decided there and then that it was time for a new phase in my life. I was going to start looking for a place of my own, where I could use my larger, noiser toys and watch pornos with abandon, and enjoy my own space. It was time.

Toys I won't bother replacing:
1. The solar-powered vibrator. I'm not sure if London is just too grey, but it never got up to full power.
2. The lipstick-shaped vibrator – looked fake, and didn't really work.
3. Ben Wa Balls – never really got the point – maybe I'm just not co-ordinated enough?
4. Strap-on apparatus – not really needed except in exceptional circumstances, and tends to scare the hell out of men.

Toys I will definitely replace:
1. Rampant Rabbit – it's a cliché for a reason.
2. Nubby G – the vibrator that trained me to have G-spot orgasms.
3. Rock Chick, and Rude Boy – the amazing hands-free vibe, and its male equivalent for prostate stimulation.

4. Magician's rope – great for bondage, just stay clear of men with lots of chest hair!

The glass dildos are lovely, but I can live without them for the time being.

# EIGHTEEN

It was the afternoon before my date with Rachel and I was nervous as hell. But it wasn't the possibility of an illicit encounter with my boyfriend's ex that filled my stomach with vomiting butterflies.

It was picking an outfit for a date with a woman that was truly nerve-racking. I know that most men don't care about fashion, but women are much harder on each other. Everyone wants a partner who looks after themselves. But women (and men) who are obsessed with appearances are far too worried about being in control to let themselves go in the sack. When my male pals ask me how to tell if someone is likely to rock their world with screaming orgasms, I advise them to seek out women who are comfortable in their own skin. My friend Michael once asked me for tips on this and I suggested he avoid overly groomed women, because too much make-up could be a sign that she'll have a different face in the morning. Manicures are fine, but avoid talons, as women with shorter nails are dirtier.

I told Michael that I remembered my first sexual experience with a woman – I had his full attention at this point – a Russian friend of mine at university. She was physically stunning, but the best thing about her was her outlook on life. She wasn't into self-denial, so we often ate chocolate cake. After midnight.

Off each other's bodies. She really was the perfect woman – if only I had been a lesbian, my love life would have been sorted years ago.

So it seemed only right that it should now be Michael who got my crisis call. I begged him to come over to examine my outfits and calm my nerves about the evening ahead. He agreed on the proviso of a cup of tea and a gossip too.

As I put on the kettle and waited for Michael to turn up I thought back to a particularly cringe-worthy first date with Marcus, a sexy Swedish trader. I had been dressed to kill. Or so I thought. I'd done a bit of spring shopping to ensure that my ensemble was dynamite. I was rocking a gold mini dress, worn with footless tights so that I resembled an extra from *Logan's Run*, minus the bouffant hair.

He turned up wearing a classic suit, and I could sense that I wasn't going to be getting lucky the minute he ran his eyes up and down my outfit. Soon afterwards, he mumbled something about 'having an early meeting' and bailed out after one drink.

It was a pretty lame excuse, one that I recognized because I've used it myself. 'Wait!' I imagined shouting as he pulled away in the cab. 'Don't you know metallics are a key trend this year?' He disappeared into the night, and never called again.

I've always known that women dress for other women, and that the dichotomy between what women consider fashion-forward and what men find sexy is more obvious than ever. I'm torn, because I do consider my style an extension of my creativity. But I want my clothes to inspire men to peel them off later, not run for the hills.

There was a buzz on my intercom so I let Michael in and shared my dilemma. So here was Michael, serial dater, lad, in my bedroom, clothes strewn all over the shop, casting a critical eye over my closet. The results weren't encouraging. He hated my 'fugly' leggings, thought my trendy ruffled blouses looked 'like something my gran would wear', and deemed my bubble skirt 'sartorial birth control'.

'I went out with a gorgeous girl with a lovely figure, but it seemed as if she was trying to make herself look as hideous as possible,' he said. 'Puffy pink skirts and bright green leggings are not whimsical and quirky,' he opined. 'They scare the hell out of men.'

The irony is that even the guys still wearing jeans-and-blazer combinations from the 1980s have strong opinions about what they hate. This season's 'sack dress' and massive sunglasses were off the menu. 'They hide a woman's face, which is deceitful,' Michael said. Baby-doll dresses were also out. 'I can't look at one without thinking of Bette Davis in *Whatever Happened to Baby Jane?*' was his view. 'Why would a grown woman want to look twelve years old?'

His advice was to 'keep it simple'. 'Wear something that you're comfortable in,' he said, 'and that you can get out of easily.'

When I finally arrived – thankfully dressed to kill in a bought-on-sale black Alexander McQueen pencil skirt and white sleeveless silk camisole – at the Charlotte Street Hotel bar and saw Rachel for the first time, I instantly felt the tension in my stomach release and knew that everything was going to be okay. She was stunning, and smiling broadly. And she was exactly my type.

I'm not sure if it's narcissism or something less sinister, but my taste in women is pretty uniform, honed through years of rifling through airbrushed magazines and lesbian porn. I like them to look picture-perfect and they have to have a similar body shape to mine, slender but not skinny.

Rachel was curvy, but in all the right places, with long wavy black hair and olive skin that made her look like a taller version of Penelope Cruz. Her prim black suit belied the fact that she was a very experimental girl. According to Jamie, they used to participate in orgies all the time. Their relationship had been completely jealousy-free, which seriously intrigued me.

I'd taken part in threesomes before, but never had one-on-one action with a girl who was as experienced as Rachel.

I needn't have worried, though, because she was warm and friendly, with a brilliant laugh. As we talked about our careers and her nightmare boss, we looked like any two girlfriends on a night out. No one knew about our dirty little secret.

'So, tell me about you and Jamie,' I said, while the remnants of the second dirty martini were starting to warm my stomach. I couldn't stop staring at her chest, then feeling my cheeks burn because I was being so obvious.

'Well, we dated all through university, and he was the only guy who understood my sexual appetite,' she said.

I plucked the last olive out of my drink and tried to suck on it seductively.

'And you didn't get jealous?'

'No, just the opposite. I actually really got off on seeing him in bed with other girls.' She slid a bit closer to me and brushed my knee. 'I'm sure he told you that I love girls too. In fact, my last relationship was with a woman. I'm probably more into women than men.'

I could feel myself getting wet, and wanting to feel her luscious lips on mine. And it wasn't because I was under the mistletoe at a crappy office Christmas party doing this for the benefit of the men – this was something I was doing just for myself.

She leaned over and brushed her lips with mine, and I kissed her back, softly at first and then with more intensity.

We were really getting into it, until we became aware of several men at nearby tables staring at us. 'Wow, it looks like Christmas has come a bit early,' one fifty-something guy in a suit slurred.

'Ew,' I said, giggling.

She took my hand. 'Let's get out of here.'

We went back to Rachel's place, where she poured me a glass of wine and sat next to me on the sofa. I slid my hands up her skirt as she unbuttoned her blouse, to reveal a pair of perfect C-cup breasts squished into a size-too-small lacy push-up bra. I kissed her neck and slid one of her nipples into my mouth, and she moaned as it hardened underneath my eager tongue.

I couldn't believe how forward I was being: I wanted to penetrate her. I was hungry.

She rubbed the palm of her hand against my knickers, which were already soaking wet. I gasped, because I couldn't wait for her to slide her fingers inside, which she did. Gritting my teeth, I almost came right there, as I mumbled something about going to the bedroom. She led me there, and on the way I dropped my skirt to the floor and kicked it into a corner.

I'd deliberately worn a flattering pair of black lace knickers, in case a thong revealed any cellulite. She stripped off her skirt and lay down on the bed, where we hugged, awkwardly, for a few seconds then we started kissing, running our hands over each other's bodies.

I was freaking out and very nervous, but slid one finger, then another, inside her and started to rub her the way I do myself when I'm home alone.

'Oh God, Cat, that feels so good,' she moaned, then twisted herself around so that she was kissing down my stomach, then softly blew her hot breath through my panties and started licking around my pussy.

I had flashbacks of all the times I'd mentally made fun of lovers' oral techniques, lying back and thinking how clueless they were, but now I felt sorry for them.

I've never had a problem with taking direction, since I know that everyone is individual. During one of my first blow jobs, my then boyfriend explained that the goal should be 'more lips, less teeth', and I've been learning ever since. But Rachel was grinding against me and her breathing was getting more and more out of control, so I sensed that I was on the right track.

I was dying, and couldn't wait any longer to taste her. I slid her G-string down and pushed a finger inside to stimulate her G-spot, pushing it in and out while I sucked on her clit, tonguing the alphabet (an old trick I'd learned from men!).

We stayed for ages in the 69 position, until I felt her tighten around my finger, then she told me she was going to come and her muscles contracted around me, and I felt her slick juices gush all around my mouth. I came a few seconds later, and if it wasn't the most intense orgasm of my, life it definitely ranked in the top five.

Sweating, breathing hard and giggling, we lay back on the bed and linked hands.

'This feels so weird,' I said.

Rachel raised one eyebrow. 'I find that very hard to believe! You felt amazing.'

'No, I mean I've been with women before but it was mostly in situations with men . . . this is new territory for me.'

'New territory is there to be explored.' She smiled salaciously, topped up my glass of wine, and opened her bottom drawer. 'I've got lots of toys that we can play with. And Jamie will be back from his travels soon, so we can do a different kind of exploration together.'

God, this girl was too good to be true.

# NINETEEN

Jamie called again a couple of nights later to find out how it had gone.

'Wow, you are a dirty little slut, aren't you?' he said, and I could tell by his heavy breathing that he was getting turned on by listening to me. 'What are you wearing right now?'

Men are so predictable. As I'd done in so many past phone sex situations, I looked down at my leopard-print tracksuit pants and bunny rabbit slippers, my bright blue clay face mask starting to leak into my eyes, and lied.

Even though I was ironing this week's clothes, I got turned on enough to start touching myself. Once Jamie had hung up my mind flitted to the guy I'd met that day.

In Jamie's absence I was biding my time by lusting after inappropriate men: the guy I sat across from on the Central Line Tube who got off at Holborn, the waiter who brought extra bread to my table, and even my dentist who I'd had an appointment with that morning.

In a way, it made sense, because I was the one lying back on the chair and he was in the power position. And while my previous dentists have tended to be grumpy old men, Julian was a thirty-something hottie with a lilting accent and dazzling smile.

We made small talk about life before he opened my mouth and stuck his fingers inside. To my astonishment, I felt a tingle down below. This came as quite a shock, because when I think of sexy men in the medical field, images of George Clooney on *ER* or plastic surgeons come to mind.

I tend to rate the sex factor of dentists down there with proctologists or chiropodists. Besides, the guy sees me in situations where I drool all over myself, which is not hot.

I wondered if I was the only one on heat who felt that the gas wasn't the only thing making me happy. So with my fingers still between my legs, I pulled my laptop up on to the bed and did a one-handed search of websites dedicated to dental fetishes. Unfortunately it was a total turn-off. Most of them looked pretty scary, and I quickly worked out that my crush had nothing to do with craving oxygen masks or having my jaws stretched apart by dental forceps.

The day after my tooth-whitening visit, I met Victoria for drinks to discuss the upcoming wedding. Red wine for her and a vodka tonic for myself. 'I'm not allowed anything that stains, otherwise I have to go back for a repeat visit,' I said, raising one eyebrow and grinning.

'Oh yeah, that's the last thing you would want,' she said sarcastically.

Victoria looked gorgeous – her already petite and curvy frame was honed to perfection. She looked really, really happy.

'God, you look fantastic, babe,' I said.

'Thanks,' she said, 'I've been working out to get ready for the wedding.'

'You must be so excited!'

'Funnily enough, I don't think that reality has set in yet. You know I've never been a girly girl when it comes to planning weddings, so I'm just assuming that everything is going to take care of itself.'

'Well, the important thing is that you've got the right groom, and he's crazy about you.' I squeezed her hand.

We then got on to the topic of the evening properly and discussed where she might have the wedding, how many guests, the reception and of course her dress. We batted ideas around for a while until Victoria changed the subject.

'Anyway, enough about me. How's the rock star?' she asked.

'The sex is great, but to be honest I don't really want it to go anywhere,' I told her. 'But I have been immortalized in song. A very, very badly written song. Anyway, he's still in Goa, finding himself, so I'm on my own for the moment.'

Though I was genuinely happy for her, I felt a pang of regret that I wasn't planning my own wedding. Suddenly I was in tears.

'Honey, are you okay? What's wrong?'

'It's JP,' I confessed. 'Although I'm supposed to be with Jamie these days, I miss him,' I said. 'And I keep replaying everything in my mind and thinking What if?'

'Oh, baby, don't cry. Amy mentioned something about this. Why don't you call him?'

'What am I going to say? He was very clear that he didn't want to see me again.'

She took my hand. 'Sometimes you have to fight for what you want.'

I laughed and wiped the tears from my eyes. 'I can't; he should be the one to come back after me. I'm not weakening myself like that.'

'Honey, this is life, not a movie. He's not going to show up under your window serenading you. That only happens in bad films. Or with the men you end up filing protection orders against. Men are simple creatures. Sometimes you have to tell them what they want.'

On my way home, walking through Soho, slightly tipsy, I thought about what Victoria had said. I'm a big believer in fate, but I also believe that you make your own luck in life. Maybe telling JP how much I loved him wasn't such a weak act after all. I unearthed my phone from the bottom of my handbag and dialled his number (I'd deleted it, but unfortunately for men I have a cracking memory for long series of numbers, including credit card details!).

But I couldn't hit call. My fingers were paralysed over the digits, hovering. I didn't feel confident enough to fake the easy breeziness that I knew would be necessary to secure a meeting with him.

I texted Jamie instead to say I was looking forward to his return soon, because I knew that he would be happy to hear from me. For now, he was the easy option, and that was all I could handle.

I guess I wasn't completely done playing games after all.

# TWENTY

I was worried that I had started obsessing about JP again, so I decided to return to my 'research' for distraction. I picked up the next book on my pile: *The Rules*. Hardly the most suitable set text for my self-imposed Anti-Rules assignment. But, frankly, I was feeling lonely, pathetic and unworthy of male companionship unless I pretended to be someone else, so I figured that it would be the perfect read.

Also, I must admit that I wanted something to make me feel more in control, even if it did mean morphing into a manipulative bitch. I would do anything to feel better.

I soon remembered why I hated it so much.

*Rule: How To Act On Dates 1, 2, and 3*
*All you really have to do on the first three dates is show up, relax, pretend you're an actress making a cameo appearance in a movie.*

*The first three dates should be like being and nothingness. Dress nice, be nice, goodbye, and go home.*

If this was the way to land a man, then I had the distinct feeling that I would be alone for ever. All I could think was, How boring!

Ever since I can remember, I've been addicted to breaking the rules. As a child my favourite question was 'Why?' and when my poor parents ran out of answers they sent me to Christian camp in the Arkansas Ozark Mountains.

I almost got kicked out in the first week for smuggling in a Depeche Mode cassette; according to the counsellors, rock and roll was 'the devil's music' and I don't think they appreciated me singing lyrics like: 'I don't want to start any blasphemous rumours/But I think that God's got a sick sense of humour/And when I die/I expect to find/ Him laughing'.

Though I'd done my share of partying in high school, I spent my first few weeks as a freshman at New York University barely venturing out except to classes and the library. I was awe-inspired but at the same time intimidated by New York's vastness and its incredible city skyline.

Soon I was in heaven as I began to explore the city, but I was still desperately lonely even if I tried to appear cool on the surface. One girl who seemed to have it all together was Erin, who ran the university fashion magazine. She had perfectly co-ordinated fashion-forward ensembles, an in-your-face attitude and huge tattoos (on her back was a giant one of Oscar Wilde flying on a sunflower, and underneath was inked: 'Each man kills the thing he loves').

I was both fascinated and terrified by her, so we never actually spoke until one day in my politics class, when she saw me thumbing through an anthology of erotic stories with a whip-wielding dominatrix on the cover.

'That doesn't look like Francis Fukuyama,' she whispered. 'What the hell are you reading?'

I blushed. 'Oh, I'm, um, just using it for research,' I said. 'I actually went to a masturbation seminar last night and I'm writing a piece on female sexuality.'

We spoke for a few minutes about Betty Dodson, the self-styled 'Mother of Masturbation' whose presentation I had been to the night before. I had been totally blown away by her candour, and the fact that she ran these seminars where she literally taught women how to get themselves off. Watching women finger themselves seemed like a pretty sweet day job. All this, and the woman was pushing seventy!

Despite being sexually active since I was fifteen, I was pretty sure that I'd never had an orgasm. In fact, I was beginning to suspect that they were part of some media conspiracy.

'She's right. You have to learn to get yourself off before you can expect any man to have a clue what to do,' Erin said matter-of-factly.

'Absolutely,' I said coolly, though I still hadn't got the hang of masturbation. I'd tried it a few times, and given up after about twenty minutes. But I reckoned that I was an 'A' student, and if I could get high marks in the classroom, I should be able to figure out how my clitoris worked.

Right before the bell rang, she invited me to a party that night on Avenue C in the East Village.

This was back in the days before clothing boutiques lined the entire area, and crack dealers still outnumbered coffee houses. I checked to make sure that we had the right address, because the building looked like it was about to be condemned.

Up at the party I noticed that the hostess had a pet rat that she kept in an aquarium. We danced until four in the morning, and Erin ended up pulling one of the guys from the party, a tall, lanky hipster who sang in a Smiths tribute band.

We all shared a cab back to my place, and when they dropped me off I leaned over to ask her discreetly if she would be okay taking a total stranger back to her house. I'd had some wild encounters in Parisian flats, but that all seemed so alien, like a weird foreign movie. This was real life.

'Are you sure that's safe?' I whispered.

'Oh yeah,' she said, smiling. 'Don't worry, baby, I keep a knife under my pillow just in case anything goes wrong.' As she winked and sped off into the night, I knew that we would become firm friends.

When I called Erin the next morning, she told me that she had no plans to see the guy again. I found her attitude to sexuality incredibly liberating, because she wasn't playing games. The city was her playground, and I wanted a piece of the action.

But her comment about getting myself off intrigued me; as Erin put it, 'If you're not sure, it didn't happen. End of story.'

That night, with Betty Dodson on the brain, I went back to the one-and-a-half-bedroom flat I shared with three other girls, and locked myself in the bathroom. I spread my legs out on the cold tile floor, pulled my panties down and arranged the lime-green bathmat so that it was underneath my ass.

Then, I started fantasizing about one of the erotic stories I'd read, about a hot thirty-something woman who encounters a nubile teenage couple fucking while she's gardening.

She strokes herself with a vibrator while the couple shags in front of her, touching the girl's tits and sliding a finger into the boy's ass as he pumps the girl from behind.

Thinking about the filthy threesome I re-wet my fingers and kept stroking my clitoris. After a while, I felt myself pulsing, and my thighs started to tremble involuntarily. Finally, with one foot wedged against the unlockable door, I brought myself to my first orgasm.

Once I knew how to get myself off, I became like a kid in a candy store, and I wanted to try every flavour.

Suddenly, the inappropriate men I'd been eyeing up didn't seem off-limits, because I didn't have to adapt the pretence of dating them just to fuck them.

I masturbated at least twice a day, at every conceivable opportunity. Forget drinking a glass of milk, an orgasm was the perfect thing to send me off to sleep, or wake me up in the morning.

I devoured sex literature, and wanted to experience pleasure in every possible permutation. Before long, I started dating a forty-five-year-old restaurant owner who was a dead ringer for George Clooney. He loved pouring champagne in my pussy and licking it out, the bubbles tingling my clitoris while I writhed in ecstasy. I was discovering sensations that I never knew existed.

At the same time as my sex life was broadening, my home life was rapidly deteriorating.

One of my flatmates was a tiny Chinese girl named Alicia who had recently found God. I couldn't really bring Erin around – this was the girl who carried Virgin Mary condoms in her handbag – because Alicia was incredibly judgemental. Every time I would come in after having a few beers, she would ask me if I had found Jesus, and before long she started leaving Alcoholics Anonymous flyers on my bed. Something had to give.

The situation came to a head one morning, when I came in, still hung-over and wearing a red micro-mini from a date with the restaurant owner, to find Alicia and her Bible study group strumming a guitar and singing 'Kumbaya'. 'Cat, don't you think it's seriously time that you re-evaluated your relationship with the Lord?' she asked me.

'Actually, Alicia, I don't think that's the relationship I need to re-think right now.' Smiling sweetly, I gave my month's notice.

Erin and I moved into a bachelorette pad in the East Village, and since we were too broke to have nice furniture we decided to make the place look as kitsch as possible. So we installed a disco ball, a leopard-print couch, and painted one wall with 'magnetic' paint that had iron filings in the mix so that we could stick up erotic magnetic poetry. I would go the fridge for a beer and find 'I slide my engorged cock into your happy gushing juicy pussy' on the door.

Life was pretty sweet, and we ended up sharing that flat for more than two years, and racked up loads of hilarious encounters and happy memories before moving into our own places. Even though I'm on the other side of the ocean now, she's still one of my best friends.

# TWENTY-ONE

They were carefree times back then in New York, as I pushed boundaries, both personally and professionally. And what better way than by nailing the boss?

As part of my journalism training, I had started an internship at an independent TV production company. Within five minutes of walking into the plush carpeted office downtown, I sensed that my immediate supervisor, Charlie, wanted to bend me over the desk.

My attraction to Charlie helped solidify my belief in pheromones when determining desirability, because, to put it bluntly, he was not a looker.

Though he had broad shoulders and a solid physique, he already had a thinning hairline at thirty, and his features were a bit off-centre rather than conventionally handsome. I'd always thought of '*jolie-laide*' as a phrase that applied to women, but it described him perfectly. His constant casual Friday wardrobe of novelty T-shirts under button-downs and Converse tennis shoes were at odds with his razor-sharp, yet self-deprecating wit. The walls of his office were lined with everything from Kierkegaard to rare Japanese comic books, and he had an encyclopaedic knowledge of pop culture.

Although we shared light-hearted banter as I slipped him his morning latte, I couldn't exactly propose that he slipped me something more substantial. Fortunately, over email one brisk autumn day, he gave me the ideal opening. 'This may be a bit inappropriate, but I was wondering if you wanted to help me research a programme,' he wrote. The rest of the email explained that he was researching 'pony people', a group of sexual enthusiasts who got off on dressing up like horses.

'Definitely,' I replied. 'I've always been a bit equi-curious.'

Later, having arranged to meet Charlie there, I turned into a back alley off Lafayette Street and thought that I must have the wrong address. Instead of half-naked sex fiends, I saw a prim-looking woman carrying a clipboard. She was wearing a dowdy pink cardigan and those old-school cat's-eye glasses on a chain that only look at home on people over fifty. 'Hi, I'm Catherine, and I'm here for the, um, horse people,' I murmured, eyes downcast.

'Go right inside, dear,' she said, patting me on the shoulder. 'Here's a flyer on our spanking seminar next Sunday.'

Inside I found Charlie, who was shifting his weight from one foot to the other and looking sheepish. 'It's pretty full-on in there,' he said. 'Are you sure you're cool with this?'

'Sure,' I said, squeezing his forearm as a corpulent guy and his lithe brunette companion, carrying a tiny saddle, breezed past. 'He's not going to ride her, is he?' I whispered. 'Talk about animal cruelty!'

We took our 'ringside' seats, and I watched in amazement as the first couple entered. A mild-mannered guy with salt-and-pepper hair appeared to be pulling a bridle. 'My name is Arthur, and this is my show pony, Starflower,' he announced.

A twenty-something blonde followed him out of the

shadows and into the 'ring', where she started prancing around in circles and whinnying.

No one in the crowd seemed to think that there was anything unusual about this – in fact, one of the men in the front row picked up her legs and investigated her haunches, as if she really were a racehorse. 'Yes, yes, she's a fine specimen,' he muttered, giving her another once-over before backing away.

'Oh. My. God. Are these people seriously getting off on this?' I whispered, as a guy wearing a thong with silver bells attached and what appeared to be a horsetail butt-plug danced around the ring.

'Cat, God, I am so sorry,' he said. 'I had no idea that it would be this intense. I thought it was some kind of meet-and-greet for new members, not a show!'

I giggled. 'Hey, you wanted raw and weird, and you got it. I think this would make one hell of a documentary!'

We watched more couples prancing through the ring, snorting and neighing, as I read the literature. Apparently the fetish is all about being nurtured and taken care of, as well as trained. To be fair, the couples did look happier and more committed than I'd been recently. Maybe it was time to start chewing on hay and change my name to Honey.

'And what is your show horse's name?' some random guy asked Charlie, staring at me as though I'd just been put up on the auction block. I could have found the line of questioning slightly more erotic had it not been posed by a sixty-something man whose flabby buttocks were clearly protruding from the derrière of his black leather chaps.

'Um, we're just visiting,' I mumbled, feeling myself blushing.

'I am so sorry,' Charlie said. 'Ready to get out of here?'

We ran for it and collapsed with laughter into the alley, with me having to hold my sides to contain my hysteria. It was only early October, but the nights were already starting to get chilly, so I wrapped my arms around myself. Yeah, I was cold, but I also wanted him to give me his jacket (this equals instant intimacy). Which, being a gentleman, he did.

'I have to apologize again,' he said. 'I promise that I would never have dragged you into that situation if I'd known.'

'No problem,' I said coyly, looking up at him. 'I'll forgive you, on one condition. You take me out for a drink, and you're buying.'

Down the street, we slipped into a wine bar and ordered tumblers of pear-flavoured eau-de-vie, which burned my stomach going down but did the trick in warming me up.

For the next two hours, we got steadily more pissed, and in between exchanging life stories kept giggling about our night. 'How far do you think their role-play goes?' I said, wiping tears of laughter from my eyes. 'Do you think that Starflower poops standing up?'

This time, when I leaned over to laugh, I very deliberately looked up and met his eyes. Then I kissed him, briefly, on the mouth. His lips stiffened in shock, but he didn't pull away. I took this as an invitation to go in for the kill, and our tongues entwined for a full five minutes.

I could feel myself getting wet, and ran my hand up his thigh, not far enough to be pornographic but enough to make him breathe harder.

'Take. Me. Home. Now.'

'Are you sure that's a good idea?'

'No,' I said. 'I've been asked that before. Usually before I do something totally awesome.'

Heart racing, I stroked his hand as he sorted out the bill and we walked the few blocks to his Greenwich Village flat mostly in silence, probably trying hard not to think about what we were planning to do. I thought about Erin, and decided that she would definitely approve.

He barely got the key in the door before we started tearing each other's clothes off, and he led me towards the bedroom. God, he was a fantastic kisser, and as he stripped me to my bra and panties in the buttery light of his bedside lamp he just kept saying, 'You are so beautiful.'

We lay down on the bed and I tried to unbutton his shirt, but he pushed my wrists together over my head and whispered, 'Not yet.' Then he started kissing my neck, in the spot behind my ear that drives me wild. I was moaning and grinding my hips into the bed; the hours of anticipation had made me crazy and I couldn't wait for him to fuck me.

He sucked my nipples one by one, kneading my breasts together, taking his time. 'Are you teasing me?' I moaned. 'I can't take much more of this.' Then, I sat up abruptly and ripped his shirt open (this was something I'd seen in a movie, and it looked really cool then, but all that happened was two buttons flew off. It was a bit anticlimactic, really).

To distract him from my failed sartorial sexual move, I unbuttoned his belt and kissed down his stomach. Judging by what I had felt while standing up in his kitchen, I was going to be in for a very nice surprise. I practically started salivating as I unearthed a thick cock that was easily eight inches long. I had the fleeting thought that what God subtracted in the looks department he had given back in the trouser department.

I deep-throated him, and he grunted while pulling my hair, roughly. 'Stop,' he said, breathlessly, 'I'm going to come any second if you keep that up. Besides, I want to taste you first.'

He sucked on my outer lips and fingered me in rhythmic strokes while working on my clit, and though I tried to stop him several times because I was self-conscious about how long I was taking he carried on licking me, keeping pressure on my thighs, and the pleasure kept coming in waves and receding until I gripped the bed-sheets and came in his mouth. It was the first time that I'd come through oral sex, and it was fucking amazing.

'Thank. You,' I breathed, as I came down from cloud nine, slowly. 'That was absolutely stunning.'

'No problem. I could do that all night,' he said, while I fidgeted with the condom he had pulled out of the bedside drawer.

'Little help, please?' I smiled sweetly at him as he looked up from between my thighs. 'I'm about as useless at this as I am at opening wine bottles.'

He smiled, slid the condom on and pushed inside me in one swift move. I could feel him pounding me while I fingered myself, and with my clit already engorged from his tongue lashings it wasn't long before I was brought to yet another resounding orgasm, and I bit his shoulder as we both fell back on to the bed.

Any embarrassment I felt at having let him see my orgasm face was cancelled when he pulled out of me without having come. 'What's the matter?' I asked.

'I don't want to come,' he told me.

'Why not?'

'This sounds stupid, but I'm afraid that if I come, this will officially be a one-night stand and you'll never come back to my bed again.' He sat up on the edge of the bed.

I put a hand on his shoulder. 'That's silly,' I said. 'I really like you.'

'Me too,' he said, stroking my cheek and looking down at me with his warm brown eyes. 'I guess I'm a bit intimidated. Or feeling guilty.'

'Why? I didn't just fall off the turnip truck, honey, and it's not like you took advantage of me.' I laughed. 'Though I would love it if you did. Again. Say, tomorrow night?'

We fell asleep in each other's arms and next morning I headed for the loo and was perusing his toiletries when I saw it, sitting ominously in the corner of his shower. It was an aquamarine, plastic eighties-style butterfly clip.

There had been another girl in his shower, and very recently. That's when I realized that I'd violated two sacred principles of romance in one night: not only was Charlie my boss, but apparently he also had a girlfriend.

# TWENTY-TWO

As I thought back to those wild days an idea crept into my mind. I was determined to stick to my Anti-Rules mission of self-discovery. Maybe my next task on the list should be to revisit the Charlie episode. To have walked blindly straight into an affair with my attached boss was something Dr Phil would probably consider worthy of an autopsy. Anyway, my rendezvous with Jean-Claude had proved an intriguing experience. Perhaps it was time to look Charlie up too.

After all these years, he was relatively easy to find. He's a movie director now, living in Los Angeles, and has done several projects with major studios in the past ten years. I wasn't surprised, since he was always so successful and driven. I actually tracked him down through blog postings from his local Democratic Party organization, where he had posted several witty responses about the lack of ethics in reality television.

'Wow, this is a blast from the past,' he emailed back. 'Great to hear that you're going to be in town. We should definitely hook up for drinks.'

'Perfect. I can't wait to catch up,' I typed, leaving out the phrase, 'and find out if you think that I may be obsessive and mentally unstable.'

On a whim, I bought an upper-class ticket from Virgin. (I justified it because they were having a sale, despite the fact that it cost about four months' rent. I figured that this might be the only time when I was more comfortable on an aircraft than at home!)

When it came to deciding which books to pack, I gritted my teeth and stuffed *The Rules* into my bag. I had promised myself I would give it a calm and objective read.

I couldn't wait to get away for a few days, and in the January gloom a warm climate seemed like the answer to my prayers.

I was excited, because Victoria's previous boss spent loads of time in LA and she travelled with him, and since then she'd raved about how much she loved the LA singles scene. 'You'll be the only smart, non-Botoxed brunette in the room. A hot writer? They will love you!' she enthused.

But I was wary, especially after I checked into my hotel, with its minimalist decor and male model door staff whose hair didn't move.

Michael gave me the phone number of one of his LA contacts who worked in the showbiz section of the paper, so on my first night I found myself at a house party in the Hollywood Hills. When I saw the sea of silicon-enhanced, perma-tanned starlets, I figured that my chances of getting laid were roughly the same as their jean size: zero.

I chatted with the owner of the house, a cute guy named Scott who ran a restaurant. 'The dating scene out here is horrific, because everyone is so full of shit and shallow,' he said. 'I'm looking for a smart girl who keeps it real.' I didn't doubt him: some of the cocktail party conversation I over-heard made Paris Hilton seem like a member of Mensa.

So I went to a corner and drank alone. I was nursing a glass of Californian white when a guy with piercing blue eyes sidled over. He introduced himself as Marc and said he was a plastic surgeon to the stars.

We had a very graphic conversation about how he sawed through bone, stretched muscles and injected silicon into the cheekbones and buttocks of aspiring actresses. 'What would you do to me?' I asked him teasingly.

'Nothing,' he said. 'There is nothing sexier than a woman who is secure about herself.'

I knew it was a line, but it worked. He asked me out to dinner the following night.

The next day, as the hours before the date ticked by, I began to freak out and pace my room. Forget the clothes, I was worried that he would be looking at my face and judging the tiny childhood scar on my forehead. Doing my make-up for him was like accessorizing for a first date with a fashion designer.

We went to a bar and ate sashimi, and I asked him why he chose to become a plastic surgeon.

'I actually work with disfigured accident victims, which is my real passion,' he said. 'Some of the kids, especially, are so brave; the other work is interesting, but kind of shallow.' Perhaps this was just a line he fed to every girl out there, but all the same, I felt like an idiot for misjudging him.

I stopped sucking in my stomach and started asking questions. Against all the odds, in the land of plastic people, I'd met someone who I had a real connection with – and he lived thousands of miles away. Just my luck!

He asked me to come home with him, and we kissed as he signalled for the bill. While we waited, I saw Scott, our host from the night before, on the other side of the room – in uniform, cleaning tables! It turned out that his claims of owning a restaurant were slightly exaggerated: he was actually a struggling actor and waiter. And his amazing house? 'It belongs to a friend of mine,' he confessed when I cornered him.

'So much for keeping it real.' I laughed. It was a shame that Scott felt he had to weave a web of lies to seem interesting. On the plus side, he had a bright future in acting ahead of him.

I met Charlie on my fourth night at the trendy bar inside the Beverly Wilshire Hotel. Within half an hour I found out that he was married, with two young sons, and had finally settled down.

'I have to ask you something,' I blurted out. 'I know this is going to sound weird, and I'm not pulling a *High Fidelity* or anything and having a mid-life crisis, but—'

'You're too young to have a mid-life crisis,' he said pointedly. 'I should know, because I've just had mine.'

'Quarter-life, third-life – whatever,' I said. 'Anyway, the point is that I've had about three break-ups in the past three years that all follow the same pattern. The relationship gets really intense very quickly, then it ends, and I'm devastated. This last one – this last one almost killed me.' I felt the back of my throat closing up and distracted myself by counting the pairs of silicon breasts on display in the bar.

'Wow, are you okay?'

I nodded, and smiled. 'I guess you think I'm totally nuts, right?'

'Yes,' he said. 'But in an amazing way. I think you are one of the most brilliant, beautiful women I've ever met.'

I remembered how he'd snared me with lines like that, even after I confronted him with the butterfly clip in the shower.

'You have a girlfriend.' I had stepped out of the bathroom and verbally blindsided him with a towel still wrapped around me. 'You lied to me.'

'I didn't lie to you, Cat. I didn't mention it because I thought that last night was a professional meeting, and then, well, you swept me off my feet.'

He smiled awkwardly, and moved towards the kitchenette to retrieve his jeans from the floor. 'I'm sorry. I guess I should have told you.'

'How long have you been seeing her?' I felt vulnerable, and used. I've never dated guys with girlfriends.

'Eight months. But it's not serious,' he added quickly.

'Eight *months*?' To my nineteen-year-old brain, that sounded like an eternity. 'Are you in love with her?'

'No, I'm not,' he said, putting his hands on my shoulders. 'Do you think you can give me some time to work this out?'

'There's nothing to work out.' I was throwing on my clothes so quickly that I put my shirt on backwards, and decided against turning it around. I buttoned my coat over it instead, cursing myself for not wearing tights. Back then, I was still learning the rules of the Walk of Shame.

'I really like you, but I'm not going to date a cheater. So let me know if and when you're free. If I'm still around.'

He sat down on the bed, looking miserable. 'Catherine, I really like you too,' he said. 'I've been into you ever since your first day in the office. You practically radiated sex.'

I smiled. 'I'll take that as a compliment. You have twenty-four hours.' I closed the door behind me with a dramatic flourish and walked to work in the previous night's clothes.

Back then, I almost got off more on the next-day call to Erin than I had in the bedroom. I thrived on drama, and couldn't wait to see how the story would end.

The next night, Charlie had called me from a coffee shop, 'just to hear my voice' before ending things with his ex over a bagel, and later that night I was back at his place. From that day on, we were a couple.

Until a few months later, when I asked if I was his girlfriend and he said he wasn't sure he wanted one. We limped along for a few weeks after that, but basically it was over. Erin, in a bid to cheer me up, pasted a huge fake orange traffic warden's 'ticket' for 'crimes against fashion' on our fridge door. Knowing that I was depressed, she had ticked 'man boobs' and 'pot belly' under Body Offences, and written: 'Loser! This is a reminder . . . you can do better!' I forgot about the ticket, until Charlie went for a beer after a guilty post-break-up hook-up at my place and never came back.

He'd later told me that the ticket had really hurt his feelings, and I'd felt awful. Erin, on the other hand, had laughed her ass off. 'Serves him right,' she'd said at the time. 'How can you feel guilty when that bastard has been messing you around all this time?'

Sitting with Charlie now at the Beverly Wilshire, I snapped back into reality and munched prawn cracker bar snacks. I shuddered to think of how many hands had dipped into the bowls before ours, and asked the question that had been on my mind for several years.

'So, the million-dollar question: Why did you dump me?'

'I didn't really dump you, Catherine . . .'

'No, you did the guy thing of stringing me along until I left. What I meant was, why wasn't I the One? You're doing me a favour here, remember? Tough love,' I added, humorously.

He looked mildly surprised, but not shocked. 'Well, it's hard to say. There were lots of reasons. I think the main one was because, even though I was thirty, I was really immature when it came to relationships. I also thought that, smart as you were, you were too young for me.'

'Oh, you were right about that,' I answered quickly. 'I'm not asking this because I think we would have worked, because I don't. You only told me that you loved me once, and as I recall you were fucking me from behind at the time.'

He looked me straight in the eye. 'I'm sorry. I actually thought about you for years afterwards, and felt really bad about how I handled the relationship. You deserved more respect, and I didn't treat you as well as I should have. What can I say? I was an idiot. And I regretted it for a long time.'

'So what was it that made you decide not to commit to me?'

'Honestly?' He drained his perfect Manhattan (I remembered that he didn't even like whiskey, but used to order the drink because it made him sound cool. I guess some things never change).

'I guess . . . I guess I never really felt comfortable with you. You were so feisty and hot and passionate and into your work, and I was crazy about you, and we had such intense conversations, and fantastic sex, but I couldn't see us doing the other stuff.'

'The other stuff? We had fantastic sex, great conversations and a connection. What else is there?'

'Well, there's sitting around on Sunday afternoon, reading the papers and letting your gut hang out. I couldn't ever see myself settling into a comfort zone with you.'

'Yeah, well, I was probably too young for that then,' I said. 'I guess I liked you so much that I wanted to be perfect in front of you.'

'I also thought, on some level, that everything was too intense to have any longevity. It felt like a fantasy. It didn't feel real.'

I dug out my reporter's mini spiral notebook and flipped it open to a blank page and titled it: *Anti-Rules – feedback from ex number 2*. 'So that's it, then? "Couldn't be comfortable in front of me"?'

He laughed. 'Are you writing this down for your book?'

I grinned. 'Don't worry, honey, I promise to mention how charming you are – under an alias of course.'

He put a hand on my wrist. 'Well, I'm madly in love with my wife, but, truthfully, I think that, hypothetically, if we'd met later I definitely could have seen things working out. With men, it's all about timing.'

I dutifully transcribed our entire conversation in the taxi, though my writing was a bit shaky after all the booze. I could also see what I hadn't at the time, that maybe Charlie had been older and wiser than me, and understood that I would never want to settle down and limit my life to one man for ever at the age of nineteen. I was too young for him, and he knew it, but he enjoyed the ride while it lasted. Case closed.

I supposed I was hoping that if I could find some kind of

pattern in these break-ups, I could stop myself from being left. But life doesn't work like that. The truth was that we just weren't the right match.

When I woke up in the morning with a wicked hangover, I looked at the paragraphs of text and saw I had drunkenly added arrows pointing to a phrase, circled several times in pen: 'Common thread: Insecure men? Or am I just picking the ones who fall for the fantasy girl instead of the real me?'

# TWENTY-THREE

I got back from LA just in time for Jamie's homecoming from Goa. It felt like he'd been gone for ever and I couldn't wait to see him. But I asked myself whether I was just buzzing with anticipation rather than genuine emotion? Would the reality be a let-down? I decided to go to airport arrivals to meet him. How I felt when he walked through the gate – that would be the test.

For all my excitement, when I clapped eyes on him that afternoon at the airport, after so many weeks, I realized instinctively that, for all our sexual chemistry, he inspired none of the deeper feelings of longing that JP had.

Even so, I rushed him into a cab before he had a chance to catch his breath. There was one thing I had definitely been pining for!

By the time we got home we were frantic, ripping off each other's clothes and grappling with each other's bodies, as we tried to pack a month's worth of fantasies into a single session. After our extremely energetic reunion between the sheets, I felt intense pleasure – followed by a shooting pain in my right eye.

Until I met Jamie, my injuries during sex were pretty much limited to carpet burns, the odd bite-mark, and, since my skin is pale and tends to blacken on impact like an over-ripe banana, no small amount of bruising. This was something else.

'Baby, the room is spinning,' I said, panicked.

'Yeah, I know, that felt totally amazing to me, too,' he said, taking my hand in his.

'No. Everything is out of focus. I can't see!'

So we got dressed, and he drove me to Chelsea and Westminster's casualty wing, which I insisted on despite it being a long way from his house. When he challenged my logic on this I brushed him off, telling him I preferred their sexual health clinic.

But at 2 a.m. the clientele was far from posh. I found myself wedged between a guy with a hacking cough and a woman with three feral children trying to choke each other. I read an out-of-date magazine with my good eye and tried not to freak out.

Finally, it was my turn, and after a brief chat with the nurse I was sent to see a young, fit doctor who was a dead ringer for my favourite film star: Clive Owen. I was shocked to recognize him as JP's doctor friend. They'd been at medical school together but his name escaped me.

I wasn't sure if he remembered who I was either and, in my predicament, I was too embarrassed to ask. After asking what medication I was on, he got to the, 'So, do you have any idea what caused this?' question.

I blushed, before blurting out that it happened when I had an orgasm.

'What I think you have here is a popped blood vessel,' he said. 'It's not that uncommon, so you shouldn't be embarrassed.'

Even in my humiliated state, I found it seriously hot that this man was taking charge. When he leaned over me to shine a light in my eye, I noticed that he had large hands with long, slender fingers. I've always been attracted to powerful men, and at that moment it felt like he held my life in the balance.

At the same time, thoughts of JP had been taking root in my mind ever since I'd arrived here. Wasn't it a bit of a co-incidence that I'd chosen a hospital located right across the street from his flat?

I tried to distract myself by fantasizing about Dr Clive ravishing me on the hospital trolley. I started making small talk about my embarrassing mishap.

'Don't worry, we see some crazy stuff in A&E with sex,' he said, and went on to describe broken penises, fractured pelvises and rogue vegetables. 'The guys who masturbate using vacuum cleaners are not just an urban myth,' he added.

Meanwhile, Jamie texted from the waiting room to say he was leaving, because he was shattered with jet-lag.

'Thanks for your concern,' I wrote back. 'What if I end up going blind?'

I knew that I was being a drama queen. The truth is, I was pulling the (mostly male) tactic of trying to start a fight because I didn't want to feel guilty about what I might do next.

'So, Miss Townsend, we're all done here,' the doctor, whose name I still hadn't discerned from his badge, said. 'You can go back outside to join your boyfriend, if you like.'

'Oh, he's not my boyfriend,' I lied (explaining the open relationship thing would just have been too complicated). I wanted to ask him if he was single. I could get taken to bed by a beautiful doctor and make JP jealous. It was an evil but strangely intriguing thought.

He went on chatting idly as if he wasn't a night doctor rushed off his feet.

I manoeuvred the conversation round to my question. 'Um, that was really interesting, what you said about sex disasters. I may do a piece on it, so would it be all right to give you a call?'

'Sure,' he said, 'I'd like that,' and gave me his mobile number.

Between the fluorescent lights reflecting off his dark hair and my damaged eye, he seemed to have a halo. Then again, everything was out of focus.

But Dr Clive was just a short-lived distraction from my deeper impulses. Because, as I walked outside and squinted, I did something really stupid and crazy. I called JP on his mobile, and on the third ring he picked up. He sounded sleepy.

'Hi, um, I know this sounds really scary and stalkerish, but I'm actually right across the street from your building just now and was wondering if you wanted to get a quick drink,' I said chirpily. Shit. This was a really bad idea – not to mention one that made no sense. It's not like I could even pretend that he's into clubbing and I thought he would be up at that hour – I knew he wouldn't. What if he was with someone else? Was I just a glutton for punishment? Maybe I had a concussion after all.

'Sure,' he mumbled. 'I'll buzz you up in what – two minutes?'

I really, really hadn't thought this through, as evidenced by the fact that my eye looked as if it had exploded.

I pushed the bell and he came downstairs to let me in, wearing the red pyjamas that I loved and looking totally dishevelled, and very sexy. I wanted to crawl under the covers with him there and then.

'Cat? What happened to you?' He cupped my chin in his hands and pulled it up to inspect my eye.

'Yeah, I was in a bar fight. But you should see the other girl!' I said. No laugh. God, that was a weak joke. 'I'm sorry, this was probably a stupid idea. I may have a concussion. That would explain the lack of judgement, and verbal diarrhoea.'

'Oh, my God,' he said. 'Are you okay? Do you want to come up and use the toilet? Or get some ice?'

'*Verbal* diarrhoea, JP! There's nothing wrong with my stomach! I just hit myself in the eye with a – door,' I said, fully realizing that his pal Clive Owen would probably tell him about my injury in embarrassing detail. I'd heard too many stories about the guy who 'accidentally' fell on to a greased-up shampoo bottle from ER doctors to have any faith in doctor-patient confidentiality.

His brow wrinkled as he looked down at me with concern. Those piercing blue eyes still made me melt.

'Actually, ice may be a good idea, though. I'm not sure that I'll survive the night. What do you think?' I smiled up at him and batted my eyelashes.

'The thing is, we'll have to be quiet if we go up. Antonia is staying in my spare room – she's taking over the flat once I finally move into my new house, and the renovations are almost finished.'

At the mention of his female friend's name, I bristled. I'd never fully trusted her, and had always suspected that she had a crush on JP – even though he had assured me over and over that he had never been attracted to her and was madly in love with me.

I have to admit, however, that Antonia brought out the bad side in me. I've never had a problem with any of JP's other female friends, even the ones he has slept with. After all, I'm friends with several of my ex-boyfriends and would never want him to censor me.

But for some reason I hated this girl on sight. Not only did I feel threatened by her, but her mannerisms were completely fake. I had a really strong gut instinct about her. But in an effort to give her a chance, I hung out with her several times, which basically involved steeling myself to be polite in the face of her bitchy exchanges. Such as when I told her that I had a book coming out, which she countered with, 'Oh, I hear that they have a chick-lit computer program that could basically write these things for you. They're pretty formulaic, aren't they?'

I know I'm not Tolstoy, but this was pretty low. I looked to JP in shock, but realized that most catty comments are like dog whistles, with a frequency that only female listeners can hear. Guys completely miss them.

'She can be difficult,' he admitted later, 'but underneath all the attitude, she's really nice.'

I think all men secretly fantasize about two women cat-fighting over them, which then turns into a threesome. Unfortunately for the boys, this only happens in movies.

She was one of those sinewy women with eighties-style shoulder pads and big hair who I called a 'man-eater', not because she was overtly sexy but because I suspected that in the event of a plane crash she would be slicing into JP's thigh before he even lost consciousness. She seemed constantly hungry for attention, and was one of those girls who never had any female friends, which she blamed on the fact that she's 'just too pretty and successful', and other girls are jealous.

We're not jealous. She's just a bitch.

'No, don't worry,' I said, 'I don't want to cause any problems. I'll just go home and crash.' I wanted to go upstairs and light a match under her hair sprayed helmet head, thus causing her face to explode into flames, and roast marshmallows over her burning carcass. Instead I smiled, pretending to be the demure and rational picture of health.

'Well, you'll probably need major surgery, but I think you'll survive,' he said, as I shuffled my feet. 'How's married life?'

My face fell and he quickly apologized, then chatted for a couple of minutes.

'Well, it was great to see you, Cat,' he said, giving me a quick hug. 'I hope you feel better. Stay away from those bar fights, okay?'

I started to walk away while he held the door. But thinking about Erin recently made me wonder when I'd stopped being brave. If I could do it sexually, then I could do it emotionally as well.

'JP?' I put my foot back in the door, fully intending to ask him casually, 'Would you like to have a drink with me some time?'

Instead, what came out was, 'I would love to see you again. I miss you.'

He looked down at the floor, then directly into my eyes. I could hear the blood pounding in my ears.

'I miss you too,' he said. 'Look, I'm about to go away for a couple of weeks. How about I give you a call when I'm back?'

I avoided asking him if the trip was business or pleasure, though I was dying to know. Instead, I tried to allow fate to take its course and leave it up to the universe when I saw him again.

'It's a date,' I said, squeezing his hand as he took mine.

# TWENTY-FOUR

Okay, so the whole Zen-master leaving it up to the universe thing lasted about ninety minutes, after which I tossed and turned all night, and as soon as the clock struck a decent hour, called Victoria to obsess over every microsecond of my conversation with JP.

First thing the next day we hit Crazy Homies and ordered Bloody Marias, which, since they have tequila rather than vodka as a base, Victoria calls 'the crack cocaine of breakfast beverages'.

'The problem with karma is that it takes way too long to work,' she said, skewering an olive.

Now I had worked through all my dating guides, I had started to read Amy's copy of the Tao, books on meditation, and even something called *Facing Love Addiction*, which was hitting pretty close to home. I was carrying around a dog-eared copy and highlighting bits on the advice of my therapist.

Victoria picked it up and read random passages, apparently amused. '"What a healthy relationship looks like,"' she said. '"Each of you is responsible for learning to experience and express your reality in moderation. Neither of you expects the other person to tolerate extreme expressions of reality." No make-up sex? Sounds fucking boring to me. Where's the passion without the drama?'

'You can have passion without the drama,' I said, pouring

Tabasco sauce liberally into my meal in a glass. 'Apparently, it's all about JP and me, and our inner children.'

'What? You believe that psychobabble bullshit? What did that therapist tell you, anyway?'

I decided to save the self-help talk for Amy.

'Basically my inner child wants to kick his inner child's ass on the playground.'

'Spanking? Now that sounds more your speed.'

Victoria has always been a believer in the occult – plus she needed cheap shag-me shoes – so we headed to Camden, where she took me to a tiny witchcraft shop. The shop owner suggested a few methods to help me get rid of 'unwanted guests', and we were soon cooking up a revenge scheme to get rid of Antonia.

Like a wicked schoolgirl, Victoria teasingly persuaded me to buy a few props, including a candle that was supposed to rid my life of evil. 'Light it every night and visualize what you want to get rid of,' she said solemnly. 'But if you really want someone to go away for ever, put black salt in their shoes.'

'If I ruin her Manolos, she may kill me first.' I laughed. 'Anyway, it's not really about her. It's about me and JP. I'm just deflecting my frustration on to her. She's not so bad.'

To make me laugh, Victoria bought me a red male voodoo doll, whose body parts were labelled with the desired result so that I could tag them accordingly: a white pin under 'Win lottery' if he was a good boy, a black one stuck in the 'Migraine' region of his head if he behaved badly.

I also bought a candle adorned with glitter and specific to my star sign, Virgo, which was meant to bring love back into my life. The saleswoman, a cute black-haired girl who bore a striking resemblance to Siouxsie Sioux in the eighties, advised me to light it every night, and then spend five minutes focusing on the object of my affection.

'You actually think this works?' I asked Victoria. 'What's next, drinking chicken blood?'

We went for coffee nearby, where we chatted about a slight wobble she'd had with Mike and some more about my encounter with JP.

'I'm going to end it with Jamie,' I blurted out. 'It's been fun, but I wouldn't want to jinx things with JP by being in another relationship.'

'But you can't just wait for JP,' she cried. 'You have to get on with your life. You have to be protective of your future now, even if he isn't in it.'

'No, of course not,' I replied. 'I'll allow myself superficial distractions. But the Jamie issue has become more than that. His liberal attitude to sex is deceptive – underneath it I think he's quite emotionally needy. I'm not the right match to be taking on that burden. It's not fair on either of us to carry on with a pseudo-relationship.'

'Jesus, that makes total sense. It sounds like high time you got out of that situation. And I can see how that would be doing the decent thing there. But I have two suggestions,' she said. 'That you keep dating rather than just waiting for JP to come to his senses. No matter how hard it is. Because it's not just about you any more – you need this for research!'

'And two?'

'That you let me hook you up with my personal trainer. Trust me, he will definitely put a smile on your face!'

'Are you trying to tell me something about my lack of

motivation lately?' I playfully socked her in the arm. 'Anyway, doesn't he live in LA now?'

'Christ, you know that's not what I mean. If anything, you look too thin right now. But he's amazingly inspiring, and you know what they say about endorphins. And he's back from the States in a few weeks for a flying visit.'

I've always hated gyms, and much prefer to adhere to the Surrealist principle of 'automatic walks', where I set off with no particular destination in mind. Unfortunately, all too often they lead me to pubs. Lately, sex has been my only cardio.

Back at home, I climbed into the bathtub and used the bath oil on my fingers to bring myself to a throbbing orgasm with one hand while tweaking my nipples with the other.

Afterwards, while calm, I lit the witchcraft candle. Even though I only did it for a laugh, I did find that spending five minutes being positive soothed me, and allowed me to believe that I was focusing positive energy on the outcome of my relationships.

If JP and I ended up happily together, maybe the serenity of the ritual could be a permanent part of my life. If not, I've still got that voodoo doll . . .

# TWENTY-FIVE

That's the last time I listen to Victoria and her advice about actively dating in the name of research. Because I'm a dating columnist, I don't say this lightly, but I have been on what ranks right up there with the Worst Dates of my Life.

It'd been a while since I'd done any Internet dating. But it was February, and for the last few days I'd been staring at a fog that looked like something out of a vampire film. So I decided to stay home for the foreseeable future and reactivate my accounts on three websites. I find it strange that people are still embarrassed to admit they met online. To me, clicking on a profile is no more random than bumping into someone in a bar. Besides, I can flirt in my slippers – a definite bonus given English weather.

At first, I was thrilled when, after only four hours, I had sixty new messages. But I soon remembered why I had tired of Internet dating in the first place: the profiles all seemed to merge into one. I enjoy candlelit dinners as much as the next girl, but I'm perplexed by guys like 'Ready4therealthing' who list 'long walks on the beach' and 'soulful conversation' as interests. It's as if men have compiled a list of what they think women want, drawing inspiration only from the covers of romance novels.

I was nostalgic for Craigslist and its 'Casual Encounters' section, which I had last looked at with Jamie, where men run ads like: 'The sex toy guy: I'll supply the toys and hotel, you bring the batteries and you!' At least they are honest about what they want.

A friend who runs her own PR firm suggested that I try a website where you can hook up with sugar daddies. I'd browsed so-called 'millionaire' sites in the past, but been put off by profile headlines like: 'Do you want to drive my Ferrari?' and 'Have you ever dreamed of being Julia Roberts in *Pretty Woman*?' I can't say that my life plan ever included street-walking. Still, since I'm not a gold-digger but do value success, I decided to take a chance.

Despite my promise to restrict my hunting time to ten minutes a day, searching for new members is highly addictive. I got really excited when I saw 'WhyNotMe', a cute six-foot-four banker, so I added him to my hotlist. Within five minutes he sent me a message back: 'Loved your pic . . . I'm married, but offering an allowance of £4–£6K monthly, depending on frequency of meetings!' I politely replied that I can pay my own way, and don't date married men.

I have to say that the site was an improvement on ones I'd checked out in the past, but the vast majority of emails I got were still from grinning, fifty-something Jack Nicholson look-alikes standing next to boats and sports cars.

But after wading through tons of winks and flirts, I made contact with one cute prospect: a forty-one-year-old producer named Laurent. I emailed him to say that I was taking my love life off-line, at least for now. He wanted to keep emailing, but I took a chance and suggested that we met for a drink. The true test of chemistry has to happen in the flesh.

If all else fails, there's an airbrushed photo of a lovely man named Charles who seems very keen to contact me, and swears that we are soulmates. He's stuck in Nigeria waiting for a cheque to clear – all I have to do is send him £5,000 and we can live happily ever after. The scary thing is, he's not the least believable guy to have contacted me this week.

'Have you ever dated a married man?'

This was tricky, because I wondered if Laurent already knew about my ex-boyfriend Andrew, who I'd been madly in love with and written about extensively.

I smiled and said, 'I've dated someone who was separated, but to be honest I'm not sure that I would do that again. Unless they really had been living apart for years.'

'I was separated for six months before I started seeing my ex-girlfriend,' he began, and I knew that I was in trouble.

Laurent and I had already met once for coffee, which we all know is really a visual lie-detector test to ensure that we hadn't been sent a picture of someone ten years ago before they gained twenty stone and started wearing an eye patch.

He was actually better looking in the flesh than online, with lovely blue eyes and a nice smile. And though I've long accepted that men exaggerate height and income while women subtract years and inches from profiles, he really was six foot tall. I didn't have a 'thunderbolt moment', but he seemed fun and made me laugh.

Besides, JP had yet to call – I needed a distraction.

Laurent, who claimed to be 'in touch with his feminine side' because he had two daughters, seemed ideal at first.

In preparation for our second date, I got a full waxing and was wearing my 'lucky' fishnet stockings under a black cock-tail dress.

Midway through the appetizers, things started to go terribly wrong after I politely asked how long he had been living in his current flat.

'About six months,' he said, looking down. 'Of course, my wife got the house in the divorce. She cleaned me out, took the kids, she even took our pets from me. I bought the dogs, and she didn't ever like them. I'm asking you, as a woman, why did she have to take the dogs?'

He began to well up, and then, just as the waiter arrived to explain our main courses in detail, the dam burst and tears rolled down his cheeks. I had no idea what to do. I told Laurent I'd read that men and women both have an emotional side; it's just that boys aren't given permission to express it. I gave him a hug, while he pulled himself together and dabbed at his eyes with his napkin. I tried to imagine what my therapist would say in the situation to make him feel better. I sympathized with him, I really did, because we've all been where he was, and I was determined to let him know that he wasn't alone.

Until he dropped the next bomb.

'You know, you're exactly the kind of girl who would make my ex-wife really jealous. She's at a party right now. I don't suppose you want to come with me?'

I was totally appalled, and told him so. I couldn't believe that my judgement had been so atrocious at a time when I was meant to be fine-tuning my emotional radar.

Then, inexplicably, he tried to kiss me at the table. I pushed him off, and he actually asked me for my advice.

'Maybe instead of playing head games, you should think about what your part in the breakdown of the marriage was,

and actually talk to her about where you guys went wrong,'
I suggested. 'Stop trying to fuck with her mind and break her
down, and talk to her.'

But he couldn't stop wallowing in self-pity. If he was hoping
for a sympathy shag, however, he was out of luck; and my
libido deflated even more when he whipped out photos of his
golden retrievers. I made my excuses and left.

By the time I got home, I was emotionally drained and
sexually frustrated.

Still, I felt proud. Sarah had told me that once I got healthier,
I would stop being attracted to men who were damaged.
'When you are a baby yourself, crawling around on the floor,
you are going to meet whoever is at your eye level,' she'd said,
'because our choice of partners is totally unconscious. When
you start standing tall, these guys won't even be on your radar.'
There might have been a time when the good-looking,
charming Golden Retriever Guy could have got under my skin
and dragged me into his drama, but now I knew how to look
after myself better.

I was still horny though.

# TWENTY-SIX

I knew I had to call it a day with Jamie, because, more and more, I was realizing that I wanted to make room in my life for a more solid relationship.

We met for coffee, where I told him that I hoped we could be friends but would have to stay away from each other for a while. I said that I realized these 'flux' relationships worked for him, and maybe they had for me in my younger days, but I wanted something more defined. 'I'm sorry, babe, but I have to be true to myself, and I'm a creature of extremes,' I told him. 'The truth is, I just can't do these "in-between" relationships long-term.'

He was sad but very understanding and supportive. Unusually for me, but typically for him, I guess, he suggested one last night of parting fun, and I agreed. Why not go out in style?

I could hear his key in the door as I adjusted my black wig, and cinched my silk kimono in at the waist. I had decided to play the 'sexy Thai masseuse' that night.

Our little role-plays had started with the occasion when, in a way that was amusingly incongruous with his rock star façade, he'd come home grumpy after a spat with a jobsworth in his local library. To cheer him up, I'd jokingly started acting

163

the part of a sexy librarian determined to punish my 'reader' who'd forgotten to pay his fines.

Later that night he'd asked whether we could role-play for real. I guessed Jamie's penchant for dressing up probably pre-dated me, given his interest in leather and eyeliner, but I was a quick learner. Next time around I squeezed into a leather corset and slipped on stockings underneath my outfit, and by the time I finally jumped on him we were so turned on that the sex had been incredible. Before long I was wondering whether I had found my new calling as an actor.

Since the start of our role-play, I had been everything from a cowgirl or cheerleader to historical figures like a naughty Marie Antoinette who supposedly said of the starving peasants, 'Let them eat cake'. It had become a form of escapism, even if our performances weren't exactly Oscar-worthy.

However, I suspected that things were going a bit too far the time he texted to say that he was off to the fancy-dress shop for a pirate outfit. I wasn't sure I'd get turned on by him wearing an eye patch. What's next? I thought. A plastic parrot on his shoulder?

I've always thought that role-play is a fun way to spice up a relationship, but I wondered whether for Jamie it was too much of a substitute for regular sex. Should I have been worried that I only really became hot for him when I pretended to be someone else? I didn't want to have to get into character every time I got into bed. 'Maybe you're trying to avoid intimacy,' Victoria had said. 'Or perhaps you're just getting bored.'

She was right. But for our last big, no-holds-barred sexual blowout, it seemed the obvious formula.

That day I had just had an intense deep-tissue massage given by a very fit male therapist, and as I relaxed enough to drool into the face cradle, I couldn't help visualizing his hands exploring underneath the towel-covered portions of my body.

Believe it or not, I'm so dominant in my life and career that I'm naturally submissive in the bedroom. So, for our final encore, I wanted to experiment in a way that put me entirely in Jamie's hands. After I had had my way with him first, of course.

When he came into the living room, I told him that he was going to be the punter while I played the exotic escort girl offering 'happy endings'.

Instead of being turned on, he burst into laughter. 'So what nationality are you meant to be?'

'I was thinking Thai,' I said, taking him by the hand and trying not to break character. The hooker thing was relatively new for me. 'What, you no like my outfit?' I purred, as I led him towards the bedroom.

'Well, no offence, but you are about a foot too tall to be Thai, and that wig is heinous.'

'God, you're in a foul mood,' I said, pulling off the glossy black wig. 'What's going on? Are you okay?'

'Sorry, babe, it's just that I'm waiting to hear back from yet another producer about our record deal. We were supposed to hear back in three days, and it's been a week.'

'Maybe they're busy, Jamie. You can't expect A&R executives to live on your time schedule. I know it's tough, but just try to be patient.'

I sat down next to him on the bed and untied the kimono. 'I have something that may cheer you up.'

I had Jamie lie down on the bed in view of the porn DVD that was 'accidentally' playing in the background. Two female flatmates were enthusiastically frolicking with the gardener – forget all this stuff about women not being visual, I prefer my porn to have minimal storylines and maximum action!

Then I made him get naked, and rubbed massage oil through my hands (unscented, of course, as I've found out the hard way that lavender and orange burn!) and sat on his back, my damp knickers pressing against the small of his back.

'Aaahhh, that feels so nice,' he mumbled softly, and after a few minutes of working out the tension between his shoulder blades I was ready to move my hands further south.

'I forgot that disc was playing,' I said innocently. 'We can turn it off if you want to.' Then, stealing the line I'd heard first from Jean-Claude, then a million times since, I added, 'We can just lie in bed and hold each other if you don't feel up to anything tonight.' I bit my lip, discreetly rocking up and down to stimulate my clit. 'Or, there's the dirty alternative.'

He turned his head around and cocked one eyebrow. 'Which is?'

'I'm the naughty masseuse, and you're in a dodgy back-street parlour,' I said, kissing the back of his neck. 'You can have anything you want. Including a very happy ending.' I had to admit that the whole servitude angle was really starting to get me off.

I reached my hand underneath his stomach and felt him suck

in his breath; he was already rock hard, and the girls onscreen were in the 69 position, which only turned him on more.

Then I worked my fingers down his spine, and when he tried to flip over I stopped him. 'No, baby, for now I just want you to relax,' I said, kissing down his back and sliding one finger gently into his arse, while the other reached around to wank him, slowly, with the oil.

He sucked in his breath again. 'Christ, that feels amazing.'

I slid my finger out and butterfly-kissed my way down his back, then gently probed his arse with my tongue, while continuing to wank him as he rolled over on his side.

We switched positions, and I had him straddle me, and continued to masturbate him with both hands. I guided his knees further up until he was straddling my chest while still wanking furiously.

'I'm close,' he muttered. 'Can I come on your tits?'

'Are you sure that you want to come on my tits?' I smiled devilishly.

'What do you mean?' he asked breathlessly.

'I mean I'd really like it if you would come on my face. It's very porn star, what do you think?'

'Are you sure?'

'I want you to treat me like the dirty whore that I am.' God, I was really getting into this. Andrea Dworkin was probably turning in her grave.

Leaning my head up, I took his cock into my mouth, and licked the index finger of my right hand at the same time. Using my saliva as lubricant, I wanked him with my left hand, while gently pushing against his arse with my finger, teasing him and sliding it in bit by bit.

At first he resisted my ministrations, but after a couple of minutes he relaxed, and started sliding down on to my hand. 'Oh, my God, this feels so fucking intense,' he said, gritting his teeth and gripping the headboard.

'I'm going to come!' he cried, and as I continued to slide my finger in and out of him, stimulating his prostate, he came in jets all over my face. The second spurt stung my eye, but I bravely carried on milking his cock for every last drop, then slid my finger out of his arse and grabbed a tissue from the side of the bed to dab at my eye.

'I'm sorry, are you okay? Did I get you?' He looked down at me and kissed my forehead lightly. Despite his concerned tone, he looked very pleased with himself.

I've never understood the male fascination with projectile streams of bodily fluid, but I've seen that look many times on the playground during childhood when boys used to see who could pee furthest in the snow.

He lay down next to me on the bed and kissed my cheek, avoiding the mess. 'God, that was incredible. Thank you. I owe you a big one!'

Heading into the bathroom to rinse my eyes out, I turned and blew him a kiss.

But later, in the darkness, I felt restless. I was going to miss Jamie but although I loved him as a friend, I knew that a relationship based on a love of drinking triple-distilled vodka and screwing – not always necessarily in that order lately – wasn't going anywhere. And I'm not very good at long-term casual dating – I'm pretty intense, so it's normally either a short-lived fling or love-at-first-sight coupling that morphs into something more serious.

The next morning, as I dressed, Jamie gave me a hug and reminded me that his door was always open. I was reassured by that, because our sexual adventures had always been fun.

But, ultimately, I don't want to have to dress up as Aladdin, ready for a dirty magic carpet ride, to make my love life interesting.

# TWENTY-SEVEN

I've been a very bad girl. After several weeks of waiting to hear from JP, stabbing voodoo dolls, and mounting sexual frustration, I found myself with two hot prospects, and only one day off. After being good and nipping it in the bud with Jamie, I figured that I was due an indulgence.

I'd already set up a meeting with Dan, a very cute PR executive, when I got a text from Brad, Victoria's ex personal trainer.

I knew Brad was only in town for one week. But I'd been so busy with work that I'd literally had to schedule loo breaks.

The only solution was to see them on the same day. I calculated that the chances of sex with Brad were higher, since his time here was so limited, so I figured I would meet him later. What I didn't count on was the amazing chemistry between myself and Dan. We met for brunch near Regent's Park, and after several Bloody Marys and a stroll we ended up falling into bed back at his place.

Over brunch, I realized that Dan was a man in transition as well: he'd just come out of a seven-year marriage, and was three weeks away from moving to New York for a new job. In short, a perfect candidate for what was to come. We fell on to the bed and I fumbled for a condom as we slipped into the missionary position, but he kept insisting that I stare into his eyes, which eventually merged into one giant Cyclops eye.

Then he asked if he could lick my arse, because apparently he was very into unreciprocated rimming. So I got on to all fours, and masturbated while he licked me from behind, which resulted in a delicious orgasm.

All in all, way too intense for never-to-be-repeated sex. Then again, maybe that was the point. In the way that it's sometimes easier to tell strangers our most intimate secrets, maybe it's less difficult to make strange requests with someone you'll never see again. Too bad, because that was one kink that I could definitely have got used to.

My orgasm was so overwhelming that I drifted off to sleep, and I woke with a jolt to discover that it was almost 6 p.m. and I had to meet Brad in town at 7. I was in north London, so nipping home for a pre-date preparation session was out of the question.

I started to panic. I've never been a cheater, so I haven't really had to deal with the logistics of disguising a recent sexual encounter. I jumped into Dan's shower to rinse off, but stopped short of washing my hair due to his lack of conditioner or a hairdryer. I felt dirty, in more ways than one.

Luckily, I always carry an emergency pair of knickers, as well as condoms. I covered the rug burn on my knees with concealer, brushed my teeth with a face towel and blotted myself with a perfume sample I'd got free from a magazine. I had to make do with men's deodorant, which smelled like one of those tree-shaped car air fresheners.

Could I get away with it? I definitely had a healthy glow. But when I met Brad in a wine bar, I was so paranoid that

I might as well have had a massive 'A' embroidered on to my top. I didn't have a commitment to Dan; in fact, we'd explicitly talked about keeping things between us casual, due to both of our recent relationship traumas and the fact that he was moving to the other side of the Atlantic (actually, I'm sure that both of these were just polite excuses for the fact that we fancied each other, but didn't really see things going further).

Still, I felt pangs of guilt, so I called Victoria from the loo. 'Do you think I'm horrible?' I asked her. 'How long should I wait between sleeping with two men?'

'If you are emotionally damaged, as long as it takes,' she said, laughing. 'Otherwise, I don't know, long enough to shower?'

She was right. If my date with Brad had been twenty hours later instead of a mere two, I wouldn't be beating myself up. So I decided to chill out and enjoy my drink, as Brad regaled me with crazy stories of LA life.

Victoria clearly knew what she was doing when she set us up – with his toned physique and wicked laugh he was definitely my type.

As the evening drew on, our body language hotted up. When he ran his hand up my thigh, I couldn't wait any longer. I smiled sweetly, raised my eyebrow and suggested we continue the party back at his. He readily agreed and so we strolled back to his swanky hotel, kissing all the way.

I realised that my earlier sex session had only whetted my appetite for more. We spent ages in the 69 position, with him licking me out and fingering my arse. I remember thinking that walking straight was definitely going to be a problem. Then I sat on top of him, already very wet, and my clit was so supersensitive that I just rocked back and forth gently until we both came.

We took a breather, and he made me a gin and tonic from the minibar, and lazily slid the ice around my nipples, until eventually we both got turned on again. We were up all night, until he raced to the airport at dawn.

On my way to work, I thought about the fact that I'd had sex with two men on the same day. Technically, the second one was after midnight, so did it count as a different day?

I thought about the link with my freelance working life. My work is all about intense bursts of activity followed by slightly worrying quiet patches. Perhaps modern work and modern dating have evolved into patterns that would be unrecognizable to older generations. But I wasn't complaining. A couple of generations back and I probably wouldn't be getting any – of either work or play.

Anyway, my 'double-date' had proved a welcome respite from an intense cerebral workout, but now it was back to the drawing board. I decided to make my encounter the subject of that week's column. It would be interesting to know what my vocal readership thought about my dating marathon. As it turned out, most of them were very supportive, especially the gay men. As one of them reminded me, a little hate mail from someone anonymous was nothing compared to being told that you were disgusting and going to hell by a member of your own family. 'The important thing is that you feel comfortable with your choices, because no one else has the right to judge you,' he wrote. 'You aren't hurting anyone, and you are being yourself, flaws and all. Be proud of who you are!' I was hugely inspired by him.

I'm happy I had the experience. When I go back to having a steady boyfriend, or JP finally gets his act together and calls, I look forward to sex on tap. Until then, I'm going to take my chances when opportunity knocks.

# TWENTY-EIGHT

I've hit rock bottom when it comes to cheesy dating guides, having worked my way through the ones I bought at Waterstone's. Not only did I download one of those 'How to Get Your Ex Back – Guaranteed!!' guides from the Internet, I actually paid twenty quid for it. I was struggling to write off this particular purchase in my mind as part of my Anti-Rules research project.

JP finally called, and asked if I wanted to have dinner with him. I tried to act nonchalant and cool on the phone, and told myself not to read too much into it because dinner was just dinner, but who was I kidding? I was overjoyed at the thought of seeing him again, because I still thought that I could fix things between us.

Before venturing out of the house to meet him, I obsessively planned every last detail. I wouldn't put pressure on him for anything, or mention our relationship, lest I scare him away.

So I found myself in that very female position of pretending that I didn't have a care in the world, while secretly wanting to throw myself on his lap and scream, 'Please love me!'

I got to the French brasserie he'd booked in good time, and fought the urge to mumble, 'Neediness, party of one,' when the maître d' told me that I was the first to arrive.

It was only 6 p.m., and I was literally the only person at the bar, so I killed a bit of time by ordering a Ketel One on the rocks. I also managed to smoke a crafty fag after I told the bartender that I was meeting an ex for the first time and he silently slipped me an ashtray.

JP came in a few minutes later, and he looked great. We stuck mostly to small talk, and he seemed very guarded.

But as the wine flowed, we started to get more comfortable, and with the merlot acting as social lubricant eventually got around to the forbidden subject of our break-up (as the guide had advised, I let him lead the conversation and was determined not to start an argument).

'I realize that I probably overreacted to what you told me,' he said. 'But it wasn't just about the marriage, Cat.'

The gulp of wine stuck in my throat. 'No?'

'No. It was everything: the column, the book – which by the way I think is brilliant – but it's not easy to have everyone reading those things about your girlfriend.'

'But you know that I was totally faithful to you. I'm probably not going to write about relationships for ever, but I love being a journalist. And I was upfront about my job from the beginning.' Don't start an argument, I told myself. Keep breathing. Keep smiling. How badly do you want this to work?

'Yes, but I thought that I was dating a journalist who went to a top US school. Not a sex columnist. And with these TV offers, and a second book, this may be your career path for life. You're not going to want to have a family for a long time.'

'Look, JP, I'm going to level with you. Before I met you, I never thought that I wanted children. But now I realize that it was because I didn't trust myself enough to be a good mum, or love someone enough to want to start a family with them. Besides, I've always wanted to get to a place in my career where I feel I've done enough before I have children. I feel that way now. I feel like, with the right person, a family could definitely happen in the next couple of years.'

I sucked in my breath in shock at what I'd just said. Since my parents' divorce, I'd always thought of children as weakening my position, leaving my border vulnerable in case of a divorce war.

But now, I was considering the possibility. I wasn't broody, but I would definitely consider children with the right person instead of running screaming in the other direction. That, for me, was progress.

I pushed my sautéed spinach and miso cod around the plate for a couple of minutes before setting my fork down to make another point.

'But I have to say, though I'm open to compromise on where my career takes me, it bothers me that you don't seem to understand how much my writing means to me.'

'I do, but really, Cat, aren't you ready to move on from that stuff? You're so smart!'

I looked up at him as he continued to tear through his steak. I'm not mad at him for saying that, I thought, because he doesn't even realize how offensive it sounds. And besides, maybe I am being too sensitive. It would be tough if the boot was on the other foot.

Breathing deeply and counting to ten, I swallowed my anger again and smiled brightly. 'I'm sure that when I settle down, the column will evolve or come to a natural end, and I'll start writing about other things,' I said.

This seemed to satisfy him, and he took my hand in his. He looked at me, and when I looked into his blue eyes, flecked with green, I melted. I felt in that instant that he did still love me, and that his occasional overreactions to the subject matter of my job were just because he was afraid of losing me. *But I never asked him to change*, the little voice inside my head kept telling me. I took another sip of vodka and told my inner child to quit whining.

For the first time, in any relationship, my primary concern was making him happy, and I really, from the bottom of my soul, wanted the relationship to work. If that meant scaling back my subject matter a bit, so be it. He paid the bill, and we made for the door. As he helped me into my coat, our lips met in a kiss that continued to spill out on to the street.

'I've missed you,' I whispered, biting his lip lightly, and then going in for another kiss.

'Me too,' he said, looking down at me. 'I love you. But I'm still confused about what to do. I suppose if we're going to make things work, we just have to go for it?'

This was a question, not a declarative sentence. But it was a start. And even though I knew that I should go home alone, I melted at his smell, the nape of his neck. I wanted to fuck him. No, it was more than that, I wanted to devour him.

We shared a cab back to his place, and I propped my feet up on his lap the way I had on our second date, and told him that I was wearing the lacy Myla stockings he loved.

Halfway to his new place, crossing Belsize Park, he pushed me away. 'Hang on a minute,' he said. 'I want you to come home with me more than anything, but I have to confess that part of me is just horny. I'm still confused.'

Part of me wanted to tell him where to stick his confusion, but I was trying to be the new, Tao-reading me, and remembering that for a long time I too had had a fear of commitment.

I couldn't be mad at him for something I'd experienced myself, now, could I?

'That's okay,' I said, sliding his hand up to rest outside my already soaking knickers. 'I'm thinking with my pussy. I have been all night.'

'Oh, God,' he moaned as he slid one finger, then two inside me, and started to push in and out.

'We're going to get in trouble.' I giggled, pushing his hand away and watching him lick his fingers.

We barely made it inside the house before racing to the stairs, where he slipped my panties off and plunged straight into my soaking pussy. After we'd got the initial urge out of our system, we paused long enough to catch our breath, at which point JP carried me through to the bedroom, my legs wrapped around him

'I've missed you so much,' I mumbled, between heated kisses. 'I've been touching myself every night thinking about you when I'm alone.'

'Me too,' he said, and our eyes met as he continued to rock gently inside me before his eyes rolled back into his head and he murmured that he was going to come. Afterwards, we both fell back, him satisfied, while I licked the sweat from his left shoulder.

He rolled over and asked me if there was anything he could do to bring me off, and even though he had all the best intentions I could tell that his eyes were half closing, and so were mine.

'I love you,' I whispered as he drifted off to sleep. Still, though, my heart hammered in my chest. I had no idea where we stood, though he'd claimed to love me and to want to be with me.

Somewhere in my mind, I was chastising myself for being so fixated on someone who wasn't sure of me. But I laid those thoughts to rest. For now, our future still had potential.

At least, in my mind.

# TWENTY-NINE

'So, what's the deal, then?'

Amy, Victoria and I were shopping for wedding dresses, a task that Victoria loathed. But her big day was looming, and with no dress we were starting to panic for her.

'Are you two back together, or not?' She emerged from the fitting room in a huge, bouffant get-up that made her look like a walking, talking cream puff.

'The truth is, I'm not sure. He said he loves me and wants to be with me, but he's confused. I don't know what to think. And frankly, I'm afraid to rock the boat and ask.'

'I think he's probably threatened by your job,' Amy said, grabbing Victoria's lengthy train so that she could accompany her to the mirror. 'If he's not used to strong women, he probably feels that he isn't good enough, doesn't have enough to offer.'

'No offence, honey, but I think he's right,' Victoria said. 'Cat, you deserve someone who knows what he wants – I mean, please! Forget what he thinks. Don't *you* know what a great catch you are?'

She turned to face her reflection and screamed. 'Jesus Christ! I look like the Stay Puft Marshmallow Man from *Ghostbusters*!'

'It's not you, baby, it's the dress,' I said, laughing. 'That train makes Diana's wedding day look understated! Did your mum suggest it?'

'Good guess,' she muttered blackly. 'I hate all of these. I told her before that I wanted something simple. I've made up my mind: we're going to do a destination wedding, in a warm climate. That way I can wear something lovely, and strapless, and get a fabulous tan.'

'That's a great idea,' I told her. 'Anything I can do to help, let me know.' Having no desire to wind her up, I didn't mention the fact that with well under a year until the big day, and a very demanding family, she might want to get booking.

I helped gather up the yards of white fabric and, as I did, I inexplicably started crying for about the hundredth time that week. I was starting to feel like Sally Field in the movie *Cybil*, who had tons of different personalities trying to integrate with each other. Apparently, my inner child was something of a cry-baby.

'Honey, don't be sad,' Amy said. 'Look, there's every reason that he'll come around. Vic didn't mean to sound harsh.'

'No, I know she's right. I am avoiding the subject, and that can't be good indefinitely. I just love him so much. And maybe, deep down, I'm afraid that he's right, and my job is a deal-breaker.'

Victoria stuck her head out from behind the curtain. 'I'm going to tell you a story, Cat. Remember when Mike and I got together? Do you know what made me decide that he was the one?'

I dried my tears, and listened.

'My mum and I were reading an article about an American café, somewhere in Texas where they have loads of guns, near your neck of the woods I think, and a crazy man with a semi-automatic gun burst into a crowded restaurant during the lunch rush and started shooting at people. So these poor little families were munching on their mashed potatoes with garlic one second, and the next instant, BAM! They were worm food. He killed, like, twenty people.'

'Wow,' Amy said sarcastically, 'sounds like a great tale of love conquers all to me.'

'Let me finish!' Victoria pulled her top over her head and continued.

'Anyway, after the SWAT team caught the guy, they were interviewing survivors, and this one woman, totally in shock, said that she was there with her fiancé, and noticed that most of the men instinctively used their body to shield their wife and children. But when the cops came and everyone started making their escape, what did her man do?' She leaned forward. 'He used her as a human shield. He put his future wife between himself and the gunman.'

I leaned against the wall for support. Amy was wide-eyed. 'No WAY!'

'Way,' Victoria said, smiling. 'And my mum, being very French, said, "Darling, there are two kinds of men in the world, the ones whose instinct is to protect you, and the ones who run for the hills at the first sign of trouble. Make sure you're with the former." I knew that I was, and that no matter what, even if we split up, Mike would take a bullet for me.'

'So that's what you're saying about JP? You think that I would be the human shield?'

'Look, I don't think he's an evil guy. I'm sure that he would protect you, after considering it for about twenty minutes and going over the pros and cons. But don't you want someone to whom that comes instinctively?'

We walked out of the wedding boutique and into the street, where I smoked a desperately needed cigarette, and we wandered into the Hummingbird Bakery for a giant piece of red velvet cake and coffee. I knew that my friends were right, and felt that they had to be cruel to be kind.

'I know that JP loves you,' Amy said kindly, as she set a cup of coffee down in front of me.

'Yeah, right,' Victoria said, rolling her eyes. 'Look, all I'm saying is, life is too short to hang out with a man who is always using a problem as an excuse not to do something. I think that if he really loved you, whatever his problems were with commitment or whatever, he would be working them out with you, not running in the other direction. You're at the point now where the ratio of heartache to happiness with this guy is skewing the wrong way, and I'm telling you that you are way too good for this.'

# THIRTY

After three more 'dates' that ended in sleepovers, one candlelit dinner cooked by me that did not result in calling the fire brigade, and two unprovoked references by him to me as his 'girlfriend', it was safe to say that JP and I were back together.

That's not to say that it had been totally stress-free. If there's any truth to the saying, 'The way to a man's heart is through his stomach,' I'm probably facing a long spell of spinsterhood.

Cooking has never been my forte. My successes in the bedroom are only outnumbered by my failures in the kitchen, where the current contents of my refrigerator are a half-eaten jar of salsa, two bottles of champagne and a withered lettuce leaf. The only thing that isn't at least six months out of date is the booze.

Once upon a time, I surprised Jean-Claude by whipping up my signature bourbon pecan pie in his kitchen. Unfortunately, after I ended up consuming two shots of Southern Comfort for every one I gave the pie, I fell asleep at the kitchen table and woke to the sound of a smoke alarm, as he tried to waft away the black smoke pouring from the oven, and dumped the charred remains in the bin.

Since then, my perfect aphrodisiac meal has been either

a) one that someone else is paying for in a fabulous restaurant, or b) anything eaten off a lover's naked body.

Still, I love a challenge. And my newspaper wanted me to do an assignment: they had asked a few of the paper's most popular columnists to prepare a dish and write about it. Naturally, my assignment was meant to be erotic. So when the *Independent*'s chef recommended my recipe based on the phallic asparagus and the oozing yolk I jumped at the chance to have a go at cooking such a sexually charged meal.

Unfortunately, since my kitchen is the size of a shoebox, JP's place was my only option. Meanwhile, JP was less enthusiastic about the idea of me cooking in his house. 'At least I have a fire extinguisher handy if anything goes wrong.' He laughed, and casually mentioned the drawer of pizza menus.

But I began to relax when I saw that there were only three ingredients: eggs, asparagus and salt. This seemed like something that even I couldn't screw up. That was before I discovered that duck eggs are the culinary equivalent of a Kate Moss-designed dress: widely advertised but impossible to find. I went to three organic grocery stores, only to be told that they had sold out. Luckily, I realized that I could substitute hen's eggs. By the time the photographer showed up I was in full-on panic mode, but he was very kind and chilled-out, and actually put me a bit more at ease.

My confidence kicked in after I managed to boil the water, and dropped in the eggs using a random wooden spoon. I had a moment of alarm when one cracked, which I suspected was not a good sign. Fortunately I had six, and only one (JP's) had to be edible.

Knife poised nervously in hand, I was about to cut the

ends off the asparagus – until the photographer helpfully pointed out that the 'woody stalks' I should be discarding were at the other end. Oops. The amount of salt wasn't listed, so I obsessed over how much to add to the pan of simmering water I had ready for the asparagus. A pinch or a handful? I guesstimated an amount and dumped it in.

The rapidly boiling brew was starting to resemble a witch's cauldron as I frantically asked JP if he had an eggcup. All he had were two espresso cups, which was close enough.

The moment of truth arrived when I cut off the egg tops, and was horrified to find that only one egg yolk was runny enough for dipping. The others were pretty much hard-boiled, so I deduced that I must have left them in the water too long.

But I gave JP the good one, after stacking the vegetables to garnish the plate like I've seen on late-night cooking shows.

Despite the chaos I managed to create in the kitchen, the end result was pretty tasty. At least his egg was; mine was a bit rubbery. I offered one to the photographer before he left, but he declined. After watching me in action, I couldn't blame him. So I thanked him, and JP and I said our goodbyes.

But JP seemed to get turned on watching me nibble the stalks, and we got pretty horny – then again, it could have been more down to the stiletto-heel-and-mini-apron combination than the chemicals in the food.

I'm no galloping gourmet, but I considered the evening a raging success. Despite the complete mess I left behind, neither of us ended up in casualty. But I have to admit that we did order pizza afterwards.

*　*　*

In these heady early days of our reunion I couldn't help feeling eager to please JP. I wasn't about to be a doormat, but at the start of a relationship I think it's hard for any woman not to paint a simplified, idealized picture of herself. Anyway, as part of this meant getting kinky, there were definite side benefits for me.

JP had once confessed to me that one of his biggest fantasies had always been to make an amateur porn film. So I found myself buying him a digital video camera. A few hours after opening the box, he was ready to roll. I was a bit sceptical, because other than the obvious trust issues raised by filming myself in such a compromising position, I was worried about suffering from performance anxiety.

Watching myself on TV is stomach-churning at the best of times, even when I'm not obsessing over the top-of-thigh overhang from my hold-ups. But despite my apprehension, filming amateur porn is something that I've always wanted to try too. However, I admit that I was a bit disillusioned after our first clumsy attempt featured mostly shots of a lone breast flashing in and out of scene!

So I downloaded a few amateur Internet porn clips to do a bit of research. I learned the importance of lighting (and not answering my mobile mid-coitus) after the green, slightly sinister grainy hue of Paris Hilton's infamous *One Night in Paris*, shot using night vision, reminded me of an episode of *Most Haunted*.

Our next hurdle was experimenting with camera placement. We found that leaving it on the bedside table the entire time looked a bit static, but relying on hand-held shots looked jumpy, and reminded me of that bit in *The Blair Witch Project* when the kids are running through the woods. Eventually we decided to do a few 'test shots' and mark the spot where we would be 'in frame' with an X. As it turned out, his bedroom bookshelf was ideal.

I also picked up a few tips online about editing software, which could be used to get rid of embarrassing noises like my growling stomach.

I ruled out eating beforehand, because I felt a bit self-conscious about being on top after consuming half a pint of pistachio ice cream. According to the pros, arching my back would help 'streamline' my stomach, but after a while I started to get dizzy.

My insecurities meant that I decided to leave my bra on for the first bit, despite JP's reassurances that I looked amazing. And there were moments when nerves took over: I was worried about pulling cartoonish faces, and the inevitable money shot.

But after a while, I realized that shooting a sex video wasn't about being waxed to perfection or having a perfectly choreographed presentation. It was about feeling sexy and adored, having fun, and doing something that JP and I could enjoy together.

So by the end, I'd stopped worrying about camera angles and started really getting into our storyline, which consisted mostly of me stripping off my knickers and masturbating in a corset and fishnets until I orgasmed, then filming me giving him a blow job, followed by us having sex from several different angles, followed by a rather explosive money shot. We finished up with more than an hour of footage, and afterwards retired to the front room to watch the entire thing play back on the TV – relationships may be fleeting, but video is for ever.

JP made popcorn, and I finally cracked open that ice cream. After focusing on sucking my stomach in all night, I was ready to let it all hang out.

# THIRTY-ONE

Even though life with JP had slotted back into place, I didn't want to entirely ditch my ongoing analysis of what made relationships tick. If anything, I felt I still had a lot to learn. In the back of my mind I wasn't completely sure of JP's deeper feelings, even though for the time being our roller-coaster sex life kept getting in the way of any serious soul-searching.

I had been assigned a piece about the female sex drive. JP was off on a business trip to New York so for once I was going to have to fall back on theory rather than practice for my journalistic investigations.

I considered my own sexual hard-wiring. I've always felt like a freak because I'm very visual when it comes to sex. Seeing JP step out of the shower, or even bend over to take out the washing, and catching a sideways sliver of toned stomach or the ripple in his calves and curve of his ass as he pulls out the whites sends me into a frenzy.

Erotic stories are great, but I prefer the dirty ones to the saccharine ramblings of romance novels: I want to see smut, not euphemisms. The only place that the phrase 'love tunnel' belongs is in a travel guide to Venice.

I went online and trawled some medical journals. According to some corners of medical science, my preferences make me weird. In studies, men and women's differences were chalked up to variations in arousal. For men, arousal leads to sex, while women are much more complicated. This is supposedly why drug-maker Pfizer's hopes of Viagra working for women were dashed – though it certainly gets me off.

Ironically, a lot of our culture's insights into male behaviour come from love rats – literally. In a study in 1989, scientists trained caged male rats to gain access to females by pushing a lever. The researchers then destroyed part of the amygdala, an almond-shaped group of neurons in the brain that have been shown in research to perform a primary role in the processing and memory of emotional reactions. The rats lost interest in pressing the lever. Yet despite this lack of motivation, they had no problem engaging in sexual intercourse when the females were placed in their cages.

So-called 'sexperts' have also added fuel to the fire by advancing the view that women need flowers and candles, and men are, basically, walking hard-ons.

Dr Pam Spurr ignited a huge debate when she said that women should learn to say yes to sex and compromise in the bedroom if they want to keep their men. She has a point, but it's not just women who need to make an effort, because I've experienced the sting of a partner's rejection too.

In every single one of my relationships, my sex drive has been greater than that of my boyfriend. A doctor friend once jokingly said that I may have too much testosterone, but as long as I'm having fun and haven't sprouted chest hair, I'm not complaining.

But the highly sexed partner has to take some responsibility as well, because sometimes we get lazy. If a guy's seduction technique is limited to pushing his partner's head down towards his nether regions, is it any wonder that sex starts to feel like a chore for his girlfriend? I've also realized that if I want more action, I have to give more no-strings-attached affection.

Like everything else, sex is all about compromise and communication. In the past, if I've been sexually rejected I've started to take it personally, and eventually stopped trying to initiate proceedings. Obviously sex isn't everything, but it is what binds two lovers together. If all I want is a cup of tea and some good conversation, I'll call my grandma.

Just as I was pondering the importance of communication, by crazy coincidence my mobile started ringing. But it wasn't my grandma calling, it was JP.

'Hi, honey, how's it all going?'

'God, it's a nightmare. The new investors we had lined up have got cold feet. I've been in back-to-back meetings and I haven't even had a moment to eat.'

It didn't sound good. As a big bloke who's in tune with his stomach, food is something of a priority for JP. The one thing he likes about his frequent work trips to New York is the super-size food over there. Chunky steaks, massive pastrami sandwiches, bagels jammed with fillings – he laps them all up.

'I'm finally back in my hotel room but I wish I was back home properly, and curled up in bed with you.'

'Baby, it's only a couple more days. Meanwhile, it sounds like you need to unwind,' I purred. 'Lie back and relax and I'll tell you about my day.'

'Mmm, that sounds like a plan.'

'Well, I've been researching that article I mentioned on

female sex drive and my brain is now aching from all the technical jargon. But it did get me thinking about what turns me on. As you know, I'm very visual and I like my eroticism down and dirty. Apparently that makes me a bit of a bloke but, well, I figure that puts us on the same page . . .'

'Interesting, go on.'

'So how about I make you up a little bedtime story of a highly, let's just say, visual nature?'

'Oh, Cat, please do,' he murmured.

So I let my imagination run wild. His job is still long and hard. But for now it's not the only thing in our relationship that is.

# THIRTY-TWO

As spring arrived and London finally blossomed, my relationship with JP felt like it was shifting up a gear. Emotionally, we had become very comfortable in each other's presence. Physically, the sex just kept getting hotter. We were experiencing the levels of kinkiness and openness I'd have associated more with someone like Jamie. But I was beginning to appreciate that erotic experiences built on true feelings could be way more passionate than any adventure Jamie and I might have had.

With JP now becoming so open to exploration in the bedroom department, I had temporarily put my soul-searching to one side and replaced it with sexual adventuring. I left the Tao books to gather dust and focused more on becoming a sexual black belt. After all the attention I'd payed to JP's fantasies, I felt it was time to focus on enhancing my pleasure. It was time for the Zen master to meet the Kegelmaster.

The scene had originated when I had been at JP's friend Jack's stag night, and a stripper began shooting ping-pong balls from her pelvis. It was a little unconventional for me to be included but I wanted to do a piece on a guys' night out and Jack had readily agreed.

I was in awe of the stripper's muscle control, and when she

was finished I asked her how she did it. 'It's all about exercising the pelvic floor muscles,' she told me. 'I can lift more than ten pounds without using my hands.'

Now, I've always believed that strengthening my core muscles will make sex more pleasurable – it's part of the reason why I occasionally do yoga – but I'd become a bit lazy about my erotic exercise routine. I only do Kegel exercises once in a blue moon, and my short-lived experiment with Ben Wa Balls came to an end after Victoria's cat once thought they were a toy and dragged them under a bed. But the ping-pong routine made me think again. 'Men are always being blamed for having small willies, but no one ever talks about how much a woman can strengthen the muscles down there,' a party guest told me. 'It makes a huge difference to sex!'

I started Googling and reading blog testimonials, including one from a woman who recently gave birth to her first child and said that a device called the Kegelmaster changed her life. Not only had she strengthened her muscles post-pregnancy, but she was now having the best orgasms of her life, including her first vaginal orgasm.

That was all the motivation I needed. So, while most of my girlfriends were hitting the gym in preparation for their beach holidays, I'd decided to focus on toning muscles further south. I bought the Kegelmaster, billed as the 'original patented progressive resistance vaginal exerciser', for £59.99 online.

When it arrived, I was sceptical. It looked like a giant curling tong. I read the instruction manual and apparently it operates through a system of steel springs, and I was meant to choose the proper level of resistance and increase it as I got more adept – just like lifting weights at the gym. At the most intense, level fifteen, the resistance would be equivalent to lifting half a stone.

I never would have thought that something that resembled a huge curling tong could give me the strongest orgasms of my life. Rock on, Kegelmaster!

Ignoring the clinical look of the device and thinking about the fantastic orgasms I would be having if I used it, I pulled back the sheets and got busy. At first, doing the routine for five minutes a day felt like the un-sexiest thing ever. But after about a week, during which I increased to thirty reps six times a day, a strange thing happened. I found that I could get turned on much more easily just by squeezing myself, even during dull business meetings.

So on my next date with JP, after he started a story about how many pull-ups his trainer had made him do at the gym, I told him about my new routine. He was intrigued, so we decided to head back to his place and strip off in the name of scientific research. The sex was amazing. I found that contracting my muscles throughout led to heightened sensitivity and a stronger orgasm. JP could feel the difference too.

I definitely have more muscle control now. I haven't had a full-blown vaginal orgasm yet, but I'm having fun practising.

Normally, this is the ideal time of year for getting frisky in the great outdoors, but when it comes to al fresco sex this summer has been a bit of a washout.

Which is why yesterday, after a boozy Sunday brunch, JP and I decided to improvise. We walked through the park near his place, and started making out near the lake. I ground myself against him and could feel how hard he was, but just as we were getting comfortable against a wall we got caught in a torrential downpour, and the spine of my umbrella snapped.

It may work in movies, but I've decided that kissing in the rain is highly overrated. It's wet and sloppy, and not in a good way. Laughing, we ran back to his house.

'Let's ditch these wet clothes,' he murmured.

'No,' I said, leading him out to his garden. 'Let's finish what we started outside.'

I was freezing, but in addition to the gooseflesh on my arms I could feel my nipples hardening, which he definitely noticed in my white T-shirt. I undid his trousers and sat on top of him. I took off my T-shirt, and the contrast between the heat coming from his naked thighs and the cold rain pouring down my bare breasts felt incredible. I could feel an explosive orgasm building – until I looked up and saw the silhouette of someone watching from the upstairs flat opposite.

'There's someone watching us,' I whispered. 'Have you ever done it in front of anyone before?'

'You are so naughty,' he whispered in response, but I could feel his thrusts getting more energetic. I suspected that we'd both harboured fantasies about being watched, which was why I was always talking dirty to him on this topic.

We came almost simultaneously, which for me is practically as rare as spotting a unicorn. Laughing, we headed inside, and as I dried off I could swear that I saw a rainbow.

All in all, it was a perfect Sunday. Lying next to him while the first of the late afternoon sun filtered through the bedroom window after the storm broke, I realized that all my daydreams about a fairy-tale ending were crap compared to the real thing. Real love, with real problems, and getting through them together, was so much better.

I had never been more in love.

'I'm ready to take this to the next level,' I said, propping myself up on one elbow.

'Really?' he said, raising one eyebrow. 'And what might that be? I'm definitely ready to live with you. You could move in tomorrow.'

My heart fluttered, because although I was very excited about living with him, I wanted to make sure that we were on a solid footing first.

'Actually,' I whispered in his ear, 'I was talking about female ejaculation.' Having done all those Kegelmaster exercises, I was ready to reap the rewards. 'I've never done it before, but apparently it's easier in long-term relationships because the woman is more comfortable.'

I rolled over on top of him, sliding my legs between his. 'And I'm definitely comfortable with you, baby.'

'That sounds amazing, sweetheart,' he said. 'What do we do first?'

# THIRTY-THREE

Both from a scientific and a personal point of view, I was fascinated by female ejaculation. I was intimidated by the long-range squirters I saw on porn videos, and had also always been worried that I would accidentally piss myself – which is so not sexy. Porn stars aside, I was fascinated by the legitimate scientific debate surrounding the so-called 'squirters' – and had just read an article in *New Scientist* that suggested that the urethrovaginal space in some women may be a remnant of the embryological prostate called the Skene's gland. Some researchers have suggested that the Skene's glands are involved in triggering vaginal orgasms, and, more controversially, enable a small number of women to ejaculate.

But I was even more fascinated by the study's other findings: basically, scientists said that women may be able to improve the sensitivity of their G-spots, and perhaps even thicken the tissue of their vaginal walls, through stimulating them.

The modification theory was backed up by a note on Rwandan women. Apparently, all the Rwandan women that the scientists interviewed were able to ejaculate, probably because they had started stretching their labia minora using plant extracts at puberty. So they had re-trained their genitals to respond to different types of pleasure.

This had certainly been my experience with orgasms in general, and my G-spot in particular: the more I stimulated it, the stronger my contractions. Yet I hadn't managed to ejaculate. But I'd certainly had fun practising so far!

But the beauty of being in what was fast becoming a long-term relationship is the ability to let yourself go, as I was discovering more and more with JP.

After positioning a movable full-length mirror width-wise in his bedroom, we climbed up on the bed and got down to business.

I'd primed myself a week earlier by buying the video *How to Female Ejaculate*, which featured a lot of shoulder-pad-wearing women with over-the-top permed hairdos that made them look like extras from eighties monster-rock videos.

Spreading a towel on the bed underneath me, I motioned for JP to get behind me. He started by fucking me in long, slow strokes, and when I kept trying to touch my clitoris he slowed down and reminded me that G-spot orgasms take longer to build.

'Stop touching yourself, baby,' he murmured.

'I don't think I can,' I moaned. I was so excited already, and dying to come.

'Well,' he said, sitting back, 'we'll have to do something about that, won't we?' He stood up and pulled a white and blue striped silk tie out of his wardrobe, then attached first one wrist, then the other, to his bedposts.

'Now, I'm going to give you a good fucking. Would you like that?'

'Yes,' I moaned. 'Fuck me like the dirty little slut I am.'

Hey, it may not be the most politically correct dialogue, but I knew that it turned him on.

He pulled out the specialty G-spot vibrator that we'd bought in a sex boutique around the corner from my flat, and slid it inside me. I gasped as I felt the specially shaped nub of the vibrator stimulate my G-spot, and he kept working the toy in and out of me while I writhed with pleasure and watched in the mirror as he wanked himself with his other hand.

After a few minutes I felt the G-spot swell up and get hard, but then I got the sensation of needing to pee. I suddenly had loads of sympathy for men who try to urinate with hard-ons. 'Oh, God,' I moaned, feeling more turned on than I ever had in my entire life. 'Baby, I feel like I have to pee, and I can't control it!'

'I just want you to come for me, baby, I don't care what happens,' he said. I could feel his fingers working over me furiously, while I strained against my silk bonds.

The video had said that I should bear down once I had the tingling sensation, so I pretended just for an instant that I was on the toilet and let myself go, and suddenly I felt the body-rocking contractions start as my entire body exploded in an orgasm.

He pulled the vibrator out just as my muscles started to clench and that's when I saw it – a tiny stream of clear liquid shot out. I squirted! I was so happy that I started to cry, and he held me.

It took me a couple of minutes to calm down and stop shaking. 'Now, baby, you've been so patient,' I said. 'What can I do for you?'

'Are you kidding? That was the biggest turn-on of my life,'

he said, spreading my legs and climbing back on top of me. 'Jenna Jameson has nothing on you!'

Later, lying on the sofa, we linked hands, and we discussed ex-relationships. 'So, you dated someone for over a decade. How come you two never got married?' I asked him.

'Are you sure you want to hear about this? That was so many years ago, I don't even think about it now.'

'I'm sure,' I said, rolling over on to my side, and patting his shoulder playfully. 'Don't worry, I can handle the truth.'

'Well, to be honest, I loved her, but it just wasn't meant to last for ever. I was never sure enough of the relationship to take it all the way.'

He traced his finger across the nape of my neck, in the spot that he knew I loved. 'It was pretty dysfunctional, actually. Anyway, even though we were together much longer, the feelings that I had for her were nothing compared to how I feel about you.'

I could feel my heart exploding inside my chest. I wanted to cry. 'So, you think that you feel more sure about this relationship?'

'Definitely. And I'll tell you something else,' he said, hovering over me as I felt my pussy aching in anticipation of round two, 'when I propose to you, I promise I'll think of something absolutely wonderful.'

As I disappeared underneath him, I knew that I could have died happy in that instant.

But as I was about to find out, there's no such thing as a happy ending – only happy chapters.

# THIRTY-FOUR

JP and I had our first big row since getting back together, which made me really stressed because I hate confrontation. While on the surface it seemed to be about my work, again, I got a sense of something uglier underneath.

It was another Sunday morning, a week later. I woke to hear him showering, then he went downstairs to make my coffee, which I loved.

He was due to meet friends for a day of shooting in the countryside but I was planning to skip it and get on with my column. By the time the coffee was ready I was already at work in front of my computer.

'Come on, it's Sunday,' he said. 'You're always working!'

'You're constantly travelling to New York for work, or to South Africa to scuba dive for ten days at a time, and I never complain,' I retorted. 'You know that Sundays are a big work day for me, because I have 4,000 words due in tomorrow, baby!' I was aware that I was being irritable, but blamed it on my current lack of caffeine. 'Okay, I'll come for a while, if you'll do something for me,' I said, kissing him softly. 'If you'll fuck me from behind, I'll stay as long as you want,' I murmured, sliding my hand down my knickers.

He bit my ear lightly, and fondled my breasts from behind as I closed my eyes. 'My pleasure,' he said, carrying me upstairs.

As soon as I arrived at the pre-shoot brunch, though, I realized I shouldn't have agreed to come for the whole day. With work on my mind I just wasn't on the same wavelength as JP's friends, who were full of relaxed chatter, surrounded on all sides by kids and chaos. Much as I loved JP's friends and wanted to have a carefree Sunday just like everyone else, I was really stressed out about my upcoming deadlines: in addition to the column, I was working on two major magazine pieces, both due the same day. Though I've always been wildly ambitious and in some ways this was what I wanted, I was a bit scared that I'd bitten off more than I could chew. In fact, I was terrified and it was making me edgy.

I managed to have a good time for the first couple of hours, but after a while my thoughts kept returning to my deadline. Not seeing an easy get-out strategy, I knew I would eventually need to sneak off so as not to break up the gathering.

I can be the life and soul of the party, but the downside is that I can also be a serious stress bunny.

The truth also was that I didn't want to tell JP then and there that I was heading off, because I was starting to get the sense that anything that didn't fit into his plans was going to be a problem. And on that day I just couldn't afford to get waylaid.

Being surrounded by his friends' kids was also a bit of a mindfuck for me, now that I had started to re-examine my attitude towards having children. I'd always insisted that I never wanted them, but being with JP, his niece and nephews and his friends' kids had made me think that loving someone enough to want to have their children could be a beautiful thing.

Through therapy, I'd realized that my absolute resistance towards having kids stemmed from a fear of being left, and being vulnerable. But I loved JP, and I trusted him. Also, I was starting to have the confidence to believe that I could actually be a good mum some day. He inspired that in me.

Nonetheless, I had to admit that toddlers still scared the shit out of me, especially the ones who were mobile but couldn't speak. If only they could be cryogenically frozen until the age of four years old . . .

I sent JP an explanatory text as I beat my retreat.

Back at his house, I let myself in, relishing the feeling of his key on my keyring. I then wrote my column, using my artistic licence and jokily finding inspiration in that morning's mayhem.

*I could feel the panic attack starting as the slavering beast lunged towards me while I was having brunch with my sometime boyfriend JP and his friends. But it wasn't a pit bull that had my adrenalin rushing; it was his friends' three-year-old, Oscar. This wouldn't be a problem for most people, but I've never had a maternal instinct in my life. Even as a child, I always preferred the company of adults. I don't coo at babies, I run from them.*

When JP came back, I could tell that he was pissed off about my sudden departure, but he just turned on the TV and zoned out. I hate passive aggressiveness, so I decided to get the issue out in the open.

'Hey, babe, I'm sorry that I had to bail out early, but I had lots to do.'

He grunted.

'Look, are you annoyed with me for some reason?'

He looked over the top of the *Financial Times*. 'Not really. I just don't know why you always have to be the first to leave when we're out with my friends.'

I sat down next to him. 'Honey, don't overreact; it's not normally like that. I'm on a deadline right now but my workload will ease up in a few weeks and I can take time off.'

He sighed and wrinkled his brow. 'You always say that, but it's always about work with you.'

Stung, I said, 'But you know how passionate I am about my writing. I know how important your career is to you.'

'But you are obsessed!'

'This from a guy who spends a week out of every month abroad? You have got to be kidding me!' I felt my face flush, and for the first time with JP I was pissed off at him, properly, but as usual I turned my anger inward.

'Look, honey, we're both really into our work, and that's probably one of the reasons why we love each other. Right?' I shook his shoulder playfully, and looked him in the eye. 'Can't we compromise, please? I know you wouldn't want to date a chick with no life!'

He smiled at me, put the newspaper down and hugged me. 'Of course we can. Can I see today's magnum opus?'

I grabbed my laptop from the kitchen table and proudly

showed him the column, explained it was tongue-in-cheek, then left him to read it as I went into the kitchen to make another cup of coffee.

He came in a few minutes later with a concerned expression on his face.

'Cat, this is part of the problem.'

My smile faded as I poured in the milk. 'What do you mean? You didn't think it was funny?'

'Yes, but it's all about how much you hate kids!'

'I know that it must be hard to have a girlfriend who writes about life experiences,' I said, 'but it's only meant to be funny vignette writing, not serious political discourse!'

I was trying to see things from his point of view, and understand how he felt about what he perceived as a worrying attack on his way of life. It was only supposed to be comedy and make fun of me, really, but I tried to be empathetic.

'Honey, are you serious? Does the column bother you that much?'

He sighed. 'Of course not. You know I'm proud of you. I love you. But sometimes I worry that we want different things, and reading that just proved my point.'

'Reading the column? How so?'

'Well, you know that I want a family some day. Being rational, if you're so dead set against the idea of children—'

'*Was* dead set against the idea,' I said, sitting on the counter. 'But since I met you I've had a change of heart. I definitely want your babies.'

'Then why write about loathing them? Are you sure you're not just telling me what I want to hear?'

'JP, you do understand that this is a job, right? It's comedy writing, not Voltaire. Also, it's my job. It's part of me. It's not me!'

'You're telling me that you don't loathe kids?'

My eyes widened. 'I don't hate them. I fear them, to tell you the truth. Especially the tiny ones. When a mum says, "Do you want to hold my baby?" and you're supposed to act really excited, and then the baby starts flopping around, I get paranoid that I'm going to drop them. And yeah, I'll admit, newborns are fugly. No matter what anyone says!'

He laughed. 'And you're telling me that you want a baby when you've compared them to larvae in public?' His voice softened. 'My baby?'

'Absolutely,' I said, walking up to him and putting my hands on his chest to gaze up into his eyes. 'Fact: I can be a great mum and still hate everyone else's young kids.'

He slid one arm around my waist. 'We are going to have gorgeous children.'

I took his hand. 'You have to understand that a news-paper column is a two-dimensional representation of life, the person on the page is a character, and she's not me. You do see the difference, right?' I was teasing, but a dark cloud was starting to form in my mind.

I tried to take my mind off the fact that despite JP's age and outward stability, I seemed to be the one who was much more ready to move things forward in our relationship. He said all the right things, but he seemed to be all talk and no action. Like Victoria said, he always seemed to find problems with me, and I constantly seemed to be trying to find solutions. But now wasn't the time to bring that up.

'Look, sometimes the things you want the most are the things you are most terrified of.' I put my arms around his neck and pulled him into a kiss. 'Take me upstairs.'

# THIRTY-FIVE

After that, we had a few days apart but it didn't take me long to rationalize his behaviour and suppress my worst fears. By the time I went over for dinner a few nights later, I'd convinced myself that these niggling doubts were normal. It was tough to stick to any decision concerning JP because although he was capable of making some really thoughtless remarks, sometimes he also instinctively knew how to patch matters up by saying the right things.

We could always talk stuff through, and I felt that with these big decisions it would be unrealistic to expect perfect harmony from the start. Some topics needed mature debate and discussion. Besides, I know that I'm not easy to live with sometimes, and my chosen profession isn't the easiest pill to swallow. I'm also incredibly neurotic, over-analytical, and super-sensitive.

The next morning I knew he was late for work, but as he stepped out of the shower he looked so cute with his hair all ruffled from the towel, I had to jump on top of him.

'I have to leave, honey,' he said, laughing. 'God, I can't keep up with you.'

So I did something very naughty while he was facing the mirror and perfecting his tie – I threw the covers over me, rolled over on to my stomach and let him get a view of my naked ass as I slid on to my hands and knees.

'Please, baby?' I said, faux-begging. 'Just stay a few minutes longer?'

'Well,' he said, unzipping his fly and guiding his cock to my mouth, 'I suppose that it would be impolite to leave you without at least giving you a proper fucking first. But only—'

He gasped as I took his entire cock deep into the back of my throat. This was a skill I had mastered after watching a pneumatic porn queen called Mystique deep-throating a kielbasa sausage.

Later, I'd practised suspending my gag reflex, first with a toothbrush, and later, in an oral sex masterclass, with props like aubergines and bananas.

He put his hand on the back of my head and increased the pace of his thrusts, before crudely flipping me over and plunging into me, gripping my ass and grunting.

I moaned, and could feel the staccato rhythm going even faster. I imagined that his balls were tightening, and that he was ready to come, which sent me over the edge.

Sensing me coming, he spread my legs even wider, and with one final thrust exploded into my pussy.

We kissed, softly, and I gently pushed him out of bed.

'Get out!' I told him teasingly. 'I have a deadline, and you're already WAY late for work!'

'I know,' he said. 'I'm just trying to take my mind off the fact that tomorrow you're leaving me for Cannes.'

'It's only for three days, sweetie, and first we've got Jack's wedding tonight, remember,' I said as he readjusted his tie and smoothed his trousers down. He didn't have any obvious staining, but I loved the fact that he would smell like me all day. The sensation that I got from him was very primal.

'Pick me up at eight?' I said.

As he headed to the top of the stairs, he hesitated. 'Didn't you tell me that you were working on something to do with weddings last night?'

'Yeah, it was about the optimum time of courtship.' I turned on the shower and handed JP his briefcase. 'Apparently the rate of successful marriages is highest in people who dated for between six and eighteen months.'

'Well, it's good to know what my parameters are,' he said, raising one eyebrow. 'But I think it will be closer to six months than eighteen in our case.'

As he walked out the door, I swooned at the thought of making this practical, pragmatic guy so swept away with romance.

# THIRTY-SIX

Maybe I should have known that things seemed too good to be true in my relationship. It was less than twenty-four hours after our cheeky pre-work sex that I discovered the next hairline fracture beneath the surface. It happened in an episode that I titled in my mind 'The Cashpoint Crisis'.

I was starting to see a pattern in my relationship with JP: just when we started to get close, I would be dramatically pushed away. I don't really blame him, though, because I don't think he was even aware he was doing it. At the time, I wasn't either.

I spent the rest of the morning at JP's north London pad sending emails and blogging before I took the Tube home, so I didn't realize that I had a cash-flow problem until much later in the day. Amy and Victoria were both being sent to Cannes for work, so I went along for the ride. I had been so busy planning my outfits for Cannes and thinking about partying with the girls that I hadn't thought through more mundane issues such as money.

To cut a long story short, two expected payments hadn't come through, so instead of having £6,000 in my bank account, I had precisely £17.50. As a freelancer I was used to getting paid last, but having no cash was a problem because I really needed money to get through Cannes.

It was made worse because I didn't have a credit card, only a debit card. And I didn't want to sponge off Victoria and Amy. I knew that they would gladly lend me the money, but I also knew that neither of them could really afford to be a couple of hundred pounds short, even temporarily.

At the time, I thought the solution was obvious. I would simply ask JP. It was tough for me to ask for financial assistance, but the company who owed me money had assured me that the payment would be in my account by Monday, and apologized for the error. So I could have the money back to him by Tuesday. Not that we really discussed money, but JP made millions, so I knew that he wouldn't miss it temporarily.

I explained my money shortage to JP in a brief conversation that day, but he seemed distracted. Later that night, fifteen minutes before he was due to pick me up in a taxi, he called back.

'Listen, babe, I'm really running late,' he said. 'Can you just take a taxi and meet me there instead?'

'Normally I would say sure, sweetheart, but you know my money situation,' I blurted out, feeling embarrassed that I had allowed myself to get into such an irresponsible situation. 'And the Tube will take at least an hour, even if I wasn't wearing four-inch heels. I won't make it!'

'Okay, okay, I'll come and get you,' he said, sounding annoyed and probably hearing the approaching panic in my voice. 'Come down to the street. I'll be there in twenty.'

I raced downstairs and waited on my doorstep in my white off-the-shoulder mini-dress and the lovely Jimmy Choo sandals that he'd bought me two weeks earlier. I started to worry that he might think that I expected him constantly to bail me out financially. Then again, I had bought him a Panerai diving watch for his birthday, so surely he wouldn't think I was cheap?

I called Victoria, pacing the street, and filled her in on the situation.

'I'm just so embarrassed,' I said, 'and I don't want him to think that I'm going to be constantly expecting financial handouts!'

'Jesus Christ. You're not Northern Rock, for fuck's sake, you just need a bit of cash to tide you over until next week.'

'But he sounded so stressed. You don't think that there's a problem here?'

'Yeah, I do, and it's the fact that you don't feel comfortable enough to ask him to help you out. You would do it for a friend, wouldn't you, if you could afford it?'

'Of course, but—'

'There. You've answered your own question. I've got to run, Cat, I think one of our cats is giving birth. Let's talk about it on the plane tomorrow.'

Against a backdrop of feline screeching, I heard her cut out, just as the taxi pulled up.

Immediately I picked up on JP's discomfort. He usually said, 'Hello, gorgeous,' and kissed me. But he merely pecked me on the cheek and kept chatting to the office on his BlackBerry.

'So did you solve your little crisis?' he asked brusquely, once he'd hung up, looking out at Hyde Park racing past the window.

'Well, no, but I did confirm that I'm getting paid on Monday. So it's just the weekend that's the problem, and I really don't know what I'm going to do with no cash. I don't want to go to France if I can't afford to get cabs, and pay my share of stuff out there. It's not fair to Amy and Victoria.'

What was wrong with me? Why couldn't I just ask him for the money?

He sat in silence, then announced, 'Well, from what you've told me you're not exactly a financial wizard.'

This stung. 'Look, I chose to be a journalist and writer, which aren't careers that you do hoping to get rich,' I told him. 'Despite that, I make a really good living. It's just that it's not like being a salaried worker. Freelancers are always the last to get paid!' I was annoyed with myself that I couldn't just ask him for the cash, and angry with him for not offering it. Why was I defending my career to him again?

He shook his head and looked at me sympathetically, and I could feel myself getting enraged at his patronizing attitude. Here was a guy who had always worked for different companies, and followed a steady path of college, med school, then business school. JP would always have a job that paid well; for him it was about degrees of success.

Meanwhile, trying to make it as a writer in London was a bit like waitressing in Los Angeles, waiting for a big break that might never come, trudging home to your dirty East LA studio after taking abuse from customers who bitch you out for forgetting their wheat-free bread and looking longingly at the refrigerator magnet that says 'Even Brad Pitt had to wear a chicken suit!', a reference to the many fast-food jobs the superstar had back in the day to make ends meet.

When things got bad, I reminded myself that Stephen King had had loads of rejections before making it big, and that F. Scott Fitzgerald wrote a piece called 'The Crack-Up' when he was seriously low on cash. The idea was that it was possible to use up all capacity for emotion and be left with nothing, a concept that I'm familiar with during my darkest days.

For people whose life is their work, rejection is always personal. And painful. It's often an all-or-nothing gamble that drains you spiritually, mentally and emotionally.

JP had a cushy job, but he didn't really take too many risks. And for the first time, I felt that he loved me, but in the same way that a child falls in love with a horse, before a parent sits the child down and explains the maintenance and upkeep involved, and tells the kid that he's going to have to learn to break in a wild animal. I sensed that JP wanted to take the ride, but also that he didn't want to get thrown.

So I didn't ask him for the money. I just made some breezy comment about busking for cash at the airport by pretending to be collecting coins for charity, and tried to cheer him up as we approached the wedding reception.

Inside, I listened to Jack, the groom, say that he'd found his soulmate, the one person who loved him in spite of his flaws. I knew that I felt that way about JP, but was I sure that he felt the same about me? Did I trust our relationship enough to let him see me be vulnerable?

The next morning, before I set off for the airport, I filed an article I had been writing about dating taboos. I had to smile at the irony of my situation as I put the finishing touches to a piece which was, coincidentally, about cheapness.

I wasn't sure why, but JP's reaction to the money incident really bothered me. It wasn't about the money, it was more the fact that I wanted so much for us to be on the same team, and yet I felt, more and more, like we were opponents in a game of chess.

> *Don't fool yourself into thinking that a man who insists on splitting the bill this early on is a poster boy for women's rights. This is not about equality. It's about him missing the opportunity to show that he actually cares enough about you to invest, say, forty teeny pounds in your relationship.*
>
> *In my experience, first-date frugality demonstrates an intrinsic cheapness. The man who whips out a calculator and says, 'I had a filter coffee, you had the crème brûlée,' will be the one insisting that you choose a honeymoon destination based on Air Miles specials.*

None of the above applied to JP, who was outwardly very generous during our dates. But the next line I typed made me pause.

> *Which brings me to my next point: men who are mean with their money are usually emotionally stingy too. Ready to settle? Thought not.*

# THIRTY-SEVEN

With the Cashpoint Crisis weighing on my mind, I knew I needed some thinking time. I'd been caught up in a sexual whirlwind, which hadn't allowed me much space to evaluate underlying issues. So the trip to Cannes couldn't have come at a better time. Emotionally, if not financially.

In the end I had sent Amy a last-minute text begging for an emergency loan, rather than get into another argument with JP about lending each other cash.

When I met her at the airport and properly explained my situation, she was horrified. 'Look, I'm not trying to upset you but when I was behind with the rent last month and struggling, Richard gave me his bank card and told me to take whatever I needed. Are you sure this guy is worth it?'

'He said that he didn't know that I really needed it, and that he wasn't sure that loaning each other money was a good idea but that of course he would have given it to me if I had asked.'

I saw Amy and Victoria exchange glances. 'Doesn't it scare you that you had to tell him? Sorry, but I would want a boyfriend who instinctively wanted to help me out,' Victoria said.

I bit my lip to keep from crying.

'Look, we all know that men do stupid things sometimes,'

Amy said breezily. 'So let's just have fun and forget about it. You know JP loves you, so you just have to have faith in that for now, okay, Patience?'

This was a joke, because it was the very ironic nickname that my mum gave me as a little girl. I almost pop an aneurism when old people spend loads of time fumbling with their wallets.

Did it bother me that JP's automatic response wasn't to help me out in my hour of need? Yes. But I was determined not to let either my rocky love life or the fact that I had no cash, no plan and no party invitations spoil our girly weekend. I deserved to find a few hot leading men to flirt with – purely platonically, of course.

Unfortunately, disaster struck at the airport after the very brisk check-in girl told me that I didn't have a seat on my flight due to overbooking (my girlfriends had both very wisely used online check-in).

'Miss, you're going to have to see the staff at the customer services counter, and ask them about the status,' she said. 'There is nothing more I can do for you here.'

Normally I would have been fine, but my fight with JP had left me emotionally raw, which I decided to use in my favour.

So my girlfriends hugged me and went to board the flight, while I was left to fend for myself. The customer services desk looked like an old-school Wall Street pit, before trading moved on to the Internet. Everyone was waving boarding passes and desperately trying to attract the attention of the harried-looking young woman behind the desk.

JP really redeemed himself at this point by offering to help me in any way that he could, proving to me once again that he did have a good heart. My worry, though, was that his first instinct, in every case, was always to regard me with suspicion. I loved him so much: how long was I going to have to keep proving myself to him?

I patiently waited my turn, and when it came, instead of berating her for crap service and demanding that I be allowed on board, I explained my situation calmly. 'I know that this totally isn't your fault, but I really need to get on that plane,' I said, my voice breaking. 'I'm promoting a book, and since I officially have fifteen pounds in the bank, I'm counting on getting a ride with my friends. The next flight you guys have is so late tonight that they'll all leave me. And I don't want to be alone right now. Anyway, thanks and I really appreciate your help.' Fat, rebellious tears slid down my cheeks, and I started quietly to experience what Rhett Butler in *Gone With the Wind* referred to as a 'crying jag'. If Scarlett O'Hara, one of the most badass, tough heroines ever, could occasionally lose it, then so could I!

At the last second they called my name, and my new ally smiled at me as she slipped a business-class upgrade into my hand. I thanked her profusely, and ran like hell.

Once I got on the plane, I discovered that I was sitting one seat away from Quentin Tarantino, and in the row behind horror director Eli Roth, who was very cute in person. I sipped my champagne and wondered if my luck was finally beginning to change.

During the journey I surreptitiously read a book called *Facing Love Addiction* – between the covers of a magazine – so Quentin wouldn't spot it. My therapist had recommended it ages ago. But with JP taking up so much of my energy my Anti-Rules research had been pretty much shelved and my guides had been gathering dust. Now my doubts about JP's commitment were surfacing I decided I'd use this time away to reactivate my quest.

When we got off the plane, Quentin was whisked to the fast-track passport queue with his entourage, so I slipped on my giant sunglasses and followed them through. And that's when I realized the number one rule of Cannes: if you don't have it, fake it. I felt guilty about blagging my way through everything, but it soon dawned on me that everyone else was doing it, and I started to relax.

In fact, it seemed that everyone in Cannes was looking for the Bigger, Better Deal – in business and relationships. Despite all the stunning women, it's a testosterone-soaked environment where success is measured in terms of size – whose yacht is the biggest, whose party gets the most celebrities, who has the most money. I knew what my next column would be about: blagging.

As we piled into a taxi, I excitedly opened the brochure for our hotel, which was described as 'an idyllic hideaway nestled on the outskirts of glamorous Cannes'.

'Amy, are you sure about this place?' Victoria asked. 'The ad looks about thirty years old.'

'I think the guy posing in it has bellbottoms on.' I giggled. 'Or maybe it's just a French thing.'

The motel confirmed my worst suspicions; definitely more roach motel than fabulous suite. The rooms were tiny, dark, un-air-conditioned boltholes that resembled the third-class decks of the *Titanic*.

'When I said I wanted a hot, dirty vacation, this wasn't what I had in mind,' I said, as Amy unpacked her bag.

Victoria started spraying her perfume in circles around her. 'I'm trying to disinfect the room,' she said. 'Ew! I swear I can feel gritty stuff on the floor.'

'I suggest that we all keep drinking,' I said, pulling an aeroplane-issued mini-bottle of vodka from my handbag. 'That way we'll kill all the germs!'

My blagging column was especially timely considering that we were feigning cool while staying at the Bates Motel. Except that at least in *Psycho* the bathroom got a thorough scrubbing by the end.

After a three-hour preparation session that involved rotating the shower, one mirror and a single power outlet, we hit a glamorous rooftop party. Amy and Victoria were both carrying copies of *Sleeping Around* to do a bit of guerrilla marketing, and I told a restaurant owner about it. 'How many people have you slept with?' he barked at me, before introducing his lovely, and much younger, date as 'my soon-to-be-ex-girlfriend'.

He was horrible, but later that night, lying in my sleeping bag, wedged between a bed and the wall, I had to ask myself if I was really so different. My girlfriends and I are used to upgrading our phones, laptops and handbags every season – so why not relationships? We all have our fantasy BBD, that imaginary perfect man who ticks all our boxes, whom we mentally measure everyone else against.

On our last night, I got us invites for the amfAR party by offering to report on it for the *Independent*. There I met Nick, a high-profile film producer who, like me, hailed from the American South. Normally, I go for well-built but average-looking guys. But this one had a surfer's body and, in addition to his success, was disconcertingly good-looking. I was feeling very flustered indeed as I got him on to the subject of who he was dating, and why he hadn't settled down again after his divorce. I also told him about JP, and the Cashpoint Crisis that had been dominating my thoughts for some reason. It turned out that he was a fan of the column, and he laughed out loud as he flipped through the book.

'Do you think we're too picky?' I asked him while we watched the fireworks under the stars. 'Do you think you'll ever find your dream woman?'

'Of course,' he replied teasingly. 'All I've ever asked for was a bisexual Rhodes scholar supermodel who loves to surf. But then I got real, and dropped the education requirement. After all, I do live in LA!'

Even though I knew he was teasing, on some level I was horrified. I was relieved that I was with a guy who totally adored me as much as I did him and wasn't looking for the bigger, better deal. On the other hand, part of me worried that he couldn't handle me, or my job. The balancing act was proving more difficult that I'd thought.

'Can I give you a piece of advice?' Nick asked.

'Of course,' I said, watching, amused, as two stick-thin models, who were evidently vegetarian, spat brown foie gras truffles into their napkins after realizing it was liver fat, not chocolate.

'You need to stop going for guys who are in awe of you from the beginning. The only ones who try that hard to be everything you want are really insecure themselves, and they know that their act in the beginning is all based on bullshit. So when you fall in love with the illusion, they bail.'

'So I can't have the swept-off-my-feet feeling?'

He touched my arm. 'Of course you can. But you need someone who is strong enough to keep on carrying you. You are a very talented and gorgeous woman, and the commitment-phobe guys are fine for flings, but when you want to get serious and settle down, you're going to need a very secure man.' He leaned back, smiled, and crossed his arms.

I had to laugh. 'That's the trouble. They all seem secure in the beginning. Then it's like "I love you, you're perfect, but could you tone it down a bit?"'

'Don't you dare,' he said, smiling, before giving me a kiss on the cheek. 'It was nice to meet you, Catherine.'

When Amy and I finally stumbled out of the party, totally pissed and after 3 a.m., we couldn't find a taxi, so we peeled off our killer stilettos and started the two-mile trek over cobblestone streets towards the taxi rank.

Unfortunately, Amy's French isn't great, so when a battered-looking Renault pulled up next to us and the driver rolled down his window, she didn't hesitate before pulling open the back door and sticking her leg inside the car.

'Amy! The guy is not a minicab! Get out!' I hissed, grabbing her arm and yanking her out. She's tiny, so I won.

'But, Cat, I asked if he was a minicab, and he's telling us how much he is . . . I don't give a shit if it's forty euros, let's just get home!'

I took her by the shoulders, looked into her glassy eyes and tried to remain steady on my feet. 'No, honey, he's not telling us how much he is. He's asking us how much we are. He thinks we're hookers!'

She covered her mouth in shock, and started twirling her hair around her fingers. 'Oh, my God. Are you sure?'

By this point the creepy guy was climbing out of his car and heading towards us, and I could see that despite his slender build he was very tall and looked like he would be a formidable opponent, even if I'd been sober. My fear was blunted because of the buzz, so I was filled with righteous indignation, not just because he had insulted us, but, really, did he think he could get this dynamite brunette/blonde combination to blow him for a mere forty euros? Who did this cheap bastard think he was kidding?

Suddenly, it was on. We both started gesticulating wildly, cursing in French (funny how quickly your vocabulary comes back when you are either a) drunk or b) seething with rage) and things were about to turn ugly when a Mercedes screeched up next to us. One of the blacked-out windows slid down, and I recognized Nick.

Great, I thought. I tried to come across as the picture of class and elegance in my metallic gold Grecian dress and sweet little ringlet curls, and here I am telling some creep to go fuck himself in the ass – albeit in French.

He stepped out of the car, told the guy to get lost, and in one fell swoop ushered Amy and me inside the car.

'Thanks,' I said gratefully. 'You're my hero.'

'I'm glad I ran into you again,' he said. 'I wanted the chance to clarify what I said back there. You know that I was only kidding about the Rhodes scholar stuff, right?'

'I know,' I said, as Amy snored against my shoulder and the car climbed through the wooded hills on the outskirts of Cannes. 'It's not you. I'm just a little sensitive about the subject because I do sometimes wonder if my job will put men off –

if, like you said, they prefer to be with women who are perfect pedigree on paper instead of one with a – shall we say – rather chequered past.'

'Well,' said Nick, 'after you'd gone I thought more about our chat. I wanted to reiterate that when we find someone amazing, I think the internal debate ends. It did with my wife. She was an actress, and she had to get naked with her co-stars on a daily basis. Sometimes that was tough for me.

'But when you really love someone, you don't get to pick and choose bits of them, you take the whole package. We didn't last for ever, but her career certainly wasn't a factor in the split, and I never would have wanted her to give up her dream. Did you tell your boyfriend, "Hey, man, I love you but I'm morally opposed to stem cell research so I'll need you to stop promoting that on your website"?'

'Of course not. I love him. Period.'

Nick smiled. 'Exactly. So why are you the one who needs to change? Don't settle, Catherine.'

As we headed towards our hovel, I began to feel like the girl from the eighties movies who lives on the wrong side of the tracks, and gets her boyfriend to pick her up at the mall because she doesn't want him to see where she lives.

'Why is everything so complicated?' I asked him.

He smiled down at me as we pulled up to our hotel. Everything looked better under the cover of darkness. 'Hell, you're the relationship expert. What I meant by not settling was that, eventually, I think we all get the partner that, deep down, we feel we deserve. And you definitely deserve the best. Don't change. And don't give up your column, or your book. You are way too talented!'

We exchanged phone numbers, and I dragged Amy, still belching and mumbling, out of the car. In our room I helped her to undress and get into bed. Victoria was already asleep, with an eye mask on and, I couldn't help noticing, fully clothed on top of the sheets.

After changing into tracksuit pants and a vest top, I went outside and smoked a cigarette by the pool, which, reflected in the moonlight, actually looked very inviting.

Nick Lowe totally intimidated me. On some level, I think I'd believed that because JP totally adored me in the beginning, he was the One. But maybe his putting me on a pedestal had been a bad thing, because it meant that I could never live up to his expectations: relationships are all about compromise, and dealing with life's problems, and the cold hard truth was that JP seemed to distance himself from me or do a disappearing act every time a real problem came along.

I adored JP, but I needed him to be more communicative, and get to the bottom of his anger. For my part, I had to stop thinking that everything that went wrong in the relationship was my fault and was something I could fix. I don't mind compromising, but I'm not going to compromise myself.

I've never shied away from a challenge in my career, or in life. I believe in facing down my fears instead of letting them take me to the point of no return. Denial only makes things worse, a life lesson I learned from watching the horror film *Rosemary's Baby*. I know I was supposed to feel sympathy for Mia Farrow's character, but, come on: how much better would her life have been if she'd paid a visit to the abortion doctor instead of saying, 'Of course I'll drink a concoction made of mystery herbs every day, no questions asked! And I'm sure that all that pesky Satanic chanting going on behind my neighbours' walls is just a bridge game!'

But I'd been doing the same thing: ignoring the fears that were gestating in my own relationship. I needed to face down the beast.

I needed to talk to JP.

# THIRTY-EIGHT

Meanwhile, I arrived back from Cannes to find my home situation was continuing to get weirder. It was the middle of the night by the time I got back from the airport. When I opened the door to the flat I heard Emma moaning behind her bedroom wall.

Exhausted, I washed my face, brushed my teeth and went to bed, assuming that she was getting some action. Good for her, I thought, before drifting off into dreamland.

The next morning, wearing my white hot pants, vest top, untied bathrobe and bunny rabbit slippers, I was putting on the kettle when I sensed a presence behind me, and turned to see a huge beast of a man with shoulder-length, wild, frizzy hair who looked as though he could have been an extra in *Planet of the Apes* with no need to jump into the make-up chair. He was stark naked, save for a pair of yellow-stained tight white pants, and lazily scratched his balls while staring at me with a single bloodshot eye (his other one was looking in the other direction, possibly a lazy eye? I wasn't sure).

'Oh, my God.' I said, shielding my eyes and almost dropping the teacup. Then, more hesitantly, I asked, 'Would you like some tea?'

'Nah, thanks, got to get home,' he mumbled, then said

something else that was utterly incoherent. He disappeared into the bathroom, and I quietly slunk back to my bedroom and waited a few minutes until I heard him leave.

Though I'd been mildly freaked out by having the Unabomber in my front room, I knew that I was in no position to judge. We'd all had our coyote shags.

Then Emma poked her head out of the bedroom and mouthed, 'Is he gone?' When I nodded she raced to the front room. 'I can't believe what's just happened, Catherine! I have the worst luck with men!'

'Are you okay?'

'Yes, it's just that he did something – something really disgusting and now I can't even talk about it—'

Despite her bizarre behaviour, I felt for her. 'What happened, honey?'

'Well, we drank loads last night, he had probably twelve pints, we got back here and shagged – which to be honest was pretty forgettable – and then I woke up this morning and noticed that the mattress felt really wet.'

I furrowed my brow in confusion. 'You mean he—'

'He pissed himself! During the night. And didn't even notice, apparently. I picked a real winner, didn't I?'

We looked at each other and burst out laughing. For the first time, I felt that we'd really bonded, and was happy to be there to help her out.

Instinctively, we knew that we couldn't let the piss-stained mattress reside in our flat for another minute, so we raced down five flights of stairs in our pyjamas carrying it, and while she looked to make sure that the coast was clear I slid it over to a bin next to Jamie Oliver's Fifteen restaurant, a couple of blocks from our flat. Then we looked both ways and ran like hell.

After we'd recovered, she suggested grabbing brunch. So we slung our clothes on and a few minutes later we stumbled into a hip little café on Hoxton Square. We still couldn't stop laughing as we ordered mimosas.

'Listen, Cat, I want to apologize for things being a bit weird at home lately,' she said, as our food arrived. 'The thing is, I'm an only child, and always had a bit of a tough time at school bonding with the other kids, so I'm sorry if we've had a few awkward encounters. Hopefully things will get back to normal soon.'

'Don't worry about it,' I said, meaning it. 'The only truly insane people, in my opinion, are the ones utterly convinced that they are totally normal.'

We clinked glasses and as we chatted I noticed something odd; a guy from two tables over, who was sitting alone, kept staring at me.

'Excuse me,' he said, standing up and walking over to us, 'this isn't a chat-up line, really, but don't I know you from somewhere?'

I blushed. 'Yes, actually, I believe you are the gentleman I accidentally spilled a drink on during my very drunken wedding day. It's a long story,' I hastily added, before motioning for him to sit with us. 'Please allow me finally to buy you that drink to make up for things. This is Emma.'

'Daniel,' he said, and as the two of them shook hands, Emma sneezed, and when she fished a Kleenex out of her handbag, one of her signature dolls fell out.

'That's a very interesting design,' he said, picking it up and examining it. 'I haven't seen anything like this before.'

Emma's eyes widened. My first concern was that he might be taking the piss because I knew Emma didn't need any more grief after the mattress fiasco. But it turns out he was completely genuine.

'I know it might seem a bit strange for a bloke, but I know about this stuff. I have a shop off Portobello Road, and we mainly do dolls and toys. Did you make this yourself?' She broke into a huge grin and twirled a lock of hair around her fingers.

Within minutes they had made plans to meet again. It seemed to be a match made in heaven. I was genuinely thrilled for her; she's a sweet girl and a testament to the fact that sometimes the most heinous one-night stand can inadvertently lead directly to the man of your dreams!

# THIRTY-NINE

Cannes had clarified my concerns about JP's commitment. Even though he still said the right things, he seemed to be trying to highlight our differences, and I wondered if he was pulling the guy move of acting distant so that I would be forced to break up with him. But when I asked him point blank, he told me that he loved and adored me, and that I was the One.

With my thirtieth birthday rapidly approaching, I decided not to worry about anything heavy for the next few weeks. After all we'd been through, perhaps our relationship just needed a bit of fun. Things weren't perfect, but I was madly in love with JP. Besides, as Victoria pointed out, I do have a tendency to over-analyse things.

I broached the subject with my therapist, who was trying to encourage me to focus on myself. 'He's definitely pushing me away,' I told her, fighting back tears. 'But the tough thing is that he was so amazing for the first few months, and was the one who kept telling me that he wanted to look after me, that he wanted to marry me. I can't figure out what's gone wrong.'

She put down her pencil and looked at me. 'Have you read the chapter in *Facing Love Addiction* about love avoidants?'

'You mean about the walls of seduction? Yeah, on the plane to Cannes; and I've been trying to forget about it ever since.'

Basically, the book says that love avoidants enter a relationship using 'walls of seduction', which are designed to give the objects of their affection the impression that they are being swept off their feet without actually risking anything themselves. It's over-the-top, false closeness, because secretly they are terrified of intimacy themselves.

Then, as soon as they realize that the other person has fallen for them and expects real intimacy, they bail. Loads of men fall into this category, to varying degrees.

'When did the first problems happen?'

'After I told him that I was married; though, actually, it was a bit before that.' I told the therapist that I'd sensed JP pulling away the moment he became aware that I had a life and a career on my own terms.

'So you feel that the marriage, and the so-called "differences", could really just be an excuse?' She started scribbling again.

'Maybe,' I blurted out.

'I'm always telling my clients that if you live together and love each other it's unrealistic to believe that you'll have all your interests in common. I always say, if you live together, fancy each other, and have a fifty per cent relationship, you are doing well. It's very unrealistic to think that things are going to be ideal.'

Feeling myself start to crumble, I grabbed a Kleenex. 'I try to tell him that we do have the same core values, love each other, fancy each other, respect each other and now that I've realized children are a possibility, we both want a family some day. Isn't that enough?'

I started crying openly now, and my therapist smiled at me kindly and softened her voice. 'Believe me, I've been where you are, and there is no worse feeling in the world than having your heart broken. For a sensitive person, this type of withdrawal is just as powerful as kicking a drug habit. Love addicts and love avoidants can be attracted to each other because they have the same fears, of intimacy and abandonment.'

'But it's so weird; with JP I do feel like I have a healthy relationship on some level. I feel I'm loyal, trustworthy, no desire to cheat, great sex life, and want to compromise. It feels very adult.'

'Right. Well, in my opinion, Catherine, you are capable of having a healthy relationship, once you're in it. Your love addiction manifests itself in your choice of partners. Do you know what I mean by that?'

Slowly, something in my mind clicked into place. 'It means that even though I'm craving intimacy, and feel like I can have a healthy relationship, I'm subconsciously picking men who aren't capable of giving me either.'

I sat in silence for two minutes, and thought about dating guides again, and their patronizing answers to love. The reason they don't work isn't technical: I probably knew this information myself logically, but until I understood in my heart why, and truly believed that I wanted and deserved better, I wasn't capable of changing. I'm still not sure if I am.

Some people may be able to absorb the information by reading it in a leaflet, but others have to live it for themselves to learn it. That's why every relationship happens for a reason.

'Well, Catherine, sweetheart, our hour is up.' She walked me to the door. 'Take care of yourself, okay? I'll see you next week.'

'I thought I was in love with JP,' I told Mark. 'But I can't figure anything out any more. Everything feels so tentative.'

Mark was obsessively flipping through his sci-fi DVDs, looking for an obscure episode of the series *Lexx*, which focuses on a horny love slave female, her insect spacecraft and hapless male crew who explore the universe in search of sex. The special effects are shit, and we have to be the only two fans in the known universe.

'Look, men are pretty simple creatures. He's around, you're dating, you sleep together and you've been to see his parents. What do you want from him, blood?'

'No, it's not that. It's just that I have a gut feeling that something is wrong, that something is missing.'

'God, do you have to over-analyse everything? He seems like a pretty straightforward guy. How's the sex?'

I swatted him on the head with a DVD. 'Get your mind out of the gutter!'

Mark laughed. 'I think you should bring back Jamie. He was funny. And he had hot lesbian friends. Remind me of his drawbacks again?'

I sighed. 'You may find this hard to believe, but I do want a monogamous, conventional relationship some day. Do you think guys will still want to marry me?'

'What do you mean?' He sat down next to me on the sofa and stared at me quizzically.

'I mean, considering my past and, um, experience. I keep getting hate mail saying that men would run a mile.'

'Look, Cat, only really insecure men are into that whole Madonna/whore bullshit. Even Freud thought it was a male psychological defect, and I know you're not a fan of his! Why are you feeling ashamed of yourself? It seems to me that he's the one who walked away. It's him who should be worried about winning you back around, not you.'

'You are so wise. I'm so glad I married you.'

I asked Mark what he thought of JP.

'Honestly? I think he's a deeply insecure man. Always have, actually.'

'Why would you say that?'

He laughed. 'Look, Cat, I just don't like his whole chasing you around for months and then leaving you in limbo routine. It's bullshit, and it's immature. I know, because that's what I did a few years ago. You aren't sure of yourself, so you pretend to be exactly what the girl wants. But then you grow up. Or in his case, not.'

I swatted him on the arm. 'Silly me, and I thought he was doing all that stuff because he loved me. The funny thing is, that's exactly what someone else just told me.'

For once, Mark looked deadly serious. 'I know he loves you. You only have to look at him to see that he's absolutely crazy about you. But I think that, ultimately, he's the wrong guy for you. And you need to stop obsessing.'

Tears came to my eyes. 'The frustrating thing is, I know

he thinks that I'm selfish, and I've tried so hard to make things work.'

Mark hugged me. 'Cat, you may be self-centred at times – wait, hear me out,' he said as I bit my lip and more tears streaked down my face.

'When it comes down to the wire, you are the most generous person I know. And you're loyal as hell. You want someone who can support you and encourage you to fly with your career, not someone you have to apologize to. Put it this way: do you think that he's half as concerned for your feelings as you are about his?'

As I settled down on Mark's sofa and he put on the DVD, his words weighed heavily on my mind.

I was never really into fairy tales as a child, especially since 'happily ever after' shots of the couple running off into the sunset together didn't really answer my questions about what was going on between the sheets. But, secretly, there's a part of me that's always been waiting for Prince Charming to ride up on that white horse.

It brought to mind something I'd read in the Tao. If you work with the paradigm that life is a mirror, then all the things that you dislike in your partner are simply reflections of those aspects of your deeper self that you have not yet learned to love and accept. Maybe that's why I was so hard on JP – and also why we were drawn together. I'd been pretty terrified of intimacy myself until recently.

While I pretended to watch the space orgy, I thought about the therapy session again. Sarah had said that there are loads of reasons why her patients have difficulty letting go of an ex. During the process of elimination, I ruled out 'fear of the unknown' and 'need for control or predictability', since those aren't issues I've ever had. But 'substituting drama for closeness' was something I could definitely relate to.

After I got home later that night, my mind was racing, so I fired up my laptop. A few Google searches later, I read that some people experience extreme withdrawal symptoms when relationships end.

According to *Psychology Today*, 'Levels of phenylethylamine (PEA) – a chemical in the brain involved in the euphoria that comes with falling in love – rise with feelings of infatuation, boosting euphoria and excitement.'

That sounds like me. Then again, that also sounds like lots of women I know. Are we all dysfunctional love addicts? Is our mental 'diet' of romantic comedies where a guy appears in the last six minutes of the film to profess his love and 'save' the heroine as damaging as soda pop would be to an infant's teeth? It feels so good, but it's so unhealthy.

Then in later life these unrealistic expectations born of childhood fantasies are given a sinister new twist by dating guides. If we haven't snared and kept our Prince Charming we're taught that the blame lies with us. And we're expected to modify our behaviour or end up as the wicked witch. As if being single or having a relationship that doesn't end in lifetime marriage is a failure.

I don't consider my broken relationships failures. Actually, they were quite successful: I entered into a commitment with someone, we tried our best and discovered that it would be mutually beneficial to break up rather than get married and have children. We learned, and hopefully grew. That's what I call success!

My love life may have been hanging in the balance but at least my research project was bearing some fruit. I was separating the wheat from the chaff in terms of relationship advice and self-discovery. And working out what my deep-rooted emotional strengths and limitations truly were.

# FORTY

I was so excited! That evening was the premiere of the first show of *How to Have Sex After Marriage*. Despite JP's increasingly distant attitude, I confess that I was angling for a miracle when I slid my key in the door of his house. I was hoping that he would have filled the house with flowers and candles, and would be there to hug me and tell me how proud he was of me.

Instead, the house was silent. Still, I picked up the pile of mail from behind the door and headed into the kitchen. I'd bought two tuna steaks, which we both love and take two minutes to cook, and as a special treat I'd also bought two gingerbread cookies from my favourite cake shop. The ghost cookie was smothered in white icing, which is my favourite thing in the world. I never eat cake, only the icing, and am an unpopular guest at birthday parties due to my tendency to scalp the birthday treats. I can't help it, it's a compulsion.

Meanwhile the witch cookie, while very cute, had minimal icing, just the black outline of her pointy hat.

In my mind, I repeated my therapist's words about reviewing the situation logically and discovering if my expectations were reasonable. After all, I hadn't told JP that I hoped he would make me feel special tonight. Then again, I didn't think that

I would have to. I didn't want to be one of those people who justify every type of bad behaviour according to the past. Just because I understand why someone is treating me like shit doesn't mean that I should have to put up with it.

I went upstairs and drew myself a bath as hot as I could stand, and watched as the steam clouded up the windows. Once in the bath, closing my eyes, I drifted off to sleep, and only woke up at 8.45 to a jarring text message alert.

'I'm on my way home now but may miss the first few minutes. See you soon. JP'

I felt my heart lurch. I didn't know which was more pathetic: my constant attempts to reassure myself that everything was fine in this relationship, or his constantly disappointing me.

Still, I was determined to keep a brave face on the evening. After all, I was on TV tonight! I slipped into a pink night-dress and headed downstairs as I heard his key in the door.

He gave me a perfunctory kiss on the cheek and went into the kitchen to start dinner, while I freaked out on the sofa. Seeing myself on television was about a hundred times worse than hearing myself on an answerphone. I had to pretend that I was watching a plastic surgery reality show, so kept having to shield my eyes and felt like I was watching the whole thing through my fingers. JP brought our plates into the living room, and we ate while watching the show – though I was too nervous to take more than a few bites. Still, I appreciated the effort, and I told him so.

Despite my enthusiasm for the programme, I'd had my reservations about the sexual content, but in the end I thought that it was beautifully executed. 'You were great, sweetheart,' JP said, but seemed distracted.

We really seemed to help the couple, Rick and Megan, and I knew that I could have a positive effect on someone else's love life. Even the cheesy ending, where Rick rode towards Megan on a camel in Morocco for their second honeymoon, brought tears to my eyes, when he said something along the lines of, 'I know that she's the love of my life, and I feel like the luckiest man in the world.'

I looked over at JP to see if he was sharing the intimacy of the moment with me, but no such luck. Because immediately after the credits started rolling, JP was texting a friend.

'Do you mind having a drink with him down at the pub?' he asked, and his tone made me realize instantly that this was a rhetorical question.

'I wish that someone felt that way about me,' I said, still watching the couple embrace.

'It has to be all about you, doesn't it?' he spat. 'You can't stand that we're going to have a drink with my friend; you're so selfish that tonight just had to be all about you.' His angry tone shocked me.

I calculated several responses in my mind. The first was to tell him to go fuck himself, why shouldn't it be all about me on the night that my TV show was going out on the air, and what a sorry excuse for a boyfriend he was. The second was to pick up the glass of very expensive red wine next to him on the table and throw it in his face.

But I did neither of those things. Instead I started to cry. 'I was just talking about the show. It was so inspiring the way they worked out their issues. I would love for someone to feel so strongly about me. All you do lately is push me away. You say that you love me but sometimes it doesn't feel like you even like me.'

Then I climbed the stairs and walked into his room. I was furious, but I couldn't show it, because then he would play the 'erratic' card. It's so unfair: men can throw screaming tantrums and cry like babies, but women who do the same thing are branded psychos.

I could see why Norman Bates stuffed his mum in *Psycho*. She was such a bitch to him for so long that maybe he thought, in death, he could re-create the ideal relationship that he never had with her in life. JP was being such a shit that taxidermy seemed like a viable alternative.

Upstairs I choked back my tears and counted to ten before I calmly went downstairs again.

'Look, I'm sorry, babe,' he said. 'I've told him that we'll do it another night. I didn't mean to get angry.'

I already knew that this wasn't good enough. But somewhere, deep down, I kept hoping for the return of the nice guy who had been so conspicuous in the first few months of our relationship. I was determined not to let his behaviour spoil my night. And *I* was the one getting called selfish?

He went into the kitchen to get us another glass of red wine, and, hands shaking, I picked up my phone to find that several friends had texted me to tell me that they saw me on TV, so, without JP knowing, the two seemingly innocent and unrelated events that happened next sealed our fate. The first was Victoria texting to say that Mike had Sky Plussed the series link to the entire show. 'You were amazing! We are so proud of you! Hope JP is spoiling you rotten and taking you for champagne tonight, but let's talk tomorrow. Love Vic.'

I grabbed the remote and flicked through JP's planner, and realized that he hadn't even set it to record the show.

It's funny how, despite horrific fights or huge problems, sometimes it's the tiniest details that signal the end of relationships. I guess it makes sense: I'd always thought that the small acts of kindness like leaving 'I love you' Post-its made a relationship; in the same way, the small acts of selfishness chip away at it.

He walked back into the living room and tossed something in my lap, sliding my wine onto the table. 'Thanks for getting the food, by the way,' he said, patting me on the shoulder. 'Here, why don't you have a treat?'

I looked down to find the witch cookie I'd bought staring up at me from his hand.

JP plopped himself down and forced a smile. He'd been in the kitchen longer than it took to pour a glass, and I spotted the tell-tale signs of a white flaky moustache above his upper lip.

'Um, I thought the witch would be okay for you. I ate the one with all the icing. Sorry.'

Without a word, I went upstairs and packed my stuff. Considering that we'd been going out for several months and talked about spending our lives together, it didn't take that long. I put in make-up, conditioner, a few clothes and the odd sock, but left out the beautiful lingerie he'd bought me. I also left the porn we'd made together. I didn't think he would be cruel enough to show it to anyone else, and I wanted him to suffer watching it. If worst came to worst, at least the lighting was flattering and didn't make me look fat.

As I was packing I heard him open the bedroom door. I paused. 'JP, I have something to ask you. You've been telling me for months that you thought I was the One. Do you still feel like that?'

He sat down on the bed and sighed, avoiding my eyes. 'I love you, Cat, but I'm not sure that the relationship is working.'

'But you don't want to compromise on anything,' I retorted.

'You're right. I should be able to compromise more, but for some reason I just can't,' he said.

Acid reflux. Heartburn. Hyperventilation into a pillow.

'You mean that you won't, because you don't love me enough to try.'

'I wouldn't say that. For whatever reason, I just can't take the next step. I can't commit.'

Maybe he was infatuated with me, at some point. But the harsh reality was that he just didn't love me as much as I loved him. I was pissed off at myself, because I should have seen this one coming.

Then he said that he was sorry. He took my bag out of my hands, took me in his arms and we held each other all night. After a while I heard him begin to snore, and was angry that his sleep was undisturbed. I was dying inside, and he was sleeping like a baby.

I thought about what the therapist had said about 'walls of seduction', and how I'd loved the idea of being rescued, in every sense.

I'm so in love with the idea of having a normal relationship that I've been selling myself short. I don't want to spend the rest of my life scrambling for whatever morsels of emotion, love and time he's willing to throw my way. I want someone who loves the real me.

The next morning, I heard him dress for work and waited until he left to crack my eyes open. I was throwing the rest of my things into a bag when he raced back upstairs.

'I'm so sorry,' he said, and I think I actually saw a tear in his eye. 'I do love you. I'm confused.'

Despite myself I smiled and held his hand in mine.

I could see the company car waiting outside, so I gave him a hug.

'That's the way the cookie crumbles.'

He walked out, and I knew that he didn't understand the significance of my words. What else was new? I'd spent almost thirty years being terrified of intimacy, but now I knew that being kept at arm's length is the worst pain of all. It would have been so much easier if I'd found JP in bed with someone else, or realized that he was addicted to gay sex. Black and white are easy, while these bullshit shades of grey decisions are much more haunting.

I dried my tears, threw my overnight bag over my shoulder and left my keys, given to me so optimistically in the first flush of love, on the table.

It was ironic. He'd wanted me to have the key so badly, and then made sure that he never let me in.

Living with him would have meant a lifetime of bracing loneliness and bald cookies. I wanted to find someone who'd happily give me the whole goddamned cookie jar.

# FORTY-ONE

At least one good thing came out of that fateful night: the ratings for *How to Have Sex After Marriage* were excellent, so we were a hit. In no time at all I was back in the midst of a crazy filming schedule as we raced to meet Channel Five's reset deadline for a new series.

The distraction was a relief. And I got through the experience by telling myself that I was helping the married couples taking part in the show. But the task I did with one of the show's last participants made me have a serious light-bulb moment in my own life.

Basically, the woman's husband had had an affair, and despite the passage of more than a decade she still hadn't quite forgiven him. So their day-to-day lives were, on some level, in danger of being poisoned by resentment. She needed to let go of her anger, not just for her marriage, but for herself.

The crew drove the van loaded with equipment to a disused warehouse in Wapping, down the back of an industrial alley. Anjula met the two of us there, and we walked inside to find a long table set with loads of crockery – including cups, plates and brown and orange leaf-shaped bowls that looked like they had been sitting in some little old woman's cupboard since the 1970s.

I listened intently as Anjula explained the process. 'What

I want you to do is write down something that you are angry about on each plate, with this marker,' she said. 'Then you are going to allow yourself to feel the anger, but as you smash the plate, visualize yourself letting go.' She went on to explain that, afterwards, she would counsel the woman to allow her to come down from the emotional turmoil of the experience.

I was a bit sceptical at first, but as we all three changed into our coveralls, and pulled on padded gloves and safety goggles, I really started to get into the exercise.

Because I was meant to be having the experience as well, I marked my plates with my feelings about what had happened with JP.

'What really makes you angry?' I could hear Anjula asking, so I wrote down, 'Not prioritizing our relationship', on a white saucer, followed by 'No compromise', on another. 'Not communicating', went on a tiny saucer.

At first, we chucked the small bits tentatively, but as I saw the china smash against the concrete wall I felt something that I never allowed to surface: red, blinding rage.

'Tell yourself, in your mind, what you're throwing each bit of cutlery for,' Anjula reminded us.

'This is for being so argumentative that you never allowed me to get angry!' my mind screamed, and I could feel the veins popping out in my neck as I hurled the clear glass plate so hard against the wall that a single shard actually bounced off the wall and hit me in the chest.

Undeterred, I kept chucking, and found it very difficult not to shout at the walls. 'This is for making me walk on fucking eggshells because you were too fucking weak to tell me what the deal was between us.'

For her grand finale, the woman scooped up a giant vase, which was meant to represent the affair, and smashed it against the wall.

Inspired by her chutzpah, I grabbed a gigantic serving plate and wrote in black marker, 'FEAR OF DYING ALONE'. I wound up like a baseball pitcher and flung it with all my might, then stamped on the pieces afterward as tears filled my eyes.

Afterwards, the three of us had a salad in Pizza Express, where the woman remarked that the exercise had really helped her let go of her anger.

'I think I should start a club for women, kind of like Fight Club except that instead of beating the crap out of each other, we get to take our aggression out on plates,' I said, sipping my Diet Coke. I really wanted a glass of red wine, but thought that it might not make me appear as mentally stable as I would have liked.

I was only teasing, but later, I looked into the grey alleyway and thought what a relief the experience had been. I was so sick of trying to appear perfect.

I'm really tired of men whining about being emasculated, because they've been more than happy to have us take up the slack. Women are to blame for everything: we're expected to be well educated and career-focused, but not so much that we threaten our future husbands. If we choose to stay at home and raise children, we'd better make sure that we hover near a size zero, maintain a taut, youthful expression and never, ever 'let ourselves go', lest we be replaced by a younger model.

And the final irony: men want women who are porn stars in bed, but who have never had much sexual experience.

On top of all this, we are expected to be the great communicators, probably because the verbal centre of our brain is wired differently.

Don't get me wrong, I love men. And their attitude to perfection is one area where I think it might be a good idea for women to emulate them. On the whole, men are driven towards improving themselves, but they don't expect that they can be perfect. They also don't expect that they alone can make a relationship perfect. If something doesn't work, they are likely to shrug their shoulders and go out looking for the next conquest, not spend months and years obsessing over an ideal that may never have existed in the first place.

Men read fairy tales and laugh. Women accept them as gospel.

There was a time as a child, before I realised that fairy tales were complete bullshit, when I fell victim to their spell – in particular, *Snow White*. When I was a little girl, I remember being enthralled by the tale, and dreaming that one day, I too would be kissed by a handsome prince, awake to a proposal of marriage and live happily ever after.

Then I grew up and got real. What if the prince had commitment problems or was saving up to buy a property? As a passive woman who left her destiny entirely up to fate, poor Snow White would either have suffocated in her glass coffin or had to shack up permanently with the seven dwarfs.

I have to face the fact that I would not have waited around. I would have climbed out of the coffin, probably hooked up with one or two of the dwarfs – after my dirty mind told me that they were 'just the right height' for something – gone to school, got a law degree and sued the evil stepmother's ass off for slipping me the poisoned apple, taking the castle and everything in it.

The handsome prince might not have wanted me then. He might have been intimidated, since I would no longer be the damsel in distress. But, eventually, I'd have to believe that I would have found someone better.

If not, I would always have my castle, my education and my self-respect. No man is worth more than that.

Walking down the street afterwards, I called Victoria. 'When you move house, honey, what are you going to do with all that old crockery? I think I need it for a new project.'

# FORTY-TWO

My thirtieth birthday was a quiet affair, but it was lovely. Since in the aftermath of JP I didn't fancy a massive party, I joined Michael for an intimate dinner with some of his political media pals.

But as I looked around the restaurant and saw his coupled-up acquaintances lovingly feeding each other bites of bruschetta, I realized that I needed to find new opportunities to meet men. My social circle seemed to be getting smaller, and the guys I met through work tended to have their own preconceptions about me.

Michael and I had a good laugh about the fact that the world of politics, which he calls 'showbiz for ugly people', and sex were so entwined. After dinner we attended an auction for the Labour Party magazine *Tribune*, where one of the MPs told me he was a fan of my *Independent* column and threatened to auction me off to the highest bidder.

I told him, teasingly, that I wanted to bid for the tea for two with David Blunkett at the House of Commons. He told me that maybe that wasn't such a hot idea – Blunkett has had enough issues with feisty American brunettes!

Michael and I were having so much fun that I barely noticed when my phone beeped. It was a text from Nick Lowe wishing me a happy birthday. We'd been in touch via Facebook and there'd been some light-hearted long-distance banter. A couple of nights ago, in reply to a message of his, I had happened to mention my break-up with JP simply because it was so much on my mind. Moments later I got a second text and, as I read it, I couldn't help but smile. He reminded me that I should hold out for a guy who can handle me and invited me for a drink the next time I'm in Los Angeles. Since my next book was going to be partly set there I replied that I was doing a research trip to LA soon. Suddenly I was looking forward to it already.

Michael raised one eyebrow when he saw my grin. 'It's rude to text at dinner, you know,' he teased, 'but dish the dirt. Why are you grinning like a Cheshire cat?'

I explained it was from a guy I met in Cannes.

'Come on, name names. I once schmoozed in those showbiz circles.'

I mumbled Nick's name.

'The movie producer? I know him. I can't believe it!' he exclaimed. 'Now, you know how much of a cynic I am but I've genuinely got huge respect for that man. Is there anything in the offing between you?'

'I should be so lucky.' I sighed. 'Anyway, why would I want to date a perfect, gorgeous and totally functional man when I can obsess over the wrong one?' I laughed bitterly.

Michael shook his head. 'Look, Cat, do you want my honest opinion?'

I smirked. 'Do I have a choice?'

'If you're going to put up with a man who has so many commitment issues, he should be some kind of goddamned rock star. I could understand if JP was Keith Richards or Rod

Stewart, for fuck's sake, but I can't believe that JP has had you jumping through hoops like this. I don't think so! You're thirty now, girl; it's time to find yourself a grown-up.'

I had to laugh at Michael's pragmatic approach. 'So you're saying if I'm going to get burned, get burned by someone amazing?'

'I would go for Nick Lowe. He's handsome, charismatic and he'd totally get you. Shoot for the stars, babe.'

I did have a crush on Nick, even if I wasn't ready to admit it to myself. But Nick was a twelve-hour plane ride away, and despite Michael's insistence that he was interested in me I remained unconvinced that his messages weren't just out of politeness.

Meanwhile I needed to start looking for new opportunities closer to home.

After my resolution to find new ways to meet men, I decided to take a fresh approach, and go food shopping for more than just ready meals. I'd read loads of stories about picking up men in supermarkets, and wondered if there was any truth to the theory. I set a goal: to speak to one attractive man per shop. The results were better than I would have guessed.

In theory, supermarkets have some serious advantages: they are democratic (since everyone has to buy food), and if someone looks good in the fluorescent lighting, things can only improve on a night out. My first destination was Waitrose, where I spied a very cute man with a naked ring finger.

I was trying to think of a pick-up line when his girlfriend came from the frozen food section, wielding a giant bag of frozen peas . . . I ran the other way before she had the chance to use them as a weapon.

As men whizzed past me at the local Tesco, I realized the downfalls of supermarket hook-ups. When I'm out in bars I have the benefit of having enough time – and liquid courage – to make an approach, but in the aisles I have only about twelve seconds before they reach the checkout.

I saw a gorgeous guy in the pasta section, but I chickened out before saying anything. I followed him to the fruit and veg, where I tried to think of an approach that wouldn't involve stroking courgettes. 'Do you think they'd mind if I sampled the grapes?' I popped one in my mouth.

He looked at me in shock. 'You should be careful,' he said. 'Some bunches have spiders living in them.' He walked off. Strike one.

My next stop was Marks & Spencer in Moorgate, which was a target-rich environment, packed with loads of stressed-out City types. I spotted a good-looking guy, but hesitated once I saw his basket: it was full of fat-free products, which signals either a girlfriend at home or an unhealthy obsession with healthy eating. Either way, it's not sexy. I went home.

My destination the next night was the swanky new Whole Foods superstore. There was a beautiful man buying organic salmon fillets from the fish counter, and while we both waited to be served, I made my move. 'So, do you know anything about how to cook salmon?' I asked him. 'I'm not exactly Nigella. For the past ten months I've been using my oven for shoe storage.'

He laughed before uttering the fateful line, 'I live by myself, and I end up ordering loads of takeaways, so don't feel guilty.'

It turned out that he lived locally. And before I knew it he was asking me on a date this weekend.

I discreetly checked his purchases, which included wine, organic steaks and loads of chocolate. I was reserving judgement until the weekend, but I was definitely impressed by the size of his basket.

I had just sat down to dinner with Supermarket Guy.

'So, what kind of wine do you like?' he asked.

I'd been a bit intimidated when he had described himself on the phone as a 'bit of an oenophile' and insisted on taking me to a restaurant where the wine list in my hand was as thick as a phonebook. It was only a few weeks after JP, but I'd justified the date by telling myself that I needed to get out of the house.

'Red?' I suggested sweetly.

'Be more specific,' he said. 'Do you like big, dark tannins? Something with an oaky finish? Ripe, berry overtones?' he asked, speaking slowly as if he were talking to a child.

'I'm not sure,' I said. 'Something full-bodied?'

I'm the first to admit that I wouldn't know a barbaresco from a zinfandel. I only know that I prefer red wine to white, and can tell when a bottle is corked. Other than that, I'm pretty clueless.

I normally love learning things from the men I date. I once spent an entire evening discussing aerodynamics with a pilot, and another night on spinal injuries with a surgeon. But this guy wasn't a sommelier; he was an investment banker.

I suspected he was being overly pretentious when he wasn't content simply to swirl the very moderately priced wine he'd chosen in his glass, but insisted on spinning it like a centrifuge, then stopped, spun it again and tasted it before declaring it acceptable. And this was after he'd sent back the first bottle.

Most of my friends have a Wine Guy lurking in their past; he's the one who prides himself on rudely returning bottles more than twice, or makes a show of smelling the cork – even if it's plastic!

I've never taken wine too seriously. My first drinking experience was back in my home state of Georgia, where we bought bottles with colourful names like Strawberry Hill and Sweet Apple Wine. As we were under-age, our wine expert was the homeless guy we paid to supply our booze. I don't think he gave much thought to the varietals.

'Can you taste the hints of espresso in this wine?' my date asked.

'Maybe,' I told him, 'but I did have a Starbucks right before I came in.'

He didn't crack a smile. Several times I tried in vain to change the subject. But when I mentioned Spain, for example, he brought the subject back to his villa there, and then segued into rioja.

But WG was very hot, and I was drunk, so I tried to side with him. 'I hear that organic wines are better for hangovers, because they don't contain sulphites,' I said.

He accused me of reading 'too many women's magazines', then ordered more claret.

My problem with armchair wine 'experts' is that a) taste is subjective and b) I suspect that most of them are bluffing. But I didn't have the heart to tell Wine Guy that. So I listened to his lecture on the maturation process of vino, at the same time as feeling that I myself was ageing about five years in five minutes.

Finally, I thanked him for a lovely time and cut him loose. Even though he was hot, I didn't suggest that we head back to his for a tête-à-tête on pinot noir. I do want something full-bodied, unique and satisfying, but not from a glass.

Or perhaps I'm just not ready to date yet.

# FORTY-THREE

As if on cue, given my temporary dating desert, the *Independent* assigned me to write about not having sex for a week. It was perfect, because it forced me to consider my positions, in and out of bed, and gave me some much-needed time to reflect.

On the whole, I've always subscribed to Woody Allen's philosophy: 'Sex without love is an empty experience,' he said, 'but as empty experiences go, it's one of the best.'

But after my experience with Supermarket Guy, I realized that sleeping with some unknown guy didn't appeal. For once the possibility of deviant sex didn't feel like a core element of my lifestyle any more. It felt like the night before a detox diet, when I raid the cabinets and eat every last scrap of raw cookie dough.

When I was younger, I used to binge more often. But staring down at my temporarily distended belly, I knew it was time to cut back.

Snacking is fine, as long as it doesn't stop me from eating proper meals.

I even questioned whether it was wise to start having sex again at all. After all, my therapist had a point: I was focusing too much on the intoxicating effect of seducing men. Which was fine for a while, but now I was wondering if I should hold back a little.

One of the biggest misconceptions about me is that I'm a proponent of casual sex. Actually, it's quite the opposite: I think that casual sex is something that requires a great deal of self-esteem. In times when I'm feeling low, I tend to rely on my trusty porno and toy stash.

After every failed relationship, I wanted to be the heroine, starting a literal and metaphorical new chapter in my life – with an upbeat soundtrack. But lately, going out with my friends and dancing on tabletops isn't working. For some reason, the track isn't switching from Joy Division to Donna Summer. It's stuck on repeat.

So I was ready for the challenge when the *Independent* asked me to go cold turkey in the interests of scientific research. I even padlocked my 'secret drawer' of erotica and stopped downloading Internet porn.

My enforced abstinence did have some benefits. I knew that I wasn't going to end evenings with late-night booty calls, so I was able to focus more on my friendships. But without a sexual outlet, the most innocent conversations and images suddenly seemed erotic, from an M&S billboard to a video of a farmer milking a cow.

On day three, I went to a sex quiz at the Science Museum's Dana Centre, where the questions about female ejaculation jolted my nether regions. I knew that I was in trouble when the humorous image of two cuddly toys in a pornographic position actually made me horny. That night, I went home and ate Nutella out of the jar. Then I fished two old menthol cigarettes out of my kitchen drawer and smoked them with shaking hands. I was suffering orgasm withdrawal!

But my week of unrequited lust wasn't just physically taxing, it was mentally stressful, too; orgasm triggers oxytocin release, which makes you feel more relaxed. Sex also stimulates the immune system, and recent research suggests that regular sessions make us less vulnerable to colds and flu. And contorting your body into Kama Sutra-style positions beats yoga any day for increasing flexibility.

On day five, I decided to have a quiet night in and renew my love affair with Indian and Thai food – pretty much off-limits when I've a strenuous sex session planned. This way, at least my taste buds would get some, and it would make a change from 'sex' days, when I'll happily live on mango and slivers of sushi.

Slipping into a hot bath, I read a book on Buddhism that compares sexual desire to drinking salty water: the more one consumes, the greater the desire – and the worse one's (mental) state of health becomes. I began to realize that I had been guilty of using sex as escapism.

The good news was that I had definitely accomplished more during my abstinence. I had written loads for my new book, cleaned the flat from top to bottom and even made a trip to Ikea with Victoria (entering the mouth of the minimalist Scandinavian beast was probably the most effective passion-killer of the week).

In fact, the experience was starting to remind me of that time when I gave up coffee for green tea, and decided that in the end life was too short to live without my daily latte. I felt the same way about orgasms. Despite my attempts to distract myself by knitting, by the end of the week I was gagging for gut-wrenching relief. Physically, I was a bloated, sniffling mess. My skin was dodgy (from all the chocolate

I ate), I had gained two pounds and felt like someone in their sixties.

So at exactly midnight on the seventh day, I cracked and responded to a text from my erstwhile boyfriend Jamie. I have great respect for the Dalai Lama, but the only nirvana I wanted that night involved baby oil and strawberries.

# FORTY-FOUR

Ever since we'd gone our separate ways, Jamie and I had kept in occasional text contact. Sometimes he'd try to persuade me out for a drink but I'd always resisted. I suspected he'd only try to get back into my knickers and I feared his sexual magnetism might be too hard to resist in the flesh. Normally I'm disciplined about sleeping with someone simply because we've got history. But by this point I was ready to break with tradition and indulge in a spot of ex sex.

I felt the need for some fun after my sexual detox, but didn't want a totally random hook-up. I decided Jamie would be a good compromise so agreed to meet him for a drink. Besides, he had told me that he had some amazing news to share, which I was too curious to hear.

It was great to see him again. He was over the moon because he'd got a record deal at last, and a sizeable advance from the label. But instead of doing the smart thing and investing, he'd rented a massive loft with gorgeous polished hardwood floors in east London that he claimed 'used to belong to Duran Duran'.

He poured me a glass of wine and we sat on the floor in his unfurnished flat, chatting.

He started nuzzling my neck, but I pushed him away. I knew that I couldn't have sex with him one-on-one without visualizing JP's face, so I decided that the only way to take my mind off him, albeit temporarily, was to do something so wild that it bore no resemblance to my bedroom antics with JP.

So Jamie dared me to call Rachel, and when I kept dialling the number and chickening out he rolled his eyes and told me that he would do it himself.

I went into the kitchen, feeling my cheeks burn and wondered why I was so much more nervous around a woman I'd slept with than a man. Probably because, unlike with men, I didn't have the confidence that I'd been good in bed (though the evidence of her multiple orgasms should have told me otherwise).

Jamie followed a couple of minutes later. 'What did you tell her?' I said, fishing the tequila out of the cabinet and downing a shot to settle my stomach (I didn't want too much, as I knew that it would dull my pleasure).

'I told her that you needed cheering up,' he said, rubbing my shoulders. 'She's on her way over.'

Twenty minutes later she arrived, looking gorgeous with her long dark hair tied into a French twist, wearing a skin-tight grey dress with a pink bra strap peeking out and black patent heels. She was also carrying an overnight bag. Just the sight of her brought back so many memories from our dirty night together and made me instantly wet.

'Hi, sweetheart, I'm so sorry to hear about your break-up,' she said, enveloping me in a warm hug. Then her eyes ran over my body, and as she tossed her bag down in the living room she whispered, 'All I can say is, his loss. In every sense!'

To calm my nerves, I sipped a vodka tonic while she kicked

off her shoes and tucked her feet underneath her on the sofa. I sat down next to her.

I can't remember what banal topic we chatted about for the next ten minutes, but I remember that the first kiss happened completely naturally: Jamie went into the kitchen to freshen the drinks and she turned my face towards hers and softly pressed her lips against mine, then slid her tongue inside my mouth at the same time as she ran her hand up my thigh. Jesus, this girl didn't waste any time.

I opened my eyes a couple of minutes later to see Jamie standing in the doorway with a bottle of champagne. He came over to us but Rachel giggled and pushed him away as she stood up. 'Not yet. Why don't you pour the champagne while Catherine and I entertain ourselves for a while?'

She slid her dress down to reveal a pink and black balconette bra, and squeezed her nipples as they spilled out over the top.

I took off my sweater, and she got on her knees and helped me pull down my jeans. She exhaled, and I could feel her hot breath through my knickers, which she then peeled down and licked me, driving me wild.

I wasted no time removing the rest of my clothes, and before long we were in the 69 position, licking and sucking each other. I liked the 69 position much better with a woman than with a man, because I wasn't getting choked to death while trying to perform multiple functions. I could feel her getting tighter around my finger, and her suction was becoming less intense on my clit so I knew that she was getting ready to come. Less than a minute later, she took her mouth off my pussy and gasped, while I continued to bury my tongue into her and licked her sweet juices.

When she was finished she went back to sucking on my clit, fingering my arse at the same time, and I gritted my teeth as I burst into an orgasm. Jamie was stripped down to the waist by now, and when we both came up for air we all sipped from the same champagne glass, then Rachel poured its contents over my breasts and licked it off.

'I think the poor man has suffered enough, don't you, Cat?' she asked.

She stood up and kissed Jamie, while I unbuttoned his trousers and pulled out his, not surprisingly, hugely erect cock.

I started to give him a blow job, as Rachel slid behind him and kissed her way down his back. While I cupped his balls with one hand, she slid her tongue inside his arse as he moaned, rocking back and forth between us. He was totally helpless, which was a huge turn-on.

I could feel him tensing, but he pulled my mouth away before he came.

'I can't come yet,' he gasped. 'Besides, it's Cat's night. She's depressed, so we have to give her whatever she wants.'

What I wanted was a very specific sexual permutation that I'd never done before. So, five minutes later, we were in front of a full-length mirror and Jamie was lubing my arse with his fingers, then pushing his cock slowly in, as I moaned in anticipation.

'I'm not sure I can take it,' I said nervously, but Rachel kept fingering me, and said, between wet kisses, 'just take it slowly, sweetheart. We have all night.'

So, as she ran her hands over my breasts, and further downward, he pushed in, inch by inch, until I was completely filled, and began to rock back against him. Rachel went down on me, and as I felt Jamie grunting behind me and her tongue and fingers in my pussy, being fucked and eaten at the same time, I had the most fantastic orgasm.

In fact, I think I may have blacked out. It might have been my last night of casual sex for a while, but I wanted to make it count. I wasn't about to mistake this hook-up with Jamie for anything more than a one-off indulgence.

Tennessee Williams once said: 'We are all sentenced to solitary confinement inside our own skins, for life.'

Lately, I've been re-reading that quote every day, and know that I can't continue to use Jamie and friends as white noise to help block out the solitude that has set in since my break-up with JP.

Much as I liked Jamie, the dynamic between us was never going to be more than a bit of fun, the piped-in Muzak that serves as background noise.

# FORTY-FIVE

The next morning, I met Victoria for an early lunch and listened to her plans for her upcoming wedding, which thankfully did not include me wearing a hideous lime-green ruffled taffeta torture device.

She'd specified black dresses for the bridesmaids, and we're going to be picking our own – a true testament to the triumph of friendship. They wouldn't match exactly, which she insisted would look 'much cooler and more fashionable'. I knew better than to argue with Victoria about anything concerning fashion. Besides, after using photos of myself in past bridesmaids' dresses as dart practice, I was thrilled with the arrangements.

'Wow, you're letting us pick flattering outfits? Isn't there something in the brides' rulebook against that?' I teased her.

'I'm not one of those people who needs to make herself look better by making sure that everyone else looks like shit,' she said, grinning.

'Wow, I thought that that was one of the privileges of the big day. Not that you need to,' I added quickly. 'You look gorgeous. Really radiant. I've never seen you this happy, and it shows.'

I meant it, despite the fact that my happiness for her was tinged with a bit of jealousy. We handled it in the only way we knew how: I was totally honest about my lust for a relationship like hers eventually, and she was equally frank about wanting my career success. It's the only way to make sure that the green-eyed monster doesn't go on a rampage.

'Thanks, sweetie,' she said, squeezing my hand. 'But I've been so caught up in this wedding that I forgot to ask about you – how are you holding up?'

'Well, I've got a new theory: let's say that the dating game is like the housing market, and you are living in a gorgeous flat that you've put your heart and soul into. The real value may stay the same, but suddenly there are loads of articles in the papers telling you that the market is going to crash. So you panic, and worry that you won't be able to attract the buyers. Then you end up accepting an offer that is way too low.'

She ordered a straight vodka martini from the hot French waiter.

'You cannot seriously buy into this crap, Cat. People writing this shit feed on fear. If you were anorexic, it wouldn't be healthy to visit a pro-ana video gallery with pictures of Nicole Richie, now, would it? You have to censor what you see.'

'I can't,' I said. 'Maybe it's because I just turned thirty, or maybe because of JP, I'm not sure. But I was researching this piece on gold-diggers, and I happened upon a feature about Seventy Thirty, that website that charges like twelve grand a year to set up millionaires with clients.'

'What pearls of wisdom did they come up with?'

'The one that sticks in my mind is the quote from one of the professional matchmakers, who says that there is an "optimum relationship window" between the ages of twenty-eight and thirty-two.'

'Uh-huh,' she said, signalling the waiter for another drink

for me, without asking. 'And your point is?'

'My point is that what if all those years I spent chasing new experiences should have been spent being sensible and settling down with a husband? If what she says is true, my window is half shut!'

Seeing my deadpan expression, she softened her tone. 'Seriously, honey, that's just crazy. Speaking from experience, I can tell you that relationships aren't perfect. You know if you had settled down earlier, you might have ended up cheating. Or getting stuck like Andrew, where the marriage dies after five years but you're trapped there because of children. I mean, would you have wanted to settle down with any of your exes for ever?'

'No,' I said, shaking my head. 'No way.'

'Exactly. Besides, there's no cut-off when it comes to love,' she said, squeezing my hand. 'But if it adds to irrational fears, I would suggest that you stop reading this stuff.'

Easy for you to say, I thought, then immediately put the notion out of my head. For the thousandth time, I reminded myself that the fact that Victoria was in a functional and happy relationship did not mean that her life was magically 'sorted'.

She was spot on about my fears. Call me naïve, but I'd always assumed that the right person was just around the corner, and I've loved every bump in the road of my journey. But lately I'm tired of the ride, feeling nauseous, and the pit-stop gas-station candy, totally devoid of nutritional value, isn't working any more.

I'm tired of driving. I'm ready to get off.

It seemed that my Anti-Rules research task had taken a temporary nosedive. I suddenly couldn't stop reading this inflammatory material but instead of criticizing its limitations, now I was sizing myself up according to its crazy standards.

'I can't stop,' I told Victoria. 'If there's that much of it out there, I need to know if it's true, if it's something that resonates with people. It's part of my job.'

After Victoria left, I took an hour to read the Sunday papers, which had always been one of the great pleasures of my weekend.

However, it was rudely interrupted by a smug couple at the next table. She was wearing an artfully dishevelled blonde ponytail, and, by the looks of it, one of her sandy-haired boyfriend's cute sweaters.

'You're so wrong about that movie,' she said, playfully swatting his arm. 'Matt Damon is a totally believable action hero! He could easily have done James Bond!'

'Sorry, darling, but Daniel Craig was the obvious choice. They needed a much harder villain, and there's no way that Damon could have pulled off a British accent. He's far too bland.'

She giggled, then he rubbed some foam from her coffee off her nose, and kissed her. I know that this was an uncharitable thought, but at that instant I wished for the scalding-hot coffee to splash into his face, temporarily blinding him, and while he screamed and flailed the tiny romantic lit candle on their table would fall onto her coat, setting her alight.

It's not that I wished the couple any harm; in fact, in my heart of hearts I normally like to see reminders that there is happiness out there somewhere.

Only my heart still feels like it's surrounded by broken glass, which threatens to stab me and spill arterial blood at any slight lurch, reminding me of my precarious mental state.

I remembered how JP had constantly interrupted my train of thought when we were reading the papers to harp on about a columnist in the *Financial Times* who he loved. He had such a passion for interest rates, and we used to get into those cute but sickly sweet play fights that probably made me the envy of every single woman in the café, who were all simultaneously praying that the earth swallowed us whole.

In-your-face happiness can be hard, and makes me realize why so many women side against men and blame the entire gender for their unhappiness.

If I could only convince myself that all men were shits, or that relationships equalled pain, then I wouldn't have to face the ugly reality staring me in the face over eggs Benedict, which was that not all men leave. It was just that JP left me.

But even with all the pain, I knew that I would do it all again in an instant. And if I've learned anything in my life, it's not to take anyone for granted. Despite what the bullshit Rule books say, no matter how you play your cards, even the strongest relationships can end; no one is safe from that. And getting left is not the end of the world. Even if it does feel like it sometimes.

Enough wallowing, I thought. I needed a new direction. It was time to step up my game with the Anti-Rules and tackle the final frontier of self-exploration.

# FORTY-SIX

It was a grey autumn afternoon, the kind where the obscured sun makes midday feel like 5 p.m., when I threaded through several labyrinth-like back alleys into the basement of a west London Presbyterian church for my first-ever Sex and Love Addicts Anonymous meeting.

The much younger sister of Alcoholics Anonymous, Sex and Love Addicts Anonymous began in the mid-seventies as many AA members became aware that their relationship problems warranted a separate set of meetings. Like the other subgroups of AA – Narcotics Anonymous, Overeaters Anonymous, Gamblers Anonymous, et cetera – SLAA adopts a twelve-step structure, which includes recognizing a higher power and admitting powerlessness over your 'addiction' – in my case, my ex.

'For someone who is love-addicted, going through a break-up feels like going through withdrawal,' my therapist had told me. She was right: I'd had splits before but never anything like this. Even though I'd really loved JP, the magnitude of my depression astonished me. There were moments when I literally felt that I would sell my soul in return for him coming back to me and telling me that he'd reconsidered, and wanted to be with me after all.

There were several folding chairs, and, horror of horrors,

a podium at the front, where I imagined that people shared their tales of how they once cut up their ex-husband's clothes and ran over them in the drive, or something similar.

Inside, the ratio of men to women and the slight air of sadness and desperation reminded me of a speed dating event, except that everyone was crying. In my experience, they usually wait until they've left speed dating for that. There were about three women for every man. Among my fellow confessors was a heavy-set black woman, who cried into her coffee the entire time, an older man with silver hair, several women my age and a very hot, curly-haired man with a South African twang who was wearing workout gear – I figured that he was either a courier or had come straight from the gym.

Suddenly, my throat was dry, and I headed to the water fountain behind the South African. As he leaned over to take a drink, I couldn't help thinking of other ways to help him work up a sweat. I wondered if he was a sex or a love addict. I'm definitely on the love addict end of the spectrum, especially considering my relationship with JP. I also wondered if you could crack a walnut between his arse cheeks.

The cynic in me suspected that some of the men here might just be trying to get laid. After all, what better place to find a potential one-night stand than a sex addicts' meeting? He wouldn't even have to shell out for cocktails first.

Despite all the literature about 'surrendering myself to a higher power', I could feel that I was probably going to hell.

None of my sexual behaviour has ever been compulsive: in fact, it's during the times I feel most calm and self-centred that I seek out the most sexual partners. But when love gets thrown into the mix, all bets are off.

I gigged to myself, partly out of nervousness, and approached a professional-looking brunette who appeared to be about my age.

'Hi,' I said, extending my hand. 'I'm Cat, and this is my first time here. I was just wondering if you find the meetings helpful?'

She forced a smile. 'I'm Emily,' she said. 'And yes. I've only been to three so far but I just did step one with my therapist.'

'Step one?' I said, confused.

'Admitting that I'm powerless over my addiction and calling on a higher power to stop it,' she said.

'Oh, right,' I said, grabbing a Styrofoam cup from the table. 'Well, I'm not sure if that applies to me. I don't always feel powerless over love, but I've had a hell of a time getting over my last relationship.'

'I used to think that too,' she said. 'Then I realized that I was in love with the idea of being in love. No matter how distant my ex was, I always went back for more. After about two sessions my therapist told me it wasn't healthy love, it was obsession. But it still took me a while to come here.'

I've always thought of obsession as Glenn Close, huddled in a dark room in *Fatal Attraction*, hissing that she would not be ignored, before going apeshit and boiling a kid's rabbit.

Emily and I moved to the folding chairs and sat down. 'So what made you come to meetings, Cat?' she asked.

'It's funny, but something in the literature about SLAA really hit me, the part where they say that in a healthy relationship, the ratio of my giving x should be equal to his giving y, or something like that. Basically a good relationship involves give and take.'

'So his x wasn't equalling your y?'

'Hell, no. He took x, y, z and the rest of the alphabet!'

It was a pretty lame joke, but it broke the ice. Soon I'd heard the tale of her ex, Bernard, the evil Frenchman who slept with several of her friends.

'When I hear stuff like that, it makes me think that JP wasn't that bad,' I admitted. 'He never would have cheated on me.'

She put her hand on my arm. 'He withdrew emotionally, though, didn't he? With work, and never making time for you? I think that's just as bad. Maybe even harder, because Bernard was such an asshole by the end that it just got ridiculous. I had to throw him out. It must have been much harder to be abandoned mentally. That's torture.'

As I sipped my burned coffee and munched some rather stale ginger biscuits while waiting for the meeting to start, I thought about the romantic novels I'd read and idealized as a child.

The first casualty was *Jane Eyre*, which was always one of my favourites. For years, I mooned over the romantic tale of the plain girl who fell for her emotionally unavailable boss. After the pesky matter of his insane wife who secretly lived in the attic was resolved – that is, after she torched herself and blinded Mr Rochester – the couple was blissfully reunited at the end, with Jane Eyre having pocketed her long-denied inheritance, and holding her newborn son.

On an adult reading, it became clear that Jane Eyre was a love addict terrified of the abandonment and cruelty she'd suffered as a child, so she picked an emotionally distant man. She only managed to 'snag' him when he was broke, blind and totally dependent on her. Some happy ending.

The Brontë sisters definitely had it in for women. Catherine and Heathcliff ended up dead, and even though he treated his wife horrifically, he magically reformed for Cathy because he pined for her. Of course this isn't how real life works.

Men who have deep emotional scars and resort to cruelty will keep doing the same thing over and over again in their new relationships. But we women keep hearing the message: 'If I'm the One, he will change.' Sorry, but I don't want to be a ghost on the moors before I get to have a committed relationship. It's time to take action.

On the other hand, I was terrified at the loss of control. I didn't want to be labelled an addict.

By accepting the premise, 'We admit that our lives have become unmanageable,' was I giving up my free will? I had responsibility over my actions, and for a long time had loved my sex life, warts and all (not literally, of course. I've always used condoms).

On the other hand, lately my failed relationship with JP had been eating away at me. I had a broken heart, and it wasn't getting any better.

I just wasn't getting over it. And every time I remembered an extract from *He's Just Not That Into You*, I got more upset, because, for once, believing that the right man would come along didn't actually solve my problem.

After years of going through man after man, some of whom, I can assure Greg Behrendt, the author lame enough to call women 'Superfox', were very into me, I wondered if another man was what I needed right now.

As I chatted with Emily, I couldn't help meeting the South African's gaze. Damn, was he hot. But I didn't need any distractions, so I crossed my legs and kept my eyes forward as the chair started the meeting by reading the Twelve Steps of the SLAA.

My palms were sweaty as people began to 'share', though being new I was spared the indignity of baring my soul.

I still wasn't sure about this whole thing. I did find myself in some of the '40 Questions for Self-Diagnosis for Love and Sex Addicts', but I also found anybody who's ever loved. 'Do you find yourself unable to stop seeing a specific person, even though you know that seeing this person is destructive for you? Do you get "high" from sex and/or romance? Do you have sex or "relationships" to try to deal with, or escape from, life's problems? Do you find yourself in a relationship that you cannot leave?'

Well, yes, but that covers all my friends and everyone I know as well. I also wasn't sure about sharing my most intimate fears with strangers. It's funny, but I found the idea of sharing my fantasies about the South African bending me over and taking me from behind, slamming into me as the stale ginger biscuits ground into my sweaty stomach, preferable to telling them the truth: that I was afraid of ending up alone.

Sharing sexual conquests is one thing, because I can always walk away afterwards. Sharing intimacy is much, much harder. I've had my brave front for a long time and it's saved my life more than once.

'I'm Pam,' a forty-something woman was saying, while everyone responded with the monotone, 'Hi, Pam!' 'and I'm a sex and love addict. I haven't had a great week. I obsessed over running into my ex, because I knew that we would be at the same work function, and was so hurt when I saw him with someone else. For days I planned how I would act at the party. I just felt that I needed him in my life so badly. But even though I still feel sad, I'm not feeling self-loathing.'

Jesus, Pam and I could be clones. But wasn't obsessing over our exes a normal part of human behaviour?

According to the group, both yes and no. My problem was that I was so attached to the fantasy that I failed to see the ugly reality. JP's actions had been suggesting for months that he wanted out of the relationship but I'd held on to my dreams. Had I fallen for a fantasy or a real person? Could I even tell the difference any more?

I got a few useful nuggets from my first meeting – namely, that no one person can define any other person, and that people are not unique but replaceable.

Over-analysing with my girlfriends wasn't cutting it any more. Besides, I was convinced that a lot of my acquaintances were full of shit anyway. 'You can't define yourself by a man,' one of them told me, while in the same breath admitting that she'd just quit her job because her husband, who had already isolated her from family and friends, wasn't comfortable with the mother of his future children working. I needed some healthy examples.

I already knew the script, but I wanted to mean the words, not just say them. I wanted to rediscover the confidence in myself that, somewhere along the road, I'd lost. And I wanted to hold a good old-fashioned Nazi-style book-burning of every shitty dating guide telling me that I needed to change myself to land a man.

Maybe I shouldn't blame dating guides. Happy endings sell. In fact, the nuptial-centric literary device was one that

Shakespeare used at the end of all his comedies: after a play full of confusion, gender-bending and identity blurring, he pairs up his characters at the end, they all get married, and they live happily ever after.

Which continues to send the message to women everywhere: no matter how successful or cool you are, if you're not happily coupled, there's no happy ending. You're just biding your time until the right guy comes along.

Logically, I know that life doesn't work like that. Some people are happy never getting married, some are miserable and lonely. Not to mention the very high divorce rate, meaning that relationships are constantly in flux.

I knew this in my head. But my heart was saying something different.

So when my turn came, I volunteered to share.

'My name is Catherine, and I'm a love addict,' I said, not even waiting for the chorus response before plunging on.

'Until today, I couldn't figure out why I couldn't get over my last relationship. But I think it's because I wanted to be good enough to be the One for him. I think I wanted to prove, on some unconscious level, that I was good enough to get someone to marry me. So I was desperate to keep my ex no matter what.

'I loved him.' I wiped the tears from my eyes. 'But he wasn't giving me what I deserved. He knew it, and I knew it. I was staying with him partly out of fear. I wanted the fantasy so badly that I wasn't seeing the reality. And the reality was ugly.'

I breathed out, and felt tears filling my eyes again. 'But not any more. I'm going to have to rely on myself. The guy on the white horse is not going to show up, and if he did, I wouldn't want him anyway. I don't *want* to be the damsel in distress.'

Emily smiled and patted my knee, and we exchanged numbers and hugged on the way out.

'That was hard,' I said. 'That meeting was totally different to what I expected. I thought there would be loads of pervy men talking about hookers.'

'I think that most of those guys come on Thursdays,' she said.

Although I did the sharing and hugging, the cynic remains. If I ever go to that meeting again, I'm totally taking my trusty hand sanitizer.


During my session with my therapist afterwards, I asked her if I would ever regain the highs I'd had during my hook-up with JP.

'I'm all for healthy love and intimacy,' I told her, 'but I also want to have the earth-shattering sex, and intensity, and feeling of being swept off my feet. Do you think that's still a possibility?'

'Definitely,' she said, pen poised in hand. 'But I have to warn you that things may never go back to the way they were.'

'What do you mean?'

'When you find love like that, it's the difference between taking an E and climbing the Himalayas to the peak and looking out over the summit. One is a temporary rush, the other feeds your soul, because you know that you've done the hard work to get there yourself, and it stays with you for ever.'

It wasn't about men. It was about me. I couldn't be scared of change, even if it meant not for ever being the commitment-phobic woman who writes about her adventures. I couldn't always be, on some level, waiting for the right guy to complete me. To be really happy, I would have to let go of that fantasy.

I had to stop hiding from my destiny. I was ready meta-phorically to strap on my backpack and climbing shoes and become a sexual Sherpa. It may be the road less travelled, but in the end it will be totally worth it.

# FORTY-SEVEN

I decided to go to Victoria's wedding sans date, though I did fly there with Mark, since his girlfriend Samantha was taking a late-night flight due to work commitments, and he had to be there earlier to complete his best man duties. Even if, with Victoria's practical and simplistic attitude towards nuptials, i.e. 'the wedding is way more important than the marriage ceremony', those duties were meant to be minimal. She didn't even want Mark there the night beforehand as there wasn't going to be a rehearsal, so we were free to get pissed together.

I was also panicking a bit about the fact that JP was probably going to be attending the reception at least, since, through a random family connection, he's technically Mike's second cousin. But I was trying not to think about that, or how I would feel if he showed up with a date. It was Victoria's day, and I had to stay focused.

Mike's family is Catholic, and Victoria had fallen in love with a church in Dublin. So much for her tropical destination wedding! I'd only been to Dublin once before, and had fallen in love with its gorgeous city centre and small-town feel.

On our Ryanair flight, Mark and I were also toasting each other with cheap white wine for another reason: to mark the occasion of our divorce papers coming through.

And we weren't the only ones celebrating: we were surrounded by a group of drunken chav teenagers, clearly heading towards a wedding of their own. The girls were wearing hideous vinyl lavender bridesmaids' dresses with corsage flowers that looked big enough to eat their heads, and the boys were making the most of the '2 for 1' Jell-O shots served in plastic pouches.

'I can only hope that Victoria's special day will be this classy,' I whispered as one of the ruddy-faced boys kicked the back of my seat.

'Be nice,' Mark said, clinking his plastic glass against mine. 'They're just excited. It's the biggest day of their lives.'

I smiled at him. 'Do I detect a change of heart from someone who once compared marriage to "being imprisoned in a domestic gulag"?'

'Well, that's the reason why I wanted to hurry the divorce along a bit – not that I don't love being married to you, sweetheart – but I'm going to pop the question to Samantha.'

'I'm so happy for you! I suspected you might be next,' I told him. 'I think we all suspected; she's amazing.' I gave him a half hug. But a small part of me thought, Will I soon be the only singleton left?

As we discussed the logistics of rings, I remarked at how far Mark had come.

'I thought you said you wanted to be a player for ever,' I said. 'You're the one who always has the movie *Swingers* in your DVD player.'

'Yeah, but I realized two things,' Mark said. 'Saying "You're so money!" and screwing cocktail waitresses in random trailers is cool when you're twenty-four, but I'm going to be forty soon. Guys who go trawling for chicks after a certain age and never commit aren't cool. They just end up looking pathetic.'

'Wow, I'm actually surprised that men think like this. I thought it was women who had cornered the market on obsessing over the biological clock. What about men ageing like a fine wine?'

I rolled my eyes as I said this, and Mark laughed.

'No guy really believes that. We're all terrified of growing old alone, and most of us don't have the money or the inclination to be Michael Douglas, running around with those tiny kids, his wife having to worry about pushing him along in a wheelchair with one hand and the buggy with the other.'

'So men aren't constantly obsessed with the younger model?'

'Honey pie, most men would love to fuck the younger model. But they know that having her on their arm for any length of time won't make them feel younger, it will make them feel older.'

I reclined my seat all the way back to fight the incessant kicking and stayed focused on Mark.

'Okay, let me ask you something else. Even if I don't like a guy that much, and I'm not sure if I want children, some dark corner of my mind always does a computer image of what our faces would look like blended if we ever had kids. Is that weird? Do men do that?'

He laughed. 'Men don't need to do that. We just visit their mums to check that they aren't fat, gross and wearing a Vicky Pollard tracksuit. Meeting Mum is like looking twenty years into the future.'

I giggled as the pilot announced that we were descending into Dublin. 'Good to know that you're still in touch with your shallow side.'

'And, Cat, you know how hot I think your mum is!'

Suddenly, the plane lurched, and felt like one of those race-car simulators I used to ride in when I was a child.

'You seem very calm, considering how much we've been bouncing around,' Mark said, grabbing my forearm and trying to unnerve me. 'I know how much you hate flying. Aren't you scared? Why aren't you panicking and putting nail marks in my hand?'

'Honestly? I make peace with the plane every time I get in, and when I hand over the boarding pass, and smile at the flight attendant, I'm thinking that if it's my day to die then I'll deal.'

He raised one eyebrow. 'Seriously?'

'Well, no. In all honesty I would probably shit myself and run around screaming. But at least I'm living life and going places, not staying put because I'm terrified of getting on a plane. If I did that I would probably be one of the fifty-two people injured in the UK each year from using a teapot.'

'Where do you come up with this shit? Is that even a real statistic?'

'My point is, and I learned this from JP,' I said, putting up my tray table and preparing for landing, 'that stagnant does not equal stable.'

'That's a good headline. You should totally use that in your next column!'

After the plane landed in Dublin, Mark and I checked into our hotel, the Clarence. I was surprised at how basic it was, considering all the hype about the fact that it was owned by

Bono, but I was excited to see the river below, and to have a bit of time to myself.

I love staying in hotels alone. But I had overslept the morning of the flight after downing half a bottle of red wine the night before when I'd meant to have only a glass, which I'd been doing a bit too much of lately. Consequently, I'd packed a load of crap, and other than my bridesmaid's outfit I had a total of three dresses, all of which were strapless, no strapless bra, and exactly one sock.

I took a hot shower, letting the bathroom fill with steam and closing my eyes.

I dressed in the jeans and vest top I'd worn on the plane and strolled out into the streets, wandering through the market stalls and cobblestone streets of Temple Bar, a neighbourhood that seems to exist only for tourists. The little tea houses and pubs have always reminded me of a movie set.

I wandered up to Brown Thomas department store, and rifled through the racks of sale clothes. Most of the designer separates were clearly picked over, but nestled among the Day-Glo yellow rejects I found it: a black, asymmetrical-hem Givenchy dress that nipped in at the waist, in size small.

Even on sale, the price tag was 375 euros, but I knew that I had to have it, especially after I tried it on and it fitted perfectly.

I put the dress on hold and walked down the street in search of a coffee shop, trying to justify the dress purchase to myself.

I soon came up with a reason: because I didn't marry the wrong guy. Between the gift, the flights, bridesmaid's dress and hotel I'd happily spent more than £1,000 celebrating Victoria's union with Mike. Unfortunately, there's no such thing as a single's registry, so I decided that the killer black dress was the next best thing.

I was on my way back to the store, listening to *Journey* on my iPod, thinking that I should be celebrating my life choices instead of constantly lamenting what I don't have, when I ran directly into a man talking into his mobile phone, and looked up to see Andrew.

It took my eyes a couple of seconds to register, because even though I'd always known that Andrew lived part-time in Dublin, I'd never seen him outside London. I always find it disconcerting to see people away from their usual environment, but maybe that's just because I'm so crap at recognizing faces.

'Hi!' he blurted out, then ended his call and enveloped me in a full-body hug. 'Cat, it's so great to see you! What brings you to Dublin?'

'Well, Victoria's wedding is tomorrow, so I'm just – well, I'm aimlessly wandering, actually, doing a bit of soul-searching. I'm thinking of dropping a few hundred quid on a dress and wondering if I can justify it. What are you up to?'

'I'm just leaving the gym – I swim every day now – and was about to go to the office. Can I buy you a coffee?'

Instead, he accompanied me to the store to give me a second opinion, which was hugely favourable, and waited by the till while I bought the dress.

'I could buy it for you,' he suggested teasingly.

'I don't think that would be appropriate.' I handed my card to the saleswoman and prayed for a miracle. Even though I knew that I had money in the bank for once, thanks to the book, I still broke out into a sweat about spending that much money. I guess old habits die hard.

'Seriously,' he said, pulling out his wallet. 'I never got you a birthday present. It would be an honour.'

His blue eyes twinkled, and he turned towards the petite, red-haired salesgirl who was looking at him adoringly.

I took the hand brandishing an American Express Platinum Card and pushed it away. 'No, really, I want to do this for myself.' The next words tumbled out. 'If you really want to get me a gift, you can come with me to the wedding tomorrow. I would love to catch up with you, and you could see some old friends.'

He turned back to me. 'It's the least I can do if you won't let me buy you the dress. But won't Victoria mind?'

'No way! She totally adores you, and she told me I could bring someone if I wanted. And Mark's her best man so you'll have a male ally who you know. Besides, she's having massage and beauty treatments tonight, then she and Mike are getting a bit of chill-out time before the big party. Nothing could faze her tomorrow.'

'Isn't it bad luck to see the groom on the night before the wedding?'

'I don't think they're going by tradition; I mean, they already live together. Besides, a traditional wedding is hardly a guarantee of success. Know what I mean?' I looked at him pointedly.

He laughed nervously, and stepped back as his phone rang. It was his wife, and as he turned away to take the call I thought about how much that would have upset me in the old days, but now I was over him. I think self-awareness, not time, is what heals the wounds. Though I still pictured our naked acrobatics every time I looked at him. You can't kill chemistry.

The saleswoman wound a ribbon around my bag, handed it to me, and as the receipt printed out she leaned in conspiratorially. 'You know, you and your boyfriend are really adorable together.'

I wanted to set this poor girl straight, and tell her that the man (who, by the way, was STILL not wearing a wedding ring) was the worst case of false advertising ever. I wanted to tell her that real love wasn't about grand gestures, but everyday kindnesses, and that the reason he looked at me with such adoration in his eyes was because I represented a fantasy world apart from his marriage, where he didn't have to deal with piss and shit and changing nappies, and his problems were so all-encompassing that they were the only ones that mattered.

But I just smiled and told her to have a nice day. Who was I kidding? Part of me was still addicted to the drama.

I said my goodbyes to Andrew and went back to the hotel.

Checking my make-up in the mirror, the morning of Victoria's wedding, I knew that I'd done something really stupid.

My mistake was even more ridiculous considering the insane lengths that I had gone to in order to maintain the illusion of control by looking perfect. I was wearing the sexy, cleavage-enhancing new dress that slipped off my shoulders, my killer silver heels, and a waist-cinching belt that, through some sort of elastic wizardry, made my waist look about sixteen inches around. For some reason, even though I loved the strapless black dress I'd already earmarked for the occasion, I always regarded finding something new that fitted perfectly as a sort of good luck charm. It worked at my book launch, and hopefully would work at Vic's wedding.

Unfortunately, my red wine hangover had affected me more than I thought – in my tired haze, I had forgotten to pack the one essential that I can't live without: tweezers.

Normally, I'm plucked to porn star perfection, and have no hair on my body from the eyebrows down. I'm actually a bit obsessed with waxing, since smoothness enhances my sensitivity.

But I have a dark secret: exactly three hairs on my chin; not peach fuzz, but coarse black ones that look like they came from *The Fly*. They have been there for years, and no amount of tweezing or waxing can banish them for ever.

When I saw that two of them had sprouted I grabbed the only thing I could, the hotel razor. I knew this was a Very Bad Idea, but panicked in the same way I had that time when Victoria stopped me from almost hacking off my long hair to look like Rod Stewart.

Unfortunately, I slipped on the bath mat and sliced myself. After failing to stop the bleeding with a tissue (now I know how men feel), I knew that in the eyes of Andrew and the male guests I would morph from Beautiful Girl to Bearded Lady.

But I had to make the best of a bad situation, because I was running really late. So I took a final look in the full-length mirror and headed down to Mark's room.

Samantha poked her head out in answer to my knock. 'Cat, that dress is gorgeous!' she said.

'Thanks,' I said. 'You look amazing too.'

'You may want to check on Mark,' she whispered. 'I think he may have a case of the best man jitters. Come in.'

'Mark? Are you okay?' He walked out of the bathroom, straightening his tie. 'Actually, I think I'm more nervous today than I was at our wedding!'

'Don't worry, I'm sure that your speech is amazing,' I told him. 'Let's go, we're going to be late.'

We squeezed into a taxi and headed to Christ Church Cathedral in central Dublin. Mark was turning green, so to distract him I started chatting about Andrew.

'Really? That's great, Cat, I'm so excited about seeing him. Is anything going on?' Mark asked slyly, giving me a sideways glance.

'No! He's married, and even if he wasn't, it's definitely over between us. But I'm glad he's in my life, and that we can be friends now.'

'Well, at least it keeps the drama quotient up.' Mark laughed.

'No way,' I said emphatically. 'Unlike ours, this will be a drama-free wedding.'

'Whatever,' Mark said. 'With you and Victoria in the same room, I doubt that's possible.'

The taxi pulled up at the back of the cathedral, and Samantha went to sit at the front while I went in search of Victoria and Mark headed off to join Mike. There weren't that many guests in the church, since Victoria had managed to keep it down to close friends and family, but I could spot Russell and Vic's dad sitting in the first two rows.

Once I found Vic, powdering her nose with Amy, she seemed remarkably composed. I squeezed her hand and gave her a hug. 'How are you feeling, babe? Are you excited?'

She smiled. 'Actually, I'm really calm. I'm just a bit nervous about the Catholic ceremony, and that fact that the Holy Water may start bubbling when I touch it because I'm concentrated pure evil, but there we go!' She looked stunning in a simple, white strapless silk dress that was the antithesis of the fussy ones we'd ravaged on the racks.

'You're going to be fine.' I pulled her into a hug, and could feel her heart racing. 'Here, you can open my gift early. Think of it as your something new.'

She opened the box to reveal the silver metallic Christian Louboutin six-inch heels, and squealed with delight. 'Cat, these are gorgeous. I fucking love them!'

Several people looked around so she lowered her voice.

'Well, I know they weren't on the registry, but somehow I just couldn't bring myself to give you a serving tray or a toaster.'

'These are perfect. Thank you so much.' She kicked off the black heels that she was wearing and put the Louboutins on in their place, covering them with the bottom of her dress.

I had to laugh. 'Are you sure that you aren't going to trip in those things?'

'Darling, I live in six-inch heels, and these are fantastic. I'm wearing them.' She squeezed my hand so hard that she almost drew blood. 'Now, how are you doing? I've been so caught up with the wedding I feel like I haven't seen you in for ever.'

'Actually, I'm great,' I said, meaning it. 'I feel better than I have in ages.'

Victoria's mum came up to us and told us it was time. As I walked down the aisle, following Amy and looking at Mike waiting at the altar, I felt moved. To me, their wedding was much more meaningful because I knew that they had been together for years, had had their share of problems, including a brief split, and had got through everything together. This was the real thing. Their love wasn't based on a quick infatuation, but was a much deeper and more meaningful connection that I was sure would last a lifetime.

While attempting to walk in time to the music – never my forte – I surreptitiously checked out several men in the congregation, and winked when I passed Andrew. His presence meant that I wouldn't have to handle all the questions from Victoria's meddling relatives about why I hadn't met the man of my dreams yet.

I listened to Mike and Victoria take their vows, and knew deep down in my soul that I wanted the same thing some day. I wanted to forsake all others for someone. I couldn't believe that I was having these thoughts given my history of hedonism, but I knew at that moment, more than ever, that I actually wanted monogamy, with all its challenges.

But unlike Andrew, I wanted a marriage that kept the passion alive, and wasn't just an empty shell. Maybe I was being overly optimistic, but I wanted a partner who could appreciate the animalistic side of me while also feeding my soul.

Mark and Victoria kissed, and everyone applauded as they walked down the aisle together.

I was ready for the reception. I was definitely ready to get pissed.

# FORTY-EIGHT

At the party afterwards, Andrew and I danced, which meant that he tried to lead me and I constantly turned in the wrong direction and ended up hitting his armpit. I'm not exactly John Travolta – I can dance at a nightclub, but never could master complicated steps. Still, we were having fun, though he could tell that I was a bit distracted.

'How am I doing?' he asked.

'You're fabulous, Andrew, it's just that I totally suck and have two left feet.'

He twirled me again, and dipped me down with a flourish. 'If I told you how gorgeous you look in that dress and what I was thinking about back there in a house of God, would you get offended?'

'Doubtful,' I said, laughing. 'With those accents, you Irish boys get away with murder!' We continued to twirl.

'Mind if I cut in?' I looked past Andrew's shoulder and my heart stopped. It was JP, wearing a tuxedo and looking gorgeous, despite the fact that his cheekbones were protruding a bit more than normal. I'd suspected that this moment was coming, but nothing quite prepared me for the shock. Still, I tried to maintain my composure.

Andrew looked down at me, a bit confused, and released his grip. 'If it's okay with Cat.'

I nodded, kissed him on the cheek and took JP's hands. I tried to keep my tone light, but my heart was racing. For a couple of seconds I was literally at a loss for words, which was a new sensation for me.

'So,' I said, trying to control my quivering voice, 'how have you been?'

He smiled, and his eyes crinkled at the corners. 'Okay. Working a lot. It's a fun wedding, though they do make me a bit emotional. If you'd been the one getting married, I probably would have re-enacted the scene from *The Graduate*.'

'That's funny,' I said drily. 'But somehow, I don't think screaming and pounding the walls is really your style.'

I was so confused. One part of me was hoping that this would turn into the end of every teen movie when the guy shows up and declares his love; the other part of me just wanted the ever-elusive 'closure'.

I could see Mike and Victoria out of the corner of my eye, sitting at a table, staring. Mark and Samantha were dancing next to me, warily circling us like vultures after a slaughter. Victoria mouthed, 'Are you okay?' but I just shrugged my shoulders, pasted on a fake grin and kept shuffling my feet like an idiot.

'I've missed you,' he said. 'You look beautiful.'

Part of me was sorely tempted to melt into his arms, but I knew that this would only start our dysfunctional cycle again. It was my fault as much as his. Where would we be three months down the line?

I decided that it was time, once and for all, to stop playing games and have one final Anti-Rules moment.

Aware of all the eyes on us, I took his hand and said, 'Let's go outside.'

I stepped gingerly across the damp grass and walked underneath a giant, gnarled tree.

'I'm actually really happy that you're here,' I said, trying to channel my therapist's advice and make decisions with my head instead of my heart. 'There's something that I've been wanting to ask you for a while. Do you think that our break-up was really because you didn't want to commit, or that you didn't want to commit to me? Because I was convinced that it was circumstances around us, like my job, but in my heart I believe that if you are lucky enough to find someone to fall in love with, you count your blessings and do something every day to make the relationship better, not tear it apart.'

He looked flummoxed, unsure of what to say next. I knew that he'd probably rehearsed his lines perfectly, and this was the scene where we filled the tough gaps in conversation with hot sex. I wasn't letting him get off that easily.

At that exact moment, Andrew popped around the corner to check on me; JP grabbed my arm and I could see his face contort in anger. 'He didn't waste much time getting back into the picture, did he?'

Now I was seriously annoyed. 'JP, Andrew is just a friend; stop being so ridiculous! I'm sick of this jealousy bullshit.'

'Hey, you heard what she said. Let's go back inside.' Andrew took my forearm to try to lead me inside, which resulted in the unfortunate situation of each man pulling on one arm.

'Stop it, you guys!' I yelled, jerking back, as my left foot got caught up with my right, and I started to fall backwards into the muddy grass. JP made a grab for me which set him accidentally stumbling into Andrew. Andrew pushed him away, probably a bit harder than the situation warranted, in a break from his usual gentle nature.

'What is your problem?' JP yelled.

I was trying to push myself up, but my six-inch heels had sunk into the mud and I was literally rooted to the spot.

'My problem is that she's not your girlfriend any more, friend. And if you love her so much, where the hell have you been for the past few months?'

'Okay, that's enough.' Now, I might have imagined it would be fun to have two men fighting over me, but actually it was pretty scary. As I tried again to scramble upright I toppled forwards and was left eating dirt. Thankfully both guys stopped in their tracks and leaned down to help me up. I brushed myself off as JP apologized and gave me his handkerchief.

I dug out my heels – sadly one of them had broken – and turned to Andrew. 'Thank you for being such a great friend to me, but I need to talk to JP. I'll see you inside in a few minutes.'

Noticing that I was shivering, JP wrapped me in his jacket and enveloped me in his arms. I could feel the heat spreading all through my body, and as my breathing intensified I fought the urge to unzip his trousers and tell him to take me right then, outside, against the stone wall. I snapped out of my little fantasy, and brought myself back to reality.

Resuming our conversation, I asked him again about why he'd ended our relationship.

'So you think I pushed the self-destruct button?' He stepped closer. 'Well, maybe I did. I'm not sure why. I do love you, but I don't think that things would have worked out in the end. We are very different people.'

I smiled. 'I love you too. And you know, I was really angry at you, but you did the right thing after all. If you didn't love me in the same way, you were totally right to break up with me, because life is way too short for half-arsed relationships. I loved you unconditionally, and I want someone who loves me the same way, and I'm very excited about being free to find him. What was I thinking, trying to talk you into loving me?' I laughed.

He looked slightly confused, and gave me a hug.

'You never had to do that, because I do love you, Catherine. And I do think about you all the time and feel like there's a real connection between us. I think that we should talk.'

'There is a connection, JP. And there always will be. You are the man who made me realize that I want to have a family, which is huge. I'll never forget you for that. And I still love you too, even if you really pissed me off sometimes.'

We both laughed, and in that instant I saw the spark that made us fall in love.

The tough part was knowing that we did love each other. But I couldn't change him, so I had to let him go.

The control freak part of me wanted to chase the connection. And if this had been a scene from a dating guide, I'm sure that they would have advised me to play it cool for a few months, push him away so that his testosterone levels were increased and he got into the chase again, and maybe eventually if I was lucky enough I could get him to marry me.

No thanks. I want a relationship with someone who is my best friend, and that means being able to be myself. Nothing could be lonelier and more exhausting that having to pretend to be someone I'm not. If I don't trust my life partner to love me as I am, what does that say about how much I love myself?

'Look, I'm going back inside,' I said, and when he went to follow me, added, 'alone.'

We hugged again, and promised to stay in touch.

It was tough, because part of me wanted to give him his happy ending. It would have been amazing to walk back in to Victoria's reception with JP on my arm, the picture-perfect end to a picture-perfect day. But it wouldn't have lasted. And I was really, finally done with the drama (outside the bedroom, of course!).

Walking across the courtyard, I thought about how much I'd learned in the past year: I loved JP, but I wasn't going to waste another second of my time and energy on someone who wasn't sure of his feelings for me, when there were so many amazing people who could give me what I wanted out there – or maybe even inside the party! I felt that an enormous weight had been lifted from my shoulders.

Also, something that Sarah said was sticking in my head: she'd told me that I would be less attracted to non-committal people when I was truly happy and confident in myself, and she was right. Deep down, I knew that I deserved someone who knew what he wanted. That was real, three-dimensional love, not just head-in-the-clouds infatuation. I was finally getting a true feel for the difference between the two.

Just as the sun broke through the clouds, I felt inexplicably joyous. I'd spent all this time wondering when I would finally get my happy ending, but it had really happened a long time ago – I'd created it myself, by moving to London, forging a career and making friends. My job is weird, and it's not for everyone, but it's me, and the right man has to take me as I am.

As if on cue, I got a text from Nick Lowe. 'I'm travelling through Singapore and keep seeing your book everywhere. How much more time must I anticipate your long-awaited visit to sunny Los Angeles? I promise not to be intimidated by your impending fame when the paparazzi descend!'

I laughed, and decided to take a walk before typing a reply.

I want someone who understands and loves both sides of me – the one who wants marriage and children, and the one who wants to be spanked while watching porn.

I was done pretending and modifying elements of my personality to 'fit' relationships and prove to men why they should love me. I was also done with trying obsessively to 'control' my destiny by reading dating guides, and wondering when I was ever going to find someone.

I was always confident about my work and friends, but had my doubts whether I could sustain a long-term relationship. Now that fear is gone, and I'm ready to let fate take its course.

So I hobbled off into the sunset on a broken heel, still flawed but inexplicably overjoyed. Hopefully, some day, the next wedding I attend will be my own. For real this time.

People have always asked me why I feel the need to write about my love life, and it's not some sort of weird narcissism. I thought back to something else in the Tao, the part that says the journey is the destination. I finally understood what that meant. All the pain, the heartache of losing JP, had taught me what a strong person I could be, truly whole and happy on my own. I'm ready to let go of some of the control.

I'm ready to love myself first, and admit that I may never have the perfect relationship, do everything in the 'right' order, prove my critics wrong, or have all (or any!) of the answers when it comes to love.

Does anyone?

www.sleeping-around.blogspot.com

# ACKNOWLEDGEMENTS

There are a few people I would like to thank, without whom this book would not have been possible:

Thank you to Rowan Yapp, Nikki Barrow and everyone else at John Murray.

Thank you to my amazing agent, Clare Conville.

Thanks to my mum, my inspiration for everything – except maybe the sex stuff!

Thank you to my grandma too.

Thank you to my dad, who always supported me.

Thank you to my amazing friends – true soulmates.

Thanks to my cousin Lauren, who was the first person to take me out on the town – I pointed the finger of blame at her many times in high school, but secretly loved every second of it!

Thank you to my friend Amina Akhtar, who has regaled me for years with tales of her love life, and given me some great advice.

Thank you to Vincent Moss, for his constant advice, support and endless cups of tea.

Finally, I would like to say thank you to all the men I've dated.

CATHERINE TOWNSEND

# Sleeping Around

## Secrets of a Sexual Adventuress

Threesomes, sorbet sex, drunk dialling, multiple orgasms, girly gossip-swaps, buying silk underwear – welcome to dating the modern girl's way

Cat describes herself as 'part slut, part hopeless romantic'. Her quest is to have her cake and eat it – an intelligent dinner date followed by a passionate one-night stand; to combine sleeping around with finding a soulmate.

A candid, sexy funny take on looking for love in unexpected places and how to find Mr Right – or at least Mr Right Now.

'Sexy, laugh-out-loud funny . . . very Carrie Bradshaw'
*Observer Woman*

'A no-holds-barred account of Catherine's erotic adventures . . . lots of fun and very *Sex and the City*' *Closer*

Order your copy now by calling Bookpoint on 01235 827716 or visit your local bookshop quoting ISBN 978-0-7195-6351-5
www.johnmurray.co.uk